F^{SE}ISHING IDAHO

An Angler's Guide

Joe Evancho

Cutthroat
PRESS

PO Box 1471
Boise, Idaho 83701

AUDENTES FORTUNA JUVAT

Edited by Joseph A. Evancho, Brad Carlson and Melissa Morrison

Cover photo by Andy Anderson
Warm Springs Creek – Lost River Range above Mackay Reservoir

Evancho, Joe
Fishing Idaho, An Angler's Guide/ Joe Evancho - Second Edition
256 pages
Includes index.
ISBN 0-9649158-1-2
I. Title
LOC catalog number : 96-83077

I've decided to make up my mind

about nothing, to assume the water mask,

to finish my life disguised as a creek,

an eddy, joining at night the full,

sweet flow, to absorb the sky,

to swallow the heat and cold, the moon

and the stars, to swallow myself

in ceaseless flow.   Jim Harrison

Acknowledgments

I would like to thank the Idaho Department of Fish and Game (IDF&G) regional biologists who helped with my information gathering: Chuck Warren, Ned Horner, Tom Curet, Jim Fredericks, Dick Scully, Doug Megargle and Ed Schriever.

Thanks also to Keith Carlson, Kent Henderson, Bill Horton, Don Benedict, Bob and Sue Evancho, Mark Devine, Art Hegewald, Casey Cline and Will Reid for help with various aspects of the book.

Special thanks to Melissa Morrison, Brad Carlson and Joe A. Evancho for their editing.

Thanks to Jim Harrison for the excerpt from *Cabin Poem*, Andy Anderson for the excellent photographs and Shanna Chuma for the detailed maps.

Joe Evancho
Boise 11/2004

What's Where

Headwater

Idaho Index 6
Introduction 7
Preface 8
Management 10
Species Identification 17
Basic Equipment 28
Idaho Hatches 31
Idaho's Big 10 32
    St. Joe River 32
    Kelly Creek 33
    Lochsa and Selway Rivers 35
    Clearwater River 37
    Middle Fork Salmon River 39
    Boise River 40
    Silver Creek 42
    Henry's Fork 43
    South Fork of the Snake River 45
        Polarized Eye wear—**PRO**TIP 48

Water

Regions 51
Panhandle 53
    Kootenai River Drainage 54
    Pend Oreille River Drainage 59
    Spokane River Drainage 66
        Learning to Fish with a Fly—**PRO**TIP . 74
Clearwater 77
    Palouse River Drainage 79
    Clearwater River Drainage 79
River of No Return 93
    Main Salmon River Drainage 94
    Upper Salmon 95
    Middle Salmon 104
    Lower Salmon 107
    Little Salmon River Drainage 109
    South Fork Salmon River Drainage 111
    Middle Fork Salmon River Drainage . . 114
        Choosing an Outfitter—**PRO**TIP 124
Treasure Valley 127
    Snake River Drainage 128
    Weiser River Drainage 131

Payette River Drainage 133
Boise River Drainage 140
Owyhee River Drainage 146
Bruneau River Drainage 147
    Accessorize—**PRO**TIP 152
Magic Valley 155
    Snake River Drainage 157
    Big Wood River Drainage 164
    Salmon Falls Creek Drainage 171
        Approach—**PRO**TIP 176
Bear Lake 179
    Snake River Drainage 180
    Portneuf River Drainage 183
    Blackfoot River Drainage 186
    Bear River Drainage 188
    Malad River Drainage 192
Upper Snake 195
    South Fork of the Snake River 195
    Henry's Fork Drainage 198
    Teton River Drainage 203
    The Sinks Drainage 205
        Selecting a Drift Boat—**PRO**TIP 210
Yellowstone National Park 213
McGuire and the Moose 222
Native Lands 226
    Duck Valley 226
    Fort Hall 227
    Nez Perce Reservation 228
    Coeur d'Alene Reservation 229
High Mountain Lakes 230
    Panhandle 231
    Clearwater 233
    Central Mountains (West) 235
    Central Mountains (East) 237

Backwater

Sponsor Pages 239
Directory 244
Water Index 246
Angler's Journal 254

Idaho Index

Capitol: *Boise*
Largest city: *Boise*
State flower: *Syringa*
State horse: *Appaloosa*
Statehood: *July 3, 1890*
State fish: *Cutthroat trout*
Miles of river: *82,677*
State tree: *Western white pine*
State gemstone: *Star garnet*
State bird: *Mountain bluebird*
Miles of white water: *More than 3,100*
Number of state parks: *28*
Number of major universities: *Three*
State motto: *Esto Perpetua (Let it be perpetual)*
Number of unrestricted public airstrips: *More than 115*
Highest point: *Borah Peak - 12,066 feet*
Lowest point: *Snake River at Lewiston - 770 feet*
Meaning of Lochsa in Nez Perce: *Rough Water*
Number of state and international borders: *Seven*
Percentage of surface acres of water in lakes: *38*
Percentage in reservoirs: *41*
Percentage in rivers and streams: *21*
Species most sought after by anglers: *Rainbow trout*
Number of acres of land owned by the federal government: *33,727,051 (63.7%)*
Number of acres of land owned by the state: *2,629,633 (5%)*
Population in 1980: *880,000*; in 1990: *1,006,749*; in 2002: *1,189,992*
Number of Olympic medal winners in skiing: *Four*
Amount of money Butch Cassidy got away with when he robbed the bank in Montpelier in 1896: *$7,165*
Number of pioneer trails used by immigrants in the 1800s: *Five*
Number of feet Shoshone Falls is higher than Niagara Falls: *52*
Currency local indians received for the land at Riggins: *Two ponies and a watch*
Number of carats in a diamond found near McCall: *20*
Rank of the Frank Church River of No Return Wilderness Area in size of wilderness areas in the lower 48 states: *First*
Ratio of pickup trucks to passenger cars in Idaho (estimate): *One to three*
Oldest Idaho fishing record: *675-pound sturgeon from the Snake River, 1908*
Smallest state-record fish on the books: *Green sunfish—five ounces*
Percentage of commercial trout sold in the United States that are produced in the Hagerman Valley: *Nearly 85*
Age of bison and antelope bones and arrowheads found in a cave near Twin Falls: *Approximately 14,500 years*
Number of non-game species for which state records are kept: *Seven*
Persons per square mile in Idaho: *15.6*; in USA: *80*
Difference in length between two Idaho northern pike that weighed 38 lbs. 9 oz. each: *Three quarters of an inch*

Introduction

I left Idaho in 1958 to play football for the Detroit Lions, knowing I would return home for good someday. And though it's taken quite a while, I'm back. Over the years and in all my travels as a football player and sportscaster, my desire to return never dimmed.

As a youngster in Boise I didn't have far to go to enjoy the outdoors, and one of the things I enjoyed most was fishing. During my high school and college days, my work with the Forest Service gave me the unbelievable opportunity of spending most of my waking hours in the midst of Idaho's woods, mountains and waters.

Since then I have traveled, hunted and fished all across the North American continent. And though there are certainly a lot of beautiful places out there, none are more beautiful than those to be found right here in Idaho. That's why, when Joe told me about his book and asked me to write an introduction, I happily agreed.

This book is about more than where to catch fish in Idaho. It's filled with information about rivers, lakes, streams and reservoirs that can't be found in any other single source. It offers tips on fishing equipment and techniques. It provides access information about the areas where fish are to be found. When used with topographical or U.S. Forest Service maps, it opens limitless opportunities to not only fish Idaho, but to see its natural attractions as well—from its geological wonders to its awesome wilderness areas.

One of life's real enjoyments is sharing. Some things can only be shared with family and close friends, of course, but there are things of common interest that can sometimes be shared with others as well. To me, this book is one of those. It's a way of sharing the natural wonders of this beautiful place called Idaho with people who can appreciate it, who will enjoy its outdoor pleasures to the fullest, but who, hopefully, won't abuse it.

So use this book and enjoy yourself. And while you're out there, be careful with the fish, be kind to the land and take time to smell the syringa.

Wayne Walker

Wayne Walker
Boise, Idaho — December, 1995

Preface

If you purchased a copy of the first edition of *FISHING IDAHO, An Angler's Guide*, you hopefully found a thing or two that you didn't know about Idaho. If this is your first look at the most comprehensive guide to fishing in Idaho you are about to be introduced to one of the most remarkable states in the Union.

With this edition, we have updated the text with the most current information on species and habitat and added more useful information about the fishing possibilities in Idaho. There are three new chapters, improved maps and fly charts, as well as more information on the wide variety of game fish in the state. We've also included *ProTips* from a variety of Idaho experts on various areas related to fishing in Idaho.

Whether you live in Idaho or far away from its pristine waters and soothing sunsets, this book will show you the way to some of the finest fishing in the world.

Part one of the book introduces you to essential information that will help you use this book most effectively. Following sections will include new aspects and fresh approaches to fishing here. Idaho Department of Fish & Game (IDF&G) management terminology has been updated as well as species identification and hatch information. We've included information on various kinds of equipment for a variety of fishing opportunities.

The book is divided into ten main sections, with the geographic regions similar, but not identical to, those found in the Idaho Fish and Game regulations. These regions consist primarily of the major drainages within the state as well as Yellowstone National Park and Native American lands.

There is a brief introductory overview of each region to familiarize readers with area features and provide points of reference. There are new maps for each region, featuring important waters and waterways plus cities, towns, and major state highways. These maps give readers usable references to locations within the region.

Detailed information—such as foot trails, unimproved roads and historic areas—can be obtained from more detailed maps, such as Forest Service or Gazateers maps, and through the *Cutthroat Press Map Service* (cutthroatpress.com). In addition, many counties and municipalities either give away or sell moderately priced maps that are well detailed. Global Positioning Satellite (GPS) coordinates are included for some locations, primarily high mountain lakes. These coordinates are for general locations only.

Following the map page, each region is divided into sections defined by its prominent drainages. The Panhandle Region, for example, has the Kootenai (koot-nee), Pend Oreille (pond-oh-ray), and Spokane River drainages. Each drainage is described in some detail, providing the big picture of the area. This is followed by detailed information specific to rivers, tributaries, reservoirs, lakes and ponds within the drainage.

This format provides users with general descriptions of the numerous fishing locations throughout the state, Yellowstone National Park and selected Native American lands.

If you have a specific destination in mind, you can quickly zero in on it. For example, someone interested in fishing in the Frank Church Wilderness would go to the *River of No Return* section of the book to review the map and get general information about the area. This would be followed by detailed information about the waters and waterways within the region, fishing conditions and species of fish found there with important information that will help narrow down choices.

For someone interested in a specific body of water, say Panther Creek, the procedure is equally simple. After locating the creek in the index, go to the *River of No Return* region, study the map, and read about the river in the Middle Fork of the Salmon drainage write-up. In both cases, maps that are more detailed should be used to reach appropriate destinations.

CAVEAT: We have tried to be as accurate as possible in describing the various waters and waterways and what to expect from them. However, they can and do change from year to year, even season to season. Some streams may run dry from drought or heavy irrigation use. A reservoir that is full one year may be badly depleted the next. Logging, road construction and agriculture, though less intrusive than in the past, continue to do damage to some fish habitat. Whenever possible, we have noted those waters and waterways affected by these conditions. Reservoir acreages are listed at full capacity. Lake acreages are estimates in average water years. GPS coordinates are for general locations only.

Management

Fishing Regulations

Fishing regulations can change from year to year and region to region, depending on environmental circumstances and management objectives. These definitions are basic and will be used throughout the book. To be safe, be sure to get a copy of the most recent regulations from the IDF&G.

Family Fishing Waters (FFW)

These are special areas around the state where there is year-round fishing and general bag limits of six trout, bass or pike. There are no limits on other species, no length limits and no gear or bait restrictions.

General Management

These waters offer uncomplicated fishing opportunities with no gear or bait restriction, no size limit on trout and a 12-inch minimum for bass. These rules are often used in waters that are stocked with catchable hatchery fish.

Wild Trout

With a bag limit of two trout and no size limit, this management regulation reduces the harvest and helps maintain an area's wild trout populations.

Quality Water

This rule applies in areas where the goal is to develop larger fish by restricting harvest. The bag limit is two fish (trout or bass) and restricted size limits, depending on the location. Some waters will have a 14- or 16-inch minimum or a 12- to 16-inch slot limit where fish in those size ranges are protected from harvest. There may be gear or bait restrictions as well.

Trophy Water

This plan is used where the goal is to catch, but not necessarily keep a trophy fish. It may be catch-and-release, a two-fish limit with a 20-inch minimum or a 12- to 20-inch slot limit. There may be gear and bait restrictions as well.

Special Cutthroat Regulations

Cutthroat populations have been reduced by over-harvest, habitat degradation and the introduction of exotic species. Many waters throughout the state are catch-and-release to protect westslope cutthroat trout. In the Magic, Bear Lake and Upper Snake regions, there is a two fish limit and the fish must be at least 16 inches.

On the Border

Bear Lake—Idaho/Utah border A holder of a valid Idaho or Utah fishing license may fish all of Bear Lake except in areas closed to all fishing.

Snake River—Idaho/Oregon/Washington border A holder of a valid Idaho, Oregon or Washington fishing license may fish the Snake River from a watercraft where the river forms the border between the states. You cannot fish from the shore without a license from the particular state in which you are standing. This includes wading and fishing sloughs or tributaries on the Oregon or Washington side. The same rules apply to Oregon and Washington license holders. One license for one bag limit.

Catch-and-Release

Once a fish is caught and landed it must be released immediately and unharmed, back into the water

Electric Motors Only

Use of gasoline motors is prohibited.

No Motors

No motors of any type are allowed.

Fly Fishing Only

Fishing with a fly rod, fly reel, fly line and artificial flies. You may use a spinning reel with a fly and float.

Winter Stream Seasons

For trout it's catch-and-release though mountain whitefish and brook trout may be harvested. Gear and/or bait restrictions still apply.

Fish Salvage

When fish populations are threatened by water shortages fish salvage may be authorized by IDF&G. No salvage of fish from public waters will be allowed without approval from the Fish and Game Commission or the director or regional supervisor. During salvage operations fish may be taken by snagging, spearing, archery, dip net, seine or with hands.

Use of toxic chemicals, explosives, firearms or electricity is prohibited. All anglers must have a valid Idaho fishing license.

....

Terminology

Some specific terminology is used to describe all aspects of Idaho fishing. Following are definitions of terms that will be used throughout the book.

Warm-water:

Water that holds fish that prefer warmer temperatures, usually lakes, impoundments or slow-moving rivers. These lakes are usually below 3,000 feet, with bass, pike, panfish and fish other than trout predominant.

Cold-water:

Salmonids are the primary species here. This includes trout, char, and mountain whitefish. Usually the water is moving quickly or is very deep where the sun cannot affect its temperature.

Mixed:

Water with both properties, with potential for a wide range of fishing opportunities.

Anadromous:

Fish that are hatched in freshwater, grow for one or two years there and then migrate to the ocean. They live at sea for one to two years, on average, then return to the stream of their birth to spawn and start the cycle over again.

Catchable fish:

Stocked and wild fish of legal size.

Wild Rivers:

Essentially, wilderness.

Scenic Rivers:

River in a wild setting with some development.

Recreational Rivers:

Free-flowing rivers with the highest degree of development.

Species of concern or interest

White sturgeon, sockeye salmon, bull trout, wild chinook salmon, wild steelhead and burbot are protected in all Idaho water. NO HARVEST.

White sturgeon:

Protected. These relics of the pre-dam era are large, but sensitive to rough handling. They cannot be taken out of the water and must be released immediately.

Bull trout:

Protected throughout Idaho and adjacent waters. These fish must be released immediately.

Chinook salmon:

They are protected throughout Idaho with special regulation for the harvest of hatchery fish that are easily identified by a missing adipose fin.

Steelhead:

They are protected throughout Idaho with special regulation for the harvest of hatchery fish that are easily identified by a missing adipose fin.

Burbot (ling):

The burbot, also known as lawyer and lingcod, was once a common species present throughout North America and specifically within the Kootenai River Basin in Montana, Idaho and British Columbia. Today, within Idaho the burbot are endemic solely to the Kootenai River.

Kamloops:

A special strain of large rainbow trout brought to Idaho for sportfishing purposes. Native to Canada, these fish are stocked in northern Idaho lakes and may reach large size.

Golden trout:

Golden trout have been stocked in mountain lakes throughout Idaho to provide a unique angling opportunity. Although they can achieve large sizes (Idaho record is 5 pounds 2 ounces), they are not generally thought of as large members of the trout family. Golden trout are a bright gold color with spots near their tail.

Arctic grayling:

Arctic grayling are found around the earth at arctic latitudes and inhabit both lakes and streams. They are not native to Idaho, but have been introduced to provide fishing opportunities in some alpine lakes. Arctic grayling spawn in the spring with adults typically reaching 10-15 inches in length and can live as long as 11 or 12 years. They have sail-like, colorful dorsal fins and are well-noted for their eagerness to take a fly.

Westslope cutthroat:

These trout exhibit three life histories, depending on where they live. Some inhabit small streams all their lives, while others live in large rivers and spawn in small streams (fluvial) or dwell in lakes (lacustrine) and spawn in streams. Its historic range is from the Salmon, Clearwater, Spokane, Pend Oreille and Kootenai rivers.

Yellowstone cutthroat:

The historic range of Yellowstone cutthroat trout generally consists of the waters of the Snake River drainage (Columbia River basin) upstream from Shoshone Falls and those of the Yellowstone River drainage.

....

Maps

Maps shown at the beginning of each region are for general reference only and should be used in conjunction with more detailed maps. U.S.

Forest Service maps and U.S. Geological Survey topographical maps are excellent resources and are usually available from local sporting goods stores. For more specific information go to *www.cutthroatpress.com*.

Alpine Lakes

Idaho has more than 800 peaks that are 6,000 feet or higher. Mountain thrusts and massive volcanic activity in Idaho have created some of the most dramatic and beautiful landforms to be found anywhere. Pristine alpine lakes, hidden deep in many of these recesses, offer a variety of fishing to those anglers and adventurers seeking a true wilderness experience.

Some of these lakes have healthy populations of native species. Some are not deep enough to keep from freezing solid during the long, harsh alpine winters. Some do not have the food source or flowing water to supply oxygen for a stable fish population, but some do. Some of these high mountain lakes can be reached by roads that take you right to the fishing. Others, such as those in the Big Horn Crags or Gospel Hump Wilderness, are only accessible by trail.

Where it is necessary and feasible, IDF&G stocks some mountain lakes on a two- or three-year rotating basis. Some stocking is done by truck. Where there are no roads, stocking is done by backpack, horsepack, airplane and/or helicopter.

Stocked species include cutthroat, golden and rainbow trout and Arctic grayling. Because of the sensitive and changing nature of these fisheries, only the more prominent and accessible lakes have been mentioned. For more detailed and current information regarding fishing Idaho's alpine lakes, contact IDF&G, the regional Forest Service office or go to *www. cutthroatpress.com*. Phone numbers and addresses can be found at the back of the book.

Lodging

Depending on your bankbook, and your comfort needs, Idaho can accommodate you in a variety of ways. From Sun Valley or Coeur d'Alene (kor-da-lane), with their four-star hotels and spacious guest ranches, to out-of-the-way destinations with modest and comfortable hotels and motels, there is lodging to accommodate any budget.

The Official Idaho State Travel Guide lists overnight accommodations with brief descriptions and phone numbers. To receive an official travel guide, call 800-635-7820

There are campsites throughout the state. Some are equipped to handle motor homes while others are more primitive with no potable water available. There are 28 state parks and hundreds of national forest campsites to choose from and one or the other will be near your fishing destination. Make sure you are equipped for the site you choose.

Hospitals

With the exception of five rural areas, every Idaho community with a population of more than 2,400 is within 10 miles of a hospital. Of the three exceptions, the farthest distance to a medical center is 18 miles. Backcountry communities often have trained paramedics who can handle emergencies.

Airstrips

Editor's note: Each airstrip is placed in the regional text according to its location.

There are many places in Idaho where the maxim, "you can't get there from here" is true. Well, it used to be true. Today, backcountry flying has opened up wilderness areas to people who haven't the physical strength, or available time to travel into the hinterlands of Idaho.

The summer of 2003 was a deadly one for backcountry pilots in Idaho, especially in the dangerous Frank Church River of No Return Wilderness in the central part of the state. A total of eight pilots and passengers died for a variety of reasons. Without knowing the exact causes, it is certain, however, that going into these remote and often dangerous backcountry air strips without the benefit of an experienced pilot is a recipe for disaster.

Beginning pilots, or those without backcountry experience, should fly in with an experienced pilot flying before attempting any backcountry flying. The weather in the mountains can be extremely unpredictable and all caution should be taken when flying there. This is especially true during the hot summer months when thermals rising from narrow canyons can wreak havoc during what appears to be calm and pleasant weather. Experienced pilots don't fly in the afternoon in the summer. They either plan a morning arrival or one later in the evening when the thermals that can toss a plane around like a cork on the ocean have subsided.

....

Icons

These icons represent facilities that are available at fishing sites throughout the state. Great care has been taken to ensure the accuracy of the information. Some locations may have facilities or special motor restrictions that are not listed in this guide. Always check fishing regulations or inquire about special circumstances at a local sports shop.

 Bathrooms

 Camping

 Docks

 Boat Ramp

 Motor Restriction

 Airstrips

 Disabled Access

Species Identification

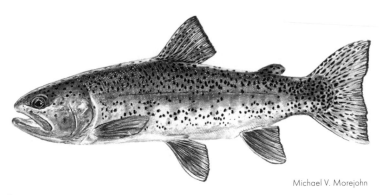

Michael V. Morejohn

Rainbow Trout NATIVE

These fish are the most sought-after species in Idaho and one of the most popular sport fish in North America. Rainbow trout prefer cold, clear streams and lakes, but they can also survive in warm-water systems where there is a source of cold, clean, water, such as a spring. They vary in their coloring but commonly have sides of silver with a blue to green back. Many have white tips on their pelvic and anal fins. Native rainbow trout differ from hatchery fish genetically but they have the same scientific name.

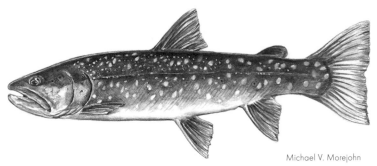

Michael V. Morejohn

Bull Trout NATIVE

Bull trout are Idaho's only native char and they are protected in all Idaho waters and must be released immediately. The bull trout population has been falling in Idaho waters for many years. A beautiful fish with an olive green body above and shading to white on their belly, they lack the worm-like markings found on brook trout. Their upper body has yellow spots with sides of red or orange spots with no spots on its dorsalfin. Tail is slightly forked. They are found throughout Idaho except in the Snake River drainage above Shoshone Falls. They are extremely sensitive to habitat degradation.

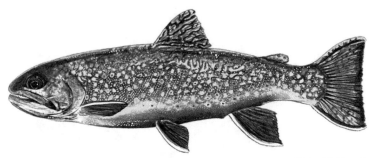

Michael V. Morejohn

Brook Trout INTRODUCED

Their original range stretched from Labrador to Saskatchewan and from Maine down to Alabama. Brook trout have a dark green or blue back that fades to a white belly. The belly and lower fins may turn bright red in spawning males and the upper body and dorsal fins have blotches or worm-like markings. Sides have pale and reddish spots usually with bluish rings. Lower fins and tail are tipped in white. The tail is square or slightly forked.

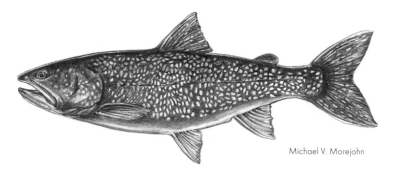

Michael V. Morejohn

Lake Trout INTRODUCED

Also know as mackinaws, these large trout were originally distributed from Labrador to Alaska in deep, cold lakes. Some have been reported to reach more than 100 pounds, but the accepted Idaho record is 65 pounds. Lake trout are dark gray or green above, with a lighter colored belly and irregularly shaped light gray spots on their back, sides, dorsal fins and tail. The tail is forked.

Splake INTRODUCED

A cross between a lake trout and a brook trout.

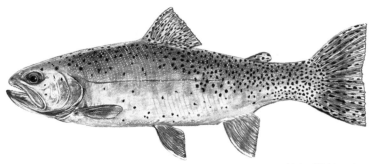

Michael V. Morejohn

Cutthroat Trout NATIVE

Ranging from coastal California to Alaska and the eastern edge of the Rocky Mountains, cutthroat trout are aggressive feeders, making them popular with anglers. Their backs are steel gray to olive green with sides that may be yellow with red or pink along their belly. Red to orange slashes on the underside of the lower jaw give the fish their name. Cutthroat in the Salmon, Clearwater and Panhandle drainages are westslope cutthroat. Cutthroat in the Snake River above Shoshone Falls are Yellowstone or Bear Lake cutthroat.

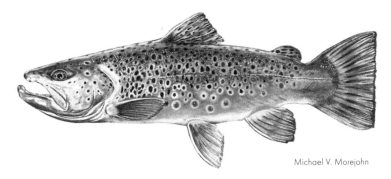

Michael V. Morejohn

Brown Trout INTRODUCED

Brown trout have become widespread since their introduction to North America around 1885 and tolerate warmer water temperatures than native trout. Their sides are light brown to yellowish with numerous brown, black and red spots surrounded by halos of blue-gray. Their backs are brown or olive with large dark spots. Their adipose fin usually has an orange border. They have few, if any, spots on the tail, which is barely forked. There are spots on their gill plates.

Idaho Fish and Game

Chinook Salmon NATIVE

Salmon hatch in fresh water, grow nearby and eventually swim to the sea where they live for a few years before returning to the stream of their birth to spawn and die. Adult chinook salmon, generally 18 to 40 inches long, have irregularly shaped black spots on their back, dorsal fin and tail. Their teeth are sharp and the inside of their mouth is black as is the gum line. Adults return to the Snake, Salmon and Clearwater rivers and their tributaries. For more information see *The Return of the Natives*, page 26.

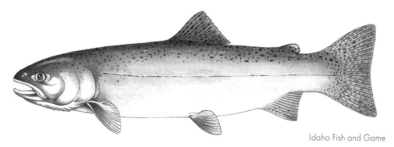

Idaho Fish and Game

Steelhead NATIVE

Steelhead are ocean-going rainbow trout, generally 18 to 40 inches in length with irregularly shaped black spots on their side, back, dorsal fin and tail. Steelhead spawn in the Snake, Clearwater and Salmon drainages. Juveniles migrate to the ocean then return as adults after one to two years. For more information see *The Return of the Natives*, page 26.

Kokanee Salmon NATIVE

These landlocked sockeye salmon have silver on their sides with a bluish-black top and white on their stomachs. The body color changes during spawning season to green heads and bright red sides. Found in large, deep lakes and reservoirs, they migrate up tributary streams to spawn from September through December. Although they are native they have been widely introduced outside their native range. Sockeye salmon are the same species as kokanee but migrate to the ocean and spend from one to two years at sea before returning to Idaho to spawn.

Coho Salmon INTRODUCED

Also known as the silver salmon, coho look like kokanee with spotting on their backs, dorsal and upper lobe of their tail fins. Attempts to create landlocked populations have been moderately successful. Attempts to re-establish anadromous populations are currently underway through Nez Pierce Tribal fisheries programs. Black mouth and gums distinguish chinook salmon from coho salmon, which have white or gray gums.

White Sturgeon NATIVE

Protected—no harvest. These large, ancient fish have a downward-pointed mouth. Their mouth has four barbels, or whiskers. These prehistoric giants grow to 10 feet in the Snake, Salmon, Clearwater, and Kootenai rivers. Prior to the construction of the dams on the Snake and Columbia, it is believed that these giants migrated to the ocean. Sturgeon in Idaho rivers still grow to be quite large.

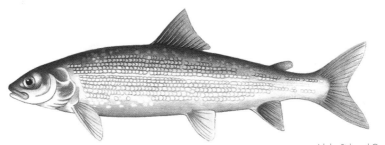

Idaho Fish and Game

Mountain Whitefish NATIVE

This under-appreciated salmonid has a light grayish back, with silvery sides a dull whitish belly and a small, toothless mouth, perfect for shoveling gravel around and sucking up water bugs. They inhabit rivers and lakes of the west slope of the Rocky Mountains. Six species of whitefish are found in Idaho.

Tiger Muskie INTRODUCED

These mouthy monsters are sterile hybrids of northern pike and muskellunge with torpedo-shaped bodies of olive green to dark gray with vertical markings on their sides. There is a 40-inch minimum size limit. They are among the most prized game fish in the world because of their reputation as ferocious fighters.

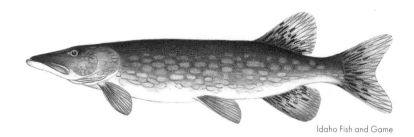

Idaho Fish and Game

Northern Pike INTRODUCED

Northern pike are known for their bulldog tenacity. They have backs of bluish-green to gray with an irregular row of light-colored horizontal spots on their sides. The most widely distributed species of strictly freshwater fish in the world, they range across all of northern Eurasia and North America and can reach six feet in length. Idaho's record is 49 inches.

Idaho Fish and Game

Bluegill, Crappie and Pumpkinseed INTRODUCED

These are the fish most people can claim as their first catch. All have spines in their dorsal fins. Bluegill have a blue spot on their gill cover and an olive to dark green back with a bluish luster. Sides are bluish with a yellow belly. Crappie have a grayish to silvery green on the head with lighter sides and a silvery white belly. They also have heavy black spotting or splotches on their body and fins. There are black and white crappie in Idaho. The maximum size of bluegill and pumpkinseed appears to be about 10 inches, with most being considerably smaller. The state record crappie is more than 17 inches. They are usually found in small lakes and ponds, or in shallow weedy bays of larger lakes.

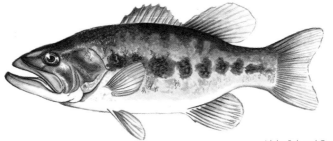

Idaho Fish and Game

Largemouth Bass INTRODUCED

The most sought-after game fish in North America, largemouth bass have a dark green back and sides and a white belly. Dark irregular horizontal bands along their sides differentiate the largemouth from its cousin, the smallmouth bass. Their upper jaw extends behind the eye.

Idaho Fish and Game

Smallmouth Bass INTRODUCED

Another popular warm-water game fish, smallmouth bass have a dark olive to brown back with bronze sides and a white belly. Dark vertical bands on their sides distinguish them from the largemouth bass. They have eyes reddish and when their mouth is closed their upper jaw does not extend behind the eye. Prefers rocky or gravelly habitat.

Idaho Fish and Game

Perch INTRODUCED

A smaller version of the walleye, perch have dark green and yellow sides with six to eight dark vertical bars. Their front fins have sharp spines. Catchable year-round, they prefer a diet of minnows and aquatic insects. They can reach 15 inches and almost three pounds. The state record is two pounds, 9.6 ounces and 15 inches long.

Idaho Fish and Game

Walleye INTRODUCED

The walleye is one of the most important game and food fish in North America. They are similar to the perch but lack vertical bars and have prominent canine teeth. Their tail's lower lobe is tipped with white. Populations exist in Little Salmon Falls Creek, Oakley and Oneida reservoirs and some Panhandle water. Walleye can reach three feet in length and weigh more than 24 pounds.

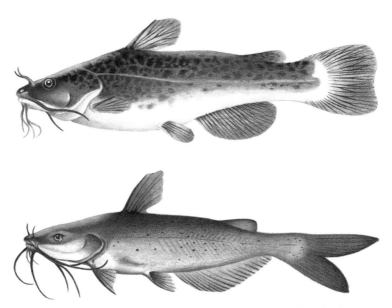

Idaho Fish and Game

Channel Catfish and Bullhead Catfish INTRODUCED

These much sought-after members of the catfish family have four pairs of whiskers, spines on their dorsal and pectoral fins and no scales. The channel catfish is the most active and popular of all catfish. They live in river channels, feed during twilight hours and move into the shallows at night. Some channel cats reach 50 to 60 pounds. A bullhead can grow to 20 inches and five pounds.

The Return of the Natives

Steelhead

Steelhead are anadromous (ocean-migrating) rainbow trout that hatch in streams and rivers and migrate to the ocean where they spend a year or two growing before returning to the streams of their birth.

There are two separate strains of Idaho steelhead. A-run fish start their journey to Idaho in June, July, or August and generally average 5-8 pounds when they return. They show up in Idaho as early as August on their way to the Salmon and Snake rivers. B-run steelies are often 12-20 pounds and they begin their run in late August or early September. Early arrivers may make it to Idaho by the end of September and continue their run through the following spring. Most fish in the B-run group travel to the Clearwater River, but some go to the Salmon River, entering small tributaries to spawn in April and May. Even though steelhead do not feed when they return from the ocean, they will strike at objects that float past them.

No other fish has adapted itself to the rigors of the spawning run as well as the Idaho steelhead. Unfortunately, wild steelhead numbers are falling and fish raised in hatcheries supplement current stocks for fishing. IDF&G said that as of the fall of 2004, the number of returning steelhead was above its ten-year average. The fish that return to Idaho are a mix of wild and hatchery-reared stocks. Special regulations protect the wild fish while letting anglers catch the hatchery stock. The Selway and South and Middle forks of the Salmon River remain free of hatchery plantings to give their wild fish freedom from competition while ensuring genetic purity.

Wild steelhead can be identified by a dominant adipose fin while hatchery-reared fish have a clipped or missing adipose fin.

Chinook salmon

Chinook salmon, also known as kings, are the largest members of the Pacific salmon family. Generally, the size of a fish that returns from the ocean depends on how long it has stayed in the ocean. Sockeye and coho salmon usually stay about a year and a half while chinook can spend as many as four years at sea.

The three sub-groups of chinook salmon in Idaho are spring, summer and fall chinook. Spring chinook migrate the farthest distance inland to spawn in tributaries to the Snake, Salmon and Clearwater rivers. Historically, chinook spawning occurred in the upper sections of Idaho's large rivers but the majority of summer chinook habitat on the Snake River has been destroyed or left inaccessible by the Hells Canyon Dam because it has no apparatus for fish passage. Fall chinook still spawn in the lower and middle reaches of the Snake River.

The Endangered Species Act protects all stocks of anadromous chinook salmon in Idaho. In 1982 chinook salmon were planted in Lake Coeur d'Alene and a healthy landlocked population was born. This popular fishery holds the Idaho state record for landlocked chinook salmon at 42 pounds.

Sockeye salmon

Sockeye salmon are a unique species of salmon because they require a lake for the first one to two years of their lives. Payette, Stanley, Alturas and Redfish lakes in Idaho once supported strong runs of sockeye. Sockeye salmon, the species most sensitive to habitat degradation, was the first fish species in Idaho to be listed under the Endangered Species Act, and are currently on the brink of extinction.

Kokanee salmon

Kokanee, which are still abundant in lakes throughout the state, are the landlocked form of sockeye salmon. Kokanee are much smaller than their ocean-going cousin, generally reaching 10-14 inches. They are important in Idaho as sport fish and as forage fish for large trophy fisheries such as Lake Pend Oreille rainbows and Lake Coeur d'Alene chinook.

Basic Equipment

Tackle and Gear

The following information will help you determine the type of fly-fishing, spinning, or bait-casting gear that will best meet your needs. In assembling your fishing gear, the most important rule is to match your equipment to the type of fishing you will be doing.

For fly-fishing in most of Idaho's streams, reservoirs and mountain lakes, a four- , five- or six-weight rod, eight-and-a-half to nine feet in length and a single-action fly reel is your best bet. The reel should hold approximately 50 yards of 20-pound dacron backing and a 90-foot fly line matched to the rod weight. For most streams, floating fly line is recommended with an eight- to 10-foot leader that tapers down to 4x or 5x.

Lake fishing from a boat, float tube or pontoon craft calls for a nine-foot (or longer), five- or six-weight rod. The reel should have interchangeable spools holding sinking lines of various sink rates. This type of subsurface fly-fishing is very popular and produces some very large fish.

Spinning equipment can range from a simple ultra-light spinning outfit (rod, reel and six- to eight-pound test line) to saltwater equipment of considerable strength for the monster sturgeon of the Snake River.

Depending on the region and the time of year, you will need a good pair of chest-high waders. Remember, temperatures in Idaho can vary greatly from region to region. While it may be 98 degrees in Boise in July, just two and a half hours away in the Stanley Basin, the temperature can dip into the 30s and even the 20s at night. Be prepared. Always carry a shell for outer covering, as well as an insulated fleece (wool or polar fleece) vest or jacket that you can add for warmth.

Polarized glasses and a good, wide-brimmed hat are a must. Both help to cut glare and aid in seeing fish in the water and flies on the water's surface. A fly section that would cover the state would be enormous. The following is a general list with some helpful hints.

Most of the mountain streams in the state can be fished successfully with hair-wing attractor dry flies throughout the summer and fall. Barring runoff and dirty water, these should be larger size flies (#10, #12) for larger water, and smaller sizes (#14, #16) for smaller streams. Examples include wulffs, humpies, trudes and elk hair caddis. Color is usually of minimal importance, although flies with white wings are easier to see in low light conditions. A wet fly package should include stone fly nymphs, bead heads and caddis larvae.

For streams subject to heavy angling pressure, such as Henry's Fork, Silver Creek and the South Fork of the Snake, you will need to match the hatch.

Lures such as Panther Martin or Mepps spinners imitate small baitfish as they flash and spin through the water. Rapalas and other floating or diving plugs imitate larger fish. Both can produce good results. There are all sorts of lures, gadgets and baits on the market today guaranteed to get you into more fish. Whether they work or not is not as important as the enjoyment you get from fishing. There is one universal truth about tactics: The best way to fish is to find a method you're comfortable with, then constantly improve that aspect of your fishing. Once you've mastered one level, there is always another to challenge you. That is the truth and beauty of the sport.

Local fishing and sporting goods shops are the best places to start when fishing an area for the first time. When asking for information, give parameters such as the kind of fishing you enjoy, how far you are willing to travel and how much time you have. Fishing ranging from good to excellent can be found throughout the state most of the year, and local experts are usually happy to share information with those who demonstrate their desire to protect Idaho's resources.

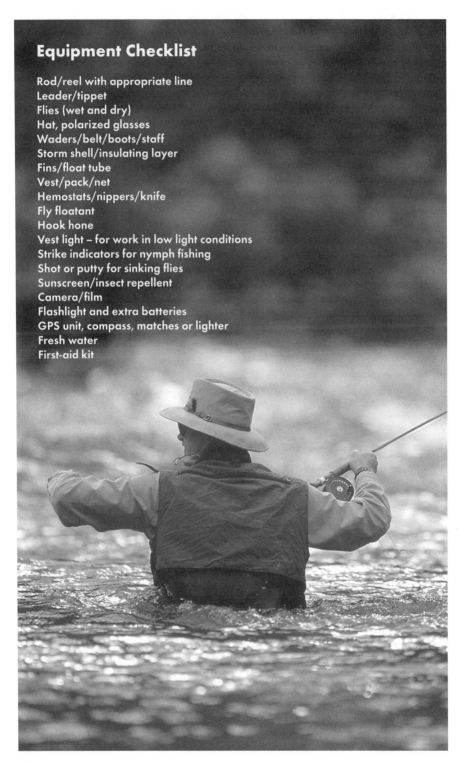

Equipment Checklist

Rod/reel with appropriate line
Leader/tippet
Flies (wet and dry)
Hat, polarized glasses
Waders/belt/boots/staff
Storm shell/insulating layer
Fins/float tube
Vest/pack/net
Hemostats/nippers/knife
Fly floatant
Hook hone
Vest light – for work in low light conditions
Strike indicators for nymph fishing
Shot or putty for sinking flies
Sunscreen/insect repellent
Camera/film
Flashlight and extra batteries
GPS unit, compass, matches or lighter
Fresh water
First-aid kit

Idaho Hatches

	STAGE	EMERGENCE	SIZE
May flies			
western green drake	dun, cripple	June - August	#10
small western green drake	dun, cripple, spinner	July, August	#14 - #16
brown drake	dun, cripple, spinner	June, July	#8 - #10
pale morning dun (PMD)	dun, emerger, spinner	June - Sept.	#16 - #20
blue-winged olive (BWO)	dun, emerger	Mar., April, Oct., Nov.	#16 - #24
tiny western olive	dun, emerger, spinner	June - Sept.	#16 - #24
tricos	dun, spinner	July - Sept.	#20 - #22
callibaetis	dun, cripple, spinner	April - Oct.	#16 - #20
pink Albert	dun, emerger	July, August	#16 - #20
Caddis			
brown / tan	adult, pupa, larva	June - Sept.	#12 - #16
gray / olive	adult, pupa, larva	June - Sept.	#18 - #20
Stone flies			
salmon fly	all	May - July	#4 - #8
golden stone	all	June - August	#8 - #12
yellow Sally	all	June - August	#14 - #18
Etc.			
midge		All season	#18 - #24
ant		May - Oct.	#12 - #18
beetle		May - Oct.	#10 - #18
grasshopper		July - Oct.	#6 - #12

Lake flies for trout

leech *(black, brown, olive, etc.)*	#2 - #14
damsel fly nymph *(shades of olive, light & dark)*	#8 - #14
scud (fresh water shrimp) *(light - med. olive gray)*	#10 - #18
midge *(black, olive, red)*	#12 - #20

Largemouth bass flies
mouse
Dahlberg diver
black leech

Smallmouth bass flies
Clouser minnow
Dahlberg diver
Stayner ducktail
marabou crayfish

Panfish flies
peacock nymph
sponge spider *(black or white)*

Idaho's Big 10

To say there are 10 top streams in Idaho is like comparing beauty, which is truly in the eye of the beholder. There are so many wonderful areas to fish that listing 10 is actually more folly than fact, though the waters mentioned here are often the ones people talk about most when they talk about fishing in Idaho.

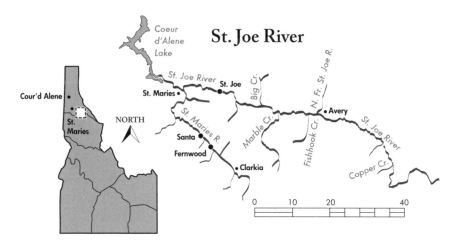

St. Joe River

The headwaters of the shadowy St. Joe gather on the western slope of the Bitterroot Mountains, then flow west to Lake Coeur d'Alene. Nearly two centuries ago, the region's beaver-rich waters drew trappers and traders. In the mid-nineteenth century, prospectors and miners left their marks as they searched for gold. They were followed by homesteaders and loggers who came for the mighty white pine and cedar. Today, the river's gin-clear waters and flashing cutthroat trout draw fishermen from across the country.

The river is open all year from Coeur d'Alene to St. Maries (with special regulations for cutthroat). However, high water during the spring can handicap fishing. In June, large cutthroat swim up the St. Joe from Lake Coeur d'Alene to feast on the massive baetis hatches, but the action can be well worth struggling with the long casts from flooded banks. Swift, deep water makes early wading risky to impossible.

As the river recedes in June and July, a variety of aquatic insects emerge, providing a cornucopia for fish and steady action for anglers. A variety of restrictions on tackle and catch limits are in place on the St. Joe to protect the fragile cutthroat population, so check the most recent IDF&G regulations.

Throughout its reach, the St. Joe offers a unique variety of fishing opportunities. Below Avery, the river flows through private lands that have been largely stripped of their timber.

Above Avery, forested slopes give meaning to the name *shadowy* St. Joe. Bass fishing is popular in the lower stretches near Lake Coeur d'Alene, while during the summer, the best trout fishing is generally above Marble Creek. From Prospect Creek upstream, the waters are reserved for catch-and-release fishing.

The St. Joe is accessed by paved road from its mouth to Red Ives. Above Spruce Tree, you walk or ride horseback. From Avery to Spruce Tree, the road is dotted with campgrounds, but summer weekend use is often heavy. Motel accommodations and restaurants are available in St. Maries. The St. Joe Lodge is operated by outfitters and accessible only by horseback or on foot. It is located about five miles above Spruce Tree. A small general store and bar are located in Avery, but no motel accommodations.

At the mouth of Marble Creek there is a display of the region's logging heritage that is well worth the stop. There are self-guided trails along this route; one to an old logging camp and steam donkey, another through a magnificent cedar grove. In addition, Marble Creek offers catch-and-keep stream fishing. A scenic alternate return to the St. Joe can be made on a paved road by way of St. Maries.

Kent Henderson

Kelly Creek

When pioneer-miner John Kelly first arrived in the region west of the Bitterroot Mountains in present-day Clearwater County, he could not imagine that his name would be linked to one of North America's most beautiful and productive trout streams.

The Kelly Creek main stem rises from the meeting of the Middle and

North forks of Kelly Creek as they flow west from the Bitterroot Mountains on the Montana border.

Its southernmost tributary is Cayuse Creek, named for the Nez Perce Indians' western cousins—the Cayuse Indians.

Cayuse Creek is also accessible by road and can also be reached by a primitive road that is only sporadically maintained, and not recommended for two-wheel drive vehicles. Check with the Clearwater National Forest for directions and road conditions before attempting this one.

While good fishing can be found right off the road along Kelly Creek, Cayuse Creek is best left to those willing to rough it with a backpack. Those willing to pay the price in sweat will find spectacular scenery, as well as excellent fishing.

Both Kelly Creek and Cayuse Creek are strictly catch-and-release fishing. Neither stream generally produces big fish, but 14-inch cutthroats are not uncommon.

The North Fork of the Clearwater, once considered one of the finest steelhead streams in the country, can provide some nice cutthroat and rainbow trout. Restrictive catch regulations applied over the past few years have improved fish populations. Black Canyon is spectacular, and, as is Kelly Creek, catch-and-release only.

While spin fishing with light lures (single barbless hooks only) can be productive, Kelly Creek and Cayuse Creek are fly-fishing waters. Standard patterns such as Royal Wulffs, elk hair caddis, caddis emergers and your favorite hopper will all work. Stimulators and other attractor patterns are often effective. Streamers imitating bait fish can provide excitement in some of the deeper pools. Hare's ear nymphs and stone fly nymphs also are effective. Take sizes in the 10 to 16 range.

Access to Kelly Creek and the North Fork of the Clearwater is dependent on snow levels. Roads are sometimes not open until late June or early July. On the other hand, in low-water years, water temperatures in mid July and throughout August can climb into the mid to high sixties, making fishing very slow. Fishing when temperatures are much over 65° F is not recommended, since fish can be fatally stressed.

Kelly and Cayuse creeks are both remote. Plan on packing in everything you will need, then packing out your leftovers and trash. There are maintained campgrounds at the Kelly Creek Ranger Station and at Weitas Creek, which flows into the North Fork of the Clearwater. Other primitive sites are also available. The nearest accommodations for food, gas, lodging and whatever else might be needed are at Pierce, Idaho, and Superior, Montana.

Be aware that since wolf reintroduction, there are active wolf packs throughout the North Fork and Kelly Creek drainages. While wolves have not attacked humans, livestock and domestic dogs have been killed by wolves. If you are lucky enough to hear or see wolves, IDF&G would love to hear about it.

Kent Henderson

The Lochsa and Selway Rivers

Both the Lochsa and Selway rivers start on the western slopes of the Bitterroot Mountains. They flow on a westerly course meeting at Lowell where they form the Middle Fork of the Clearwater River.

The Lochsa officially begins where White Sands and Crooked Fork creeks meet near the Montana border. It flows through thickly forested mountains along the northern boundary of the Selway-Bitterroot Wilderness Area. U.S. Highway 12 follows the river through rugged country, roughly along the same route as the Lolo Trail used by Lewis and Clark. The Selway flows north, then veers toward the northwest until it turns west and meets the Lochsa at Lowell. The land between the rivers is rugged, forested and wild and includes vast roadless areas.

During peak runoff, the Lochsa rushes downstream at Lowell at more than 8,500 cfs, the Selway at nearly 13,000 cfs. At the end of June, normal flow on the Lochsa at Lowell will drop to 4,000 cfs and the Selway to around 5,000. By late September, the Lochsa can drop to as low as 430 cfs, and the Selway, down to 600 cfs. Like other mountain streams in Idaho, high flows increase the difficulty for wading. It might be possible to wade the shore of some sections during high water, but great care is urged.

The Lochsa is easily accessible and is flanked by Highway 12 most of the way from Lowell to the Montana line. There are numerous campsites along the way, with pit toilets, but little else in the way of amenities. The many points of interest along Highway 12 range from a former federal work prison camp (turned into a Japanese internment camp in 1943), whose occupants built the highway, to tour loops to the Lolo Trail – the same trail used by Lewis and Clark.

The Lochsa Historical Ranger Station, 25 miles from Lowell, has one of the most complete displays of U.S. Forest Service historical materials anywhere. It's open from Memorial Day to Labor Day.

Lodging and food are available at Lowell, the Lochsa Lodge at Powell (65 miles from Lowell) and Lolo Hot Springs, just over the pass in Montana. Many rafters and kayakers run the Lochsa in the early fishing season. The Selway is secluded and hard to access, and if you want to float the river through the wilderness area, you must apply for a permit up to a year in advance. The Forest Service allows only one launch a day to protect the pristine makeup of the river through the wilderness area.

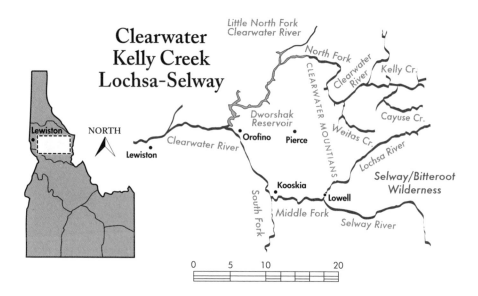

You can reach Selway Falls from Lowell by turning off Highway 12 and following the Selway for 19 miles. Though most impressive in the spring, the trip to the falls is worth the drive anytime. From Lowell to the end of the road above the falls, numerous campsites are available as well as good trails along the stream into the wilderness. A horse and hiking trail above the falls runs along highly fishable sections of the Selway and offers access to tributaries Meadow Creek and Moose Creek.

No stocking occurs in the Lochsa or Selway. Fenn Pond, at Fenn Ranger Station along the Selway, and White Sands Pond, near Powell Ranger Station on the Lochsa, are stocked with catchable trout for those wanting a trout dinner.

Large stoneflies appear in late April and early May, before fishing season begins. Smaller golden and yellow stoneflies appear during the early fishing season. Caddis are predominant for much of the season, and mayflies appear occasionally. Mayflies and caddis patterns can be used as well as hare's ear and prince nymphs through the fall. For spin fishers, flashy spinners or small spoons (barbless, single hooks) pulled along the stream bank or near midstream boulders will produce good results at the right time.

Like Kelly Creek and the St. Joe, these two streams are primarily fly-fishing water. There are special regulations for both rivers upstream from Lowell. It's artificial flies and lures only with other restrictions. Check the current Idaho fishing regulations. In a winter stream season from December. 1 to March 31, anglers can catch and release trout and harvest whitefish, on the Lochsa below Wilderness Gateway and on the Selway below Selway Falls.

Keith Carlson and Brad Carlson

The Clearwater River

The Lewis and Clark Corps of Discovery may have been the first travelers to write about the Kooskooskee, as the Nez Perce called the Clearwater River, and they were certainly the first non-natives to see the mighty steelhead and salmon that filled the river on their annual migration runs.

The Corps of Discovery opened the door for travelers to view this majestic river that flows through some of the most beautiful terrain in the world.

Flowing across the northern stretch of Idaho from Montana, the Clearwater River starts in the Bitterroot Mountains and, as in many areas of the northern portion of the state, Lewis and Clark left their mark on the area. The explorers made camp near Lenore, east of Lewiston, in late September of 1805 and spent about two weeks getting ready for the journey down the Clearwater, Snake and Columbia rivers. A historical marker acknowledges their stay.

Today the Clearwater River is synonymous with steelhead fishing in Idaho and there are two separate runs of these ocean-going rainbow trout. The A-run fish are ocean-run rainbow that have spent one year at sea living off the vast food base there, of which they are also a part being food for sea lions, whales and the like. These fish usually enter the Columbia River in July and August and arrive in Idaho about the middle of September. They head for the Snake and Salmon rivers in Idaho or the Grande Ronde River in Oregon. Under the right conditions, large numbers of A-run steelhead can arrive in late September or early October.

The B-run fish enter the Columbia in late August and, depending on river conditions, they can arrive in Lewiston in mid-October. Migratory factors such as river flows, rainfall and water temperature all play a part in the steelhead's return.

The fall is a great time for fishing the Clearwater while the water levels are low and anglers can move about the river with relative ease. When the conditions are just right, large numbers of steelhead will reach Lewiston by early September. The A-run fish provide excellent fly-fishing in September and early October before the B-run fish arrive.

Though generally smaller, the A-run fish, migrating toward the Clearwater's cooler temperatures, usually average twice the numbers of the B-run spawners. A-run fish average about seven pounds while the B-run steelhead average 13 pounds. Catch-and-release season opens on July 1, several weeks prior to the catch-and-keep season that runs through the end of April.

Historically, the best stretch of the Clearwater is from Lewiston to Orofino. It is in this 45-mile section that the *Killer Bs* are at their best, with prime time being generally around the middle of October. A clipped adipose fin distinguishes the hatchery fish, and wild fish must be released.

Spring chinook salmon fishing is usually open during May and June, depending on the number of fish returning. The average salmon taken from the Clearwater is 12 to 15 pounds with 20-pounders not uncommon.

There are several ways to ensure a successful fishing trip on the Clearwater River. They include hiring a guide with a jet or drift boat. This allows anglers to fish more than one location. Some anglers like to walk the shore or don waders and get into the water and site-fish.

Those who would like a close look at the Clearwater steelhead and salmon without wetting a line can stop at Dworshak National Fish Hatchery near Orofino—the world's largest combination producer of steelhead and spring chinook salmon. The hatchery is located at Ahsahka at the confluence of the North Fork of the Clearwater and the main stem Clearwater. It was designed by the U.S. Army Corps of Engineers and is operated by the U.S. Fish and Wildlife Service. Visitors are welcome, exhibits describe the hatchery activities and self-guided tours are available.

Overall, the Clearwater is about more than catching the big one. It is a step back from the daily grind into a world of serenity and natural beauty not often found in the world today. Wildlife such as deer, elk, turkey, mink and beaver are frequent visitors to the river. Eagles and osprey ride the air currents overhead. If you're lucky, you just might see them fishing too.

Joe Norton/Nancy C. Butler

Middle Fork Salmon River

Starting at the confluence of Bear Valley and Marsh creeks in the River of No Return Wilderness, the Middle Fork of the Salmon River is one of Idaho's great outdoor adventure attractions and the fishing is an added bonus. From the historic relics that dot the area, to the stories of the people who put those relics there, the Middle Fork offers much more than a wild whitewater ride of a lifetime. Aside from the opportunity to fish for native cutthroat trout, day trips off the waterway offer an insight to a time when the world moved at a slower pace.

Although no one can say who first navigated the Middle Fork earlier last century– if not Captain Harry Guleke in the 1920s– he certainly was one of the first. Since that time, countless rafters have made the exciting whitewater trip, not only for the excitement of boiling rapids and turbulent river runs, but also for the excellent cutthroat trout fishing.

For most modern-day adventurers, the trip down the Middle Fork begins with a phone call to an outfitter. There are companies whose sole business is providing customers with transportation, food and other comforts for the six-day journey downriver. Outfitters supply everything except sleeping bags, toiletries, clothing and personal gear.

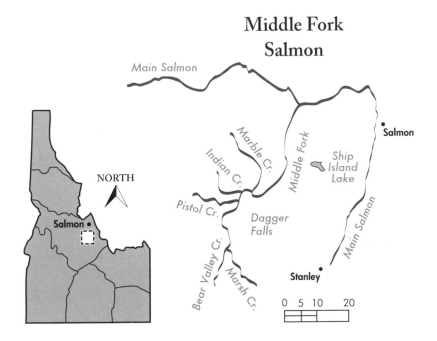

Middle Fork
Salmon

Put-in is below Dagger Falls or at the Boundary Creek launch site in a narrow section of the river. At Indian Creek the water slows down and flattens out, giving the rafters ample angling opportunity for native cutthroats. It remains gentle water until the Flying B Ranch, where the river descends and pulses quicken.

According to some outfitters, the best fishing is from Big Creek down to the mouth. Cutthroat trout are the primary species. At the right time they will readily take a dry fly. When the summer sun warms the riparian areas and grasshoppers flit through the air, hopper imitations floated through riffles or along shoreline shallows can get you into fish. If you aren't getting any action on the surface add some weight to your hopper and fish below the surface. A strike indicator will let you know when your hopper's been taken.

Besides the access below Dagger Falls, there are many mountain airstrips along the Middle Fork course. Morgan (private) is the first below Dagger Falls. Pistol Creek (private) is 27 miles downstream. The next four airstrips are U.S. Forest Service strips. They are Indian Creek, Thomas Creek, Mahoney, Lower Loon (Simplot) and beyond the private Flying B Ranch airstrip is the Bernard airfield. Flights into these airstrips require experienced pilots. Extreme precautions must be taken when flying into these mountain airstrips because weather conditions can change very quickly.

Many of the airstrips are used as a point of entry for hiking, hunting trips and float trips down the Middle Fork. For information regarding permits and general services, contact the U.S. Forest Service office in Challis, Idaho.

Boise River

The North, Middle and South forks of the Boise River begin their westward journeys in the south central mountains of the state. Their drainages are on or near the border of vast wilderness areas and are remote and rugged in their upper reaches. As they flow toward their confluence above Arrowrock Reservoir, they take on the feel and character of classic Rocky Mountain trout water.

The North Fork is the most remote of the three. It is 42 miles long and borders Elmore and Boise counties. Forest fires and the subsequent salvage logging were factors in the river altering its course after a downpour caused flash floods in the area in 1995.

The Middle Fork is a popular outdoor playground, even though the road from Arrowrock Reservoir to Atlanta can be extremely rough due to logging truck traffic. This fork begins in the Boise National Forest at about 8,000 feet and flows for 90 miles before joining the South Fork seven miles above Arrowrock Dam.

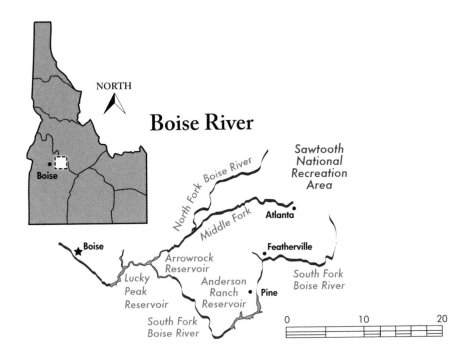

The South Fork begins in the Sawtooth National Forest and flows freely to the reservoir above Anderson Ranch Dam. The tailwater area below the dam is a popular and productive fishery. It is a medium-size stream with a healthy insect population. Spring runoff can make wading in any of the three forks difficult and not an adventure for the fainthearted. Most spring and early summer fishing is done by drift boat or some sort of vessel.

Flows are regulated out of the Anderson Ranch Dam according to irrigation needs. Usually by the end of summer, the water has receded enough to make wade-fishing a reasonable option.

The most popular water on the South Fork is below Anderson Ranch Dam, where there are special regulations that include artificial flies and lures only, as well as slot limits. The road leaves the South Fork at Danskin Bridge and a float through the canyon from Danskin to Neil Bridge has a bit of white water and some solid fishing opportunities. In the fall, kokanee salmon migrate to streams above Anderson Ranch Reservoir to spawn.

Flies include pink Alberts, a variety of caddis, blue-winged olives and stone flies. Your favorite grasshopper pattern will work when the summer sun sends the hoppers flying. Stone fly nymphs, hare's ears and prince nymphs are good wet fly patterns.

The most popular access to the South Fork is from Highway 20 north of Mountain Home. To get to the Middle Fork, take the Middle Fork Road (FR 268) off Highway 21 past Lucky Peak Reservoir. Rabbit Creek Road, east of Idaho City, is the easiest access to the North Fork.

Accommodations in the upper reaches of these regions are minimal, so make sure you have what you're going to need. If you pack it in, pack it out when you leave.

Silver Creek

Formerly the Sun Valley Ranch, the area of Silver Creek now part of the Nature Conservancy's Nature Preserve is one of the premier fishing spots in the world. People from across the state, country and globe come to Silver Creek to get a taste of this fabled and formidable spring creek, located south of Sun Valley. Ernest Hemingway used to fish and shoot in the Silver Creek area.

The ease of getting to Silver Creek belies the effort needed to succeed at *The Creek*. It is all blacktop highway until you reach the entrance of the Conservancy land. If you come from the west and travel the base of the Picabo Hills, you can get a glimpse of some of the monster rainbows as they cruise the shallow waters of Sullivan Lake. Even from the distance of a hundred yards or more, on a clear, windless day you can see the silhouettes of these fish as they gracefully and effortlessly move about the slough.

The most famous waters of Silver Creek lie on Conservancy property. One stipulation of access is that all anglers sign in at the cabin headquarters. The water is catch-and-release, fly-fishing only, with a single barbless hook. Wade fishing is the primary means of fishing, though some anglers use float tubes in areas where they are allowed.

Because the creek is spring fed, there is not the massive influx of runoff that other waters in the state see. The flow remains relatively consistent throughout the year.

There are some camping areas available off the Conservancy grounds at the Hayspur Hatchery and Point of Rocks. The facilities are minimal.

From its mouth at its confluence with the Little Wood River south of Picabo, upstream to the county road bridge near Picabo, Silver Creek is approximately 14 miles of wild rainbow and brown trout water.

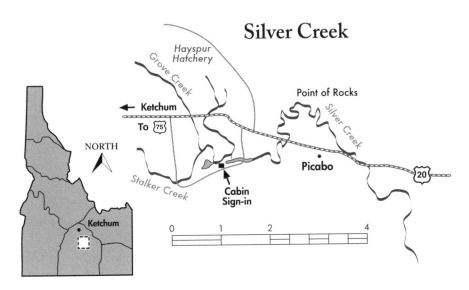

It's six miles from the county road bridge, north of Picabo, to the bridge at milepost 187. This is a quality brown and rainbow trout fishery.

The next 8.5 miles of river, between milepost 187 and the Stalker Creek bridge, is within the Nature Conservancy jurisdiction area. This section is fly-fishing only and catch-and-release.

The Conservancy water has a healthy population of large fish. Some of the brown trout grow to more than 30 inches. The area is very heavily fished. This pressure causes the fish to be very wary of anything unusual in the river or on the river bank. Therefore, these large fish are as difficult to catch as any fish in the world.

Henry's Fork

The Henry's Fork is perhaps Idaho's most famous trout stream, and for good reason. You can cast to rainbow trout of more than twenty inches as they sip tiny mayflies on or just below the surface.

From Henry's Lake outlet to McCrea Bridge it is a put-and-take fishery for catchable rainbow trout, with cutthroat, brook and cuttbow trout hybrids and mountain whitefish also present.

Island Park Reservoir (8,400 surface acres) is a put-and-grow fishery for rainbow, cutthroat and cuttbow trout hybrids and kokanee salmon. The reservoir fish population is supplemented with stocked catchable rainbow trout.

Below Box Canyon the eight-mile stretch through Harriman State

Park is catch-and-release fly-fishing only to produce trophy fish and protect spawning populations. There are trails from the rim to the river, and it's a steep climb out. The canyon rim allows for a good view of the river before descending to the water. The river can be deceptively swift in the canyon with slick rocks and a fast current. There are mostly rainbow trout with few, if any, brook trout in this stretch.

From Island Park Dam to Riverside Campground it is a wild catch-and-release fishery with some fish being larger than 18 inches. From Riverside Campground to Lower Mesa Falls it is managed under regulations that allow two fish that are not larger than 16 inches to be kept.

The 25-mile stretch from Lower Mesa Falls to the U.S. 20 bridge is managed to maintain wild populations of rainbow trout.

From the U.S. 20 bridge to Ashton Dam the river and reservoir are stocked with catchable rainbow trout. From the Ashton Dam to Fritz

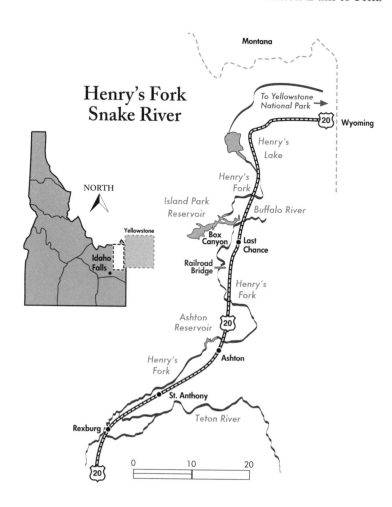

**Henry's Fork
Snake River**

(Veron) Bridge there is a spawning season closure for rainbow trout and no motors are allowed in this stretch. From Fritz Bridge to St. Anthony the fishery is managed to support natural production of rainbow and brown trout and mountain whitefish.

From St. Anthony to its confluence with the South Fork, there are 30 miles of cold-water fishery with a restricted cutthroat limit. It is managed for cutthroat trout below the Teton River with supplemental plantings of fingerling cutthroat and brown trout. Other species include rainbow trout and mountain whitefish.

In the spring, flows in excess of 2,000 cfs are not uncommon downstream from Island Park Reservoir. During the summer, the flow might drop to half that amount. The flow can go lower than 500 cfs in the fall.

Wading is possible throughout the summer but will require some strength, and perhaps a sturdy wading staff.

Hotels and restaurants are available, as are campsites that range from rustic to those with electrical hookups and showers.

Box Canyon is a three-mile stretch below Island Park Reservoir known for its large trout. Because of the ease of access, the area often has fishermen lined up along the bank.

The Railroad Ranch is primarily a rainbow trout stretch that is wadeable most of the time. Above and below the Ranch Bridge, anglers can cast to sipping rainbow along the wide, meandering river. Moose often wade the shallows downstream from the bridge as they feed on water grass that grows in large mats on the river bottom.

To get to the Ranch Bridge, park in the lot across from the mailbox and gate on U.S. Highway 20. The walk is about a mile and you might want to carry your waders rather than wear them on the hike.

South Fork of the Snake River

The South Fork of the Snake is one of Idaho's greatest treasures. After its start in Yellowstone National Park the river flows through the western edge of Wyoming before entering Idaho above the aptly named Palisades Reservoir.

Below the reservoir the river flows past deep-sided canyons, magnificent stretches of beautiful scenery and abundant wildlife, then through agricultural land until it joins the Henry's Fork. Floating the river in a drift boat with a seasoned guide is a common means of enjoying the river but, if you are not careful, the fishing can be so hypnotizing as you cast and drift you will miss some of the most spectacular scenery in the region.

In Idaho, the river flows out of Palisades Reservoir near the Wyoming border for 60 miles to the Henry's Fork. The South Fork supports the largest cottonwood ecosystem in North America. It is home to a vast array of wildlife ranging from bald eagles to moose.

In the spring, the river flow can be as high as 18,000 cfs. During July, a flow of 14,400 cfs below the dam is common. September will see the flow reduced to 5,000 cfs or less. Even though the water is considerably lower in the fall than in the spring, it is still fished primarily from a drift boat or raft.

Because the non-native rainbow trout compete with the more valued native Yellowstone cutthroat, there is no limit on rainbow trout or hybrids, and harvest of these non-native species is encouraged. To increase the rainbow trout harvest the entire South Fork is open all year. Because the area is an important wintering ground for a variety of wildlife it is important to minimize disturbance to wintering animals.

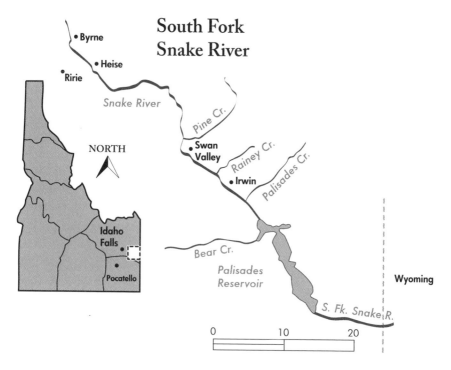

The South Fork is a very large trout stream, even by western standards. Midsummer flows are usually between 10,000 and 20,000 cubic feet per second, making the river too fast to wade, except near shore banks and broad shallow riffles. Most fishing is done with some kind of watercraft—primarily drift boats. Professional outfitters can be found throughout the valley.

If you're floating the river for the first time, with our without your own boat, a licensed guide is a worthwhile investment. Guides know the water and can help you with equipment and tactics. For example, the section of river from Conant to Heise is not for beginners. Once you've gone down the river with a guide you'll be able to use that experience to do some exploring of your own—you'll just need the boat.

The South Fork is big water and wading opportunities have to be searched out. For anglers who prefer wading, a drift boat can act as a taxi, taking you from one riffle or run to another. If you stay in the boat and float the river, you'll be able to cover much more water and see more of the beautiful Snake River country. Vertical canyon walls, hundreds of feet high, reach from the river to the sky above you. The only problem is that when you spend most of your time reeling in fish you'll miss the wonderful scenery.

Camping along the river has some restrictions and is allowed at only 15 designated sites on the river.

There is camping at Palisades Reservoir and numerous private locations along the river from Palisades to Heise. Bed-and-breakfast facilities and lodges with tackle shops and outfitters can be found throughout Swan Valley. Jackson Hole is only an hour away.

There are special regulations for the South Fork below the Snake, so check your regulations carefully.

POLARIZED EYE WEAR IS ESSENTIAL

Celebrities may wear sunglasses to enhance their image, while others consider sunglasses a fashion accessory. For knowledgeable and ardent anglers, sunglasses are critical pieces of equipment, becoming a matter of pure practicality and necessity...and they must be polarized!

The primary benefit polarized sunglasses offer is cutting glare, the bothersome result of light waves reflecting off flat shiny surfaces, such as water. Glare creates visual interference, so reducing glare from the water's surface allows an angler to see into the water. This makes your casting more accurate and productive, and locating fish easier. An angler's ability to see below the surface of the water can aid in wading and boating safety as well.

Another reason sunglasses are essential for anglers is eye protection. Polarized sunglasses guard against harmful UV (ultraviolet) rays entering the eye directly or reflected by water. This precaution protects the eyes from painful inflammation of the cornea which, with prolonged exposure, can cause potential cataract formation. Another benefit polarized sunglasses offer is the prevention of eye strain after a long day on the water, along with protecting the eyes from a less-than-perfect cast.

Solving the Polarization Riddle

Polarization is a premium feature in a sunglass lens. During the manufacturing process, a specially designed filter is sandwiched between two lenses or molded into the lens. The filter blocks horizontally reflected light waves, known as glare. The lens cleans the selected interfering light waves, providing the angler with crisp and clear vision.

Not everybody has 20/20 vision and most reputable companies offer their lenses in a prescription program that may include single vision or bifocal lenses. To ensure the highest quality, make sure it is an authentic lens program with fishing specific tints, not just stock prescription polarized lenses.

Here are a few things to look for when purchasing polarized fishing sunglasses.

There are two predominant lens materials commonly used in polarized glasses—glass and polycarbonate.

Glass:

Polarized glass lenses have the best optical quality. Generally, they are more expensive, offer the highest scratch resistance, use the finest polarizing elements and can have photochromic capabilities. A photochromic glass lens will adjust its tint density to varying UV exposures. It's darker in bright conditions and lighter in darker conditions adding versatility for the angler! Frames with glass lenses may be slightly heavier than plastic, but newer, extra thin glass lenses and a proper frame fit make it a nonissue.

Polycarbonate:

These are plastic polarized lens that are generally less expensive than glass. Polycarbonate is the undisputed champion for high velocity pursuits in the sporting world, pairing impact resistance with remarkable value.

Lens color is also an important factor in purchasing fishing glasses.

Copper: One of the most popular tints, this color provides medium contrast with increased definition and is very soothing on the eyes. Best when used in medium to bright conditions.

Amber: The yellowish tint of this lens enhances depth perception and gathers available light in low light situations. It is a higher contrast lens and best when used in medium to low light conditions.

Brown: Very popular with freshwater anglers, brown offers a nice combination of contrast and realistic color transmission. Optimum performance in medium to bright conditions.

Grey: This lens tint will give you the truest color transmission, preserving natural hues and colors. While grey is the choice for open-sea fishing, most freshwater fishermen seek lenses with more contrast. Grey works best in medium to bright conditions.

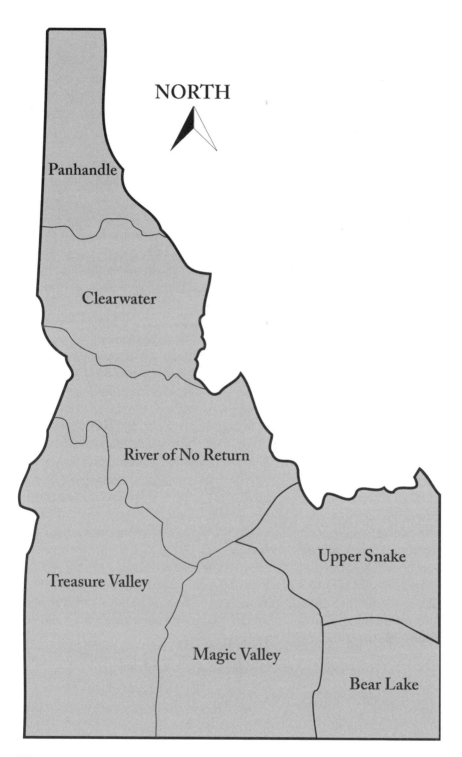

NORTH

Panhandle

Clearwater

River of No Return

Upper Snake

Treasure Valley

Magic Valley

Bear Lake

THE REGIONS

From the northern tip of the Panhandle to the southeast corner of Bear Lake, Idaho is truly an angler's paradise. The rivers, lakes, and streams of this vast and wild region offer nearly every type of freshwater fishing available. If you want to fish cold, deep lakes for large lake trout or small mountain streams for native cutthroat trout, the Panhandle has everything you need. If perch fishing is more your style, the state abounds in panfish lakes that are not only uncrowded, but also relatively easy to get to.

Stream anglers have more than enough famous water for a lifetime with Kelly Creek up in the Clearwater country, Silver Creek in Magic and the South Fork of the Snake and Henry's Fork in eastern Idaho.

Except for part of the Bear Lake Region and the Panhandle, the entire water system of the state is directly connected to the Snake River. Beginning in Yellowstone National Park, the Snake River arcs its way through the southern plains to eventually join the Columbia River in Washington State. Something as immense as the Snake River cannot be described adequately in the space available. It must be seen, felt and pondered.

As large as the Snake River is, it is only part of the Idaho fishing story. Every region in the state has water that ranges from good to excellent, along with a few surprises. These maps and regional descriptions are not how-to information. They are merely jumping-off points for further research and exploration on your part.

Some new information about high mountain lakes has been added to this edition. These areas can be dangerous, so thorough preparation must be made before venturing into these distant places.

In a day and age when the world seems to be getting smaller and smaller, a walk through an Idaho mountain meadow along a babbling brook or watching a bobber on a high mountain lake with a grandchild or a friend can make the world big again.

Panhandle

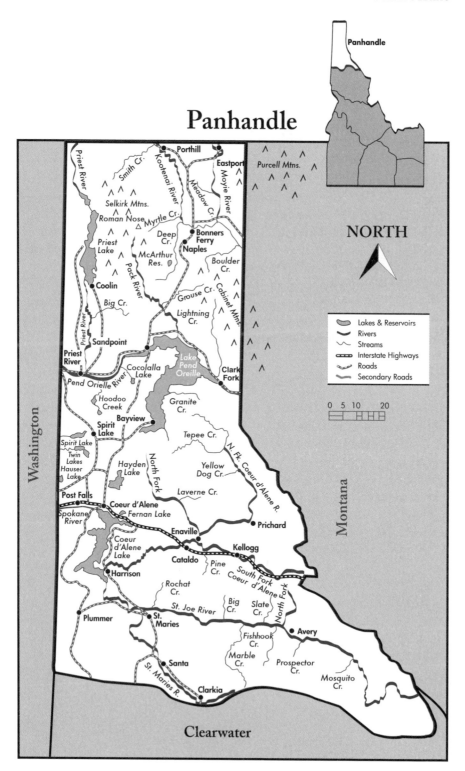

Panhandle

NORTH

Lakes & Reservoirs
Rivers
Streams
Interstate Highways
Roads
Secondary Roads

0 5 10   20

Priest River
Smith Cr.
Kootenai River
Porthill
Eastport
Meadow Cr.
Moyie River
Purcell Mtns.
Selkirk Mtns.
Roman Nose
Myrtle Cr.
Deep Cr.
Bonners Ferry
Naples
Priest Lake
McArthur Res.
Pack River
Boulder Cr.
Coolin
Big Cr.
Grouse Cr.
Cabinet Mtns.
Priest River
Lightning Cr.
Sandpoint
Priest River
Cocolalla Lake
Lake Pend Oreille
Clark Fork
Pend Orielle River
Hoodoo Creek
Granite Cr.
Bayview
Spirit Lake
Spirit Lake
Tepee Cr.
Twin Lakes
Hauser Lake
Hayden Lake
North Fork
Yellow Dog Cr.
N. Fk. Coeur d'Alene R.
Post Falls
Laverne Cr.
Spokane River
Coeur d'Alene
Fernan Lake
Prichard
Enaville
Coeur d'Alene Lake
Kellogg
Cataldo
Pine Cr.
South Fork Coeur d'Alene
North Fork
Harrison
Rochat Cr.
St. Joe River
Big Cr.
Slate Cr.
North Fork
Plummer
St. Maries
Avery
Fishhook Cr.
Santa
Marble Cr.
Prospector Cr.
Mosquito Cr.
St. Maries R.
Clarkia

Washington

Montana

Clearwater

Panhandle

The Idaho Panhandle is home to woodland caribou and grizzly bears—both endangered species. Along its rivers and streams and on its mountain slopes you can find whitetail deer, mule deer, moose, elk and black bear as well as eagles, osprey and a variety of waterfowl.

More than 100 years ago, travelers from around the world came to the region seeking fortunes mining the lead, silver and gold that lay beneath the mountains. Today, a few of the old mining towns, such as Wallace, Kellogg and Mullan remain and cater to curious visitors. At Emerald Creek near Clarkia, the U.S. Forest Service operates a pay-to-dig star garnet area from Memorial Day through Labor Day. Idaho and India are the two major locations in the world where the Idaho state gem is found.

There are three drainage areas within the Panhandle Region: the Kootenai (koot- nee) River in the northeast corner; the Pend Oreille (pond-oh-ray) River in the central section; and the Spokane River at the south end. The three rivers drain an area of more than 41,000 square miles in Washington, Idaho, Montana and British Columbia.

The region has one of the largest concentrations of lakes in the West and is home to three of the largest natural lakes in Idaho; Lake Pend Oreille (94,000 acres and 1,152 feet deep), Lake Coeur d'Alene (31,500 acres and 200 feet deep) and Priest Lake (23,360 acres and 369 feet deep). A 37-pound kamloops trout was taken from Lake Pend Oreille in 1947, and a 31-pounder was caught in 1993. The slender Panhandle produces some of the finest fishing in Idaho and state and Forest Service campgrounds are abundant.

Native species include westslope cutthroat trout, bull trout and mountain whitefish. White sturgeon and burbot are also species native to Idaho and burbot are found only in the Kootenai River. Both are protected from harvest. Introduced species include brown, brook, rainbow and lake trout, as well as kokanee, chinook salmon and Lake Superior whitefish.

All warm-water species were introduced. They include largemouth and smallmouth bass, black crappie, yellow perch, pumpkinseed, bluegill, green sunfish, bullhead and channel catfish, northern pike and tiger muskie.

If it has a tail, gills, fins and sleeps underwater in Idaho, it is probably available in the Panhandle Region.

The Kootenai River Drainage

The Kootenai River starts at nearly 11,900 feet in British Columbia's Kootenay National Park, north of Mount Assiniboine. It is impounded at Libby Dam in Montana where it forms Koocanusa Lake. From there it flows westward into northern Idaho where it meets the Moyie River, also of Canadian origin.

It is the northernmost waterway in the state and flows through the northeast section of the Idaho Panhandle—a slender strip of land bordered by Canada to the north, Washington to the west and Montana to the east. The Kootenai River enters Idaho in eastern Boundary County then heads back north into Canada to Kootenay Lake. It flows out of the lake and joins the Columbia River near Castlegar, British Columbia.

The river drains approximately 15,000 square miles and is 485 miles long. In Idaho, the topography is dominated by steep mountainous country, 90 percent of which is forested or above tree line. It drops nearly 10,000 feet in elevation as it flows through the basin.

Rainfall is normally plentiful throughout the region making it the second largest tributary to the Columbia River system in terms of runoff, though it is only the third largest in terms of drainage area. Only the Snake River contributes more volume, and does so from a much larger watershed area.

The Kootenai River drainage has native rainbow trout above waterfalls in the main river and some of its tributaries. The Moyie River trout fishery is supported by wild fish, primarily rainbow trout, with about a third brook trout populations and an occasional cutthroat trout. All other tributaries support a mix of wild, native cutthroat and rainbow trout and non-native brook trout. Rainbow trout, mountain whitefish and bull trout are present in the main Kootenai River. The main Kootenai, and some west-side tributaries, hold early spawning kokanee salmon in the late summer and fall. Some kokanee escape from the Libby Reservoir in Montana and enter the Kootenai River in Idaho.

High country lakes in the Selkirk and Purcell mountain ranges are stocked with trout fry on a two-year rotating basis. Most of these lakes have westslope cutthroat trout, rainbow or brook trout. Several lakes are reserved for golden trout and Arctic grayling. Some lakes are not stocked to maintain some fish-less, natural alpine lake ecosystems for amphibians and reptiles.

Lowland lakes offer nearly every type of warm-water fishing available in the state, including largemouth bass, crappie, bullhead, perch and

pumpkinseed. Several lowland lakes are managed for specialty warm water fisheries requiring hatchery stocking. Channel catfish are stocked in Smith Lake and Dawson Lake is stocked with tiger muskie. Bluegill can be found at Bloom, Brush, Dawson, Robinson and Smith lakes. Put-and-take rainbow trout, planted cutthroat trout and some kokanee round out the lowland-lake fishing lineup.

The majority of the waters in the Kootenai drainage produce fine fishing for trout. The Kootenai and Moyie rivers and their tributaries, as well as the mountain and lowland lakes, provide moderate amounts of high-quality fishing in a beautiful setting. Just getting to these places is half the fun.

Rivers, Lakes and other Waters

Kootenai River

From the Montana border in eastern Boundary County, to the Canadian border at Porthill, there are 66 miles of Kootenai River in Idaho. The Kootenai is big water. From the Montana line to Bonners Ferry, the river is inaccessible, cutting through steep canyons with an average drop in elevation of three feet per mile. The 47-mile section from Bonners Ferry to Porthill is slow moving with broad, meandering sections—some with holes more than 100 feet deep.

White sturgeon are found in the deep pools, and it is the only river in the state where burbot, a cod-like freshwater fish, also referred to as ling, is native. Both species, and bull trout, are protected.

Glaciers from the last ice age have created steep waterfalls on many of the Kootenai tributaries in the Purcell and Selkirk mountains. These waterfalls block upstream fish movement. Populations of small, resident trout are found above most of these barrier falls.

The Kootenai is primarily a cold-water fishery containing rainbow and cutthroat trout, mountain whitefish, kokanee salmon and bull trout.

There are more than 100 miles of accessible tributaries to the Kootenai River holding rainbow, cutthroat and brook trout. There are more than 300 miles of tributary waters that are inaccessible or difficult to reach. Species in these reaches include rainbow, cutthroat and brook trout. In some tributaries below Bonners Ferry waterfalls limit fish movement.

Westside Tributaries

Ball, Boundary, Deep, Long Canyon, Mission (eastside), Myrtle, Parker, Smith and Trout creeks all have short, productive runs before they enter the Kootenai River. Myrtle and Smith creeks have barrier falls near their mouths. Numerous tributaries drain the Selkirk and Purcell mountains and either flow directly into the Kootenai River or merge with larger tributaries.

There are about 130 accessible miles of tributary water on the Kootenai and they are remnants of a retreating glacier that scoured out a steep-sided valley, leaving significant waterfalls that block upstream movement of fish. These relatively short streams have rainbow, cutthroat, bull and brook trout. Some kokanee are present. Smith Creek is wild rainbow and cutthroat trout water. Myrtle Creek has good brook trout fishing above its barrier falls. The canyon sections have beautiful scenery, but access is difficult.

Moyie River

This river is the Kootenai River's largest tributary, although a natural 80-foot waterfall and a dam approximately one-and-a-half miles from its mouth separate most of the Moyie from the Kootenai, dividing it into two areas. There are 25 miles of the Moyie River in Idaho and above its confluence with Meadow Creek, it is a relatively flat stream with a few pools and several small tributaries to provide spawning habitat. The river is wild rainbow trout fishery with some cutthroat, brook and bull trout. The river there is flanked by a partially improved road.

The eight miles of river below Meadow Creek is steeper and looks more like classic trout water with much better trout habitat. There is a dirt road paralleling this section and Deep and Meadow creeks have enough good spawning habitats to provide a good wild trout fishery. These two creeks produce the wild fish for the Moyie River. Access is very limited.

There are approximately 35 miles of accessible Moyie River tributary water that is managed as a wild trout fishery with cutthroat, rainbow and brook trout above Meadow Creek.

Round Prairie Creek

There are no facilities at this tributary to the Moyie River that is populated with brook trout. It enters the Moyie River north of Sinclair Lake.

McArthur Reservoir (200 acres)

This Boundary County reservoir is an IDF&G waterfowl management

area. It is primarily a warm-water fishery for perch, brook trout with some largemouth bass and pumpkinseed. It is open all year. Deep Creek, below McArthur Reservoir, has limited fishing for wild rainbow trout. Most of the land is private, so access is limited. Elev.: 2,080 feet.

Robinson Lake (60 acres)

This Boundary County lake has put-and-take rainbow trout as its major cold-water species with some wild brook trout present. Warm-water species include bluegill and pumpkinseed, and it is managed as a quality largemouth bass fishery. Elev.: 2,638 feet.

Smith Lake FFW (30 acres)

Stocked rainbow trout are in this Boundary County lake along with largemouth bass, bullhead catfish, pumpkinseed and hatchery channel catfish. Elev.: 2,986 feet.

Brush Lake (29 acres)

This is a mixed fishery located in Boundary County. Primarily a cold-water fishery with stocked rainbow trout. Warm-water species include largemouth bass, bluegill and pumpkinseed. Elev.: 2,995 feet.

Perkins Lake (60 acres)

This warm-water fishery in the Kaniksu National Forest has large-mouth bass, pumpkinseed, black crappie, yellow perch and bullhead. Elev.: 2,628 feet.

Dawson Lake (35 acres)

This warm-water fishery located east of Smith Lake in the Kaniksu National Forest is regularly stocked with tiger muskie with a 40-inch minimum size limit. Other important species include largemouth bass, black crappie, yellow perch, bluegill, pumpkinseed, bullhead and channel catfish. Elev.: 2,966 feet.

Bonner Lake (23 acres)

This Boundary County lake is managed as a quality trout fishery with restricted season, gear, size and bag limits. There is no limit on largemouth bass and pumpkinseed.

Periodic treatment is performed to maintain a quality fishery for trout as needed. Westslope cutthroat trout were stocked in the 90s and various strains of rainbow trout were stocked as well. Elev.: 2,480 feet

Kerr Lake (30 acres)

This is a warm-water fishery in Boundary County west of Copeland with largemouth bass and pumpkinseed and no facilities. Elev.: 1,785 feet

Solomon Lake (10 acres)

This northeast Boundary County cold-water lake provides fishing for legal-size hatchery rainbow trout in the Kaniksu National Forest. There are no facilities. Elev.: 3,358 feet.

Bloom Lake (20 acres)

This cold-water lake east of McArthur Lake is located within the Kaniksu National Forest on private land, but public access is currently allowed. The lake is stocked with put-and-take rainbow trout and holds pumpkinseed and bluegill. There are no facilities. Elev.: 2,988 feet.

Sinclair Lake FFW (three acres)

This is a cold-water lake near Eastport, stocked for year-round fishing with catchable rainbow trout. There are motor restrictions on this tiny lake in the Kaniksu National Forest. Elev.: 2,540 feet.

Alpine Lakes

There are approximately 20 fishable alpine lakes in the Kootenai River drainage totaling 260 acres of water. These lakes are stocked to provide fishing consistent with fish capacity and angling pressure.

Westslope cutthroat are used exclusively for cutthroat stocking. Some lakes are reserved for grayling and golden trout. Rainbow trout are stocked in some lakes while lakes with naturally reproducing brook trout populations are not stocked.

The Pend Oreille River Drainage

Lake Pend Oreille, Idaho's largest natural lake, lies at the heart of the Pend Oreille drainage, which encompasses 24,000 square miles in Idaho and Montana. The lake itself is 43 miles long with 111 miles of shoreline and with a depth of 1,152 feet it is the fifth deepest in the nation.

The Kalispell Indians lived in the region and as late as the 1930s Sandpoint was the site of a gathering of Kalispell, Kootenai and other tribes where they held horse races, played traditional games and kept their culture alive.

During World War II more than 300,000 enlisted men passed through the Farragut Naval Training Station at Bayview. The Navy continues to perform tests at the station at Bayview at the tip of the lake's southern arm.

Several species have been introduced to the drainage over the years, including Lake Superior whitefish, tiger muskie, channel catfish, lake, brook, brown and kamloops rainbow trout and kokanee salmon. Both channel catfish and tiger muskie are hatchery-supported fisheries. Several species are the result of unintentional introductions from Montana including kokanee, smallmouth bass, northern pike and walleye.

At the same time, some of the native species have been dwindling. Population growth, urban development and man's historic impact on the land, all upsetting to the natural balance of wild habitat, have had some negative impact.

Cutthroat numbers have declined, especially populations that spend their adult life in Lake Pend Oreille. Bull trout were listed as threatened under the Endangered Species Act in 1998, but Lake Pend Oreille's bull trout population is considered stable. Several significant efforts are underway to increase bull trout numbers in Lake Pend Oreille.

There are more than 14 kinds of game fish to be found in the Pend Oreille drainage. Its hundreds of miles of streams and rivers and thousands of acres of lakes, ponds and reservoirs offer some unique fishing opportunities.

In the 1960s, mysis shrimp were introduced into Priest Lake as a food source for kokanee. The initial effect was positive and several record-size fish were taken from Priest Lake in the 1970s. The shrimp also proved to be an excellent food for the lake trout, spurring an increase in the number of small mackinaws. Because of the collapse of the kokanee population in 1975 the Priest Lake fishery is now dominated by lake trout.

The kokanee population in Lake Pend Oreille also has declined, but for different reasons. Deeper winter drawdowns to enhance hydropower generation downstream in the Pend Oreille and Columbia rivers nearly eliminated shoreline spawning beds for wild kokanee. A depressed kokanee population was vulnerable to increased predation by rainbow, lake and bull trout and significant fishing regulation changes were made in 2000 to reduce the predator population and protect kokanee spawners.

Harvest levels for kokanee have dropped from around 1,000,000 annually during the 1940s through the mid 1960s to a complete closure in 2000. The kokanee are a food source for trophy rainbow and bull trout. Fortunately, kokanee numbers were rebounding in 2004.

Rivers, Lakes and other Waters

Lake Pend Oreille (94,000 acres)

Lake Pend Oreille is fed by more than 200 miles of tributary streams, a shoreline of nearly 111 miles and a maximum depth of 1,152 feet. Rainbow trout are managed to produce trophy fish and are maintained with special regulations.

Lake Superior whitefish were successfully introduced in 1889. In the early 1900s, eastern brook trout were planted there as well, and are now present in some of the watershed's tributaries. Following that success, lake trout were planted in the 1920s, but made no real impact on its sport fishing until the 1990s. Kokanee salmon that had been planted in Montana's Flathead Lake in 1916 migrated to the lake during the winter flood of 1933.

Today, Lake Pend Oreille is one of the most important fisheries in the U.S., and its trophy fish attract anglers from around the world. Two world-record fish have been taken from the lake—a Gerrard rainbow trout in 1947 (kamloops), weighing in at 37 pounds and a bull trout taken in 1949 that weighed 32 pounds. The lake produces some kamloops rainbows in the 20-pound range and some large lake trout as well.

Pend Oreille cutthroat trout are managed as quality species with restrictive regulations. Lake trout are managed with no limit and a commercial rod-and-reel fishery to maintain their abundance at a low level to minimize their impact on more desirable species. Kokanee salmon historically provided a yield fishery and will again as recovery progresses. Lake Superior whitefish are numerous, but very few anglers know how to catch these tasty fish.

Some tributaries provide limited fishing for smaller wild rainbows and cutthroat trout. Largemouth and smallmouth bass, crappie, yellow perch and northern pike are all found in the warm-water regions of the lake. Walleye are now increasing in abundance in both the Clark Fork River and the bays of Lake Pend Oreille.

Pend Oreille River

There are 23 miles of flowing river and 760 surface acres of water in this mixed, though insignificant, fishery. Annual water level fluctuations of more than 11 feet create a warm, slack water reservoir in the summer and a cold flowing river in winter. Species found in the river include rainbow, brown and cutthroat trout, largemouth and smallmouth bass, crappie, perch, pumpkinseed, bluegill and bullhead.

Hoodoo Creek

Hoodoo Creek features 11 miles of trout water with brook, brown, cutthroat and rainbow trout. The creek feeds and empties Hoodoo Lake and there are no facilities.

Clark Fork River

There are 11 miles of this river in Idaho in the Kaniksu National Forest. Bull trout and kokanee are managed with conservation regulations. Cutthroat trout are managed with Quality/Wild management rules and rainbow trout are a trophy species. Brown trout, mountain whitefish and walleye are managed with general regulations. Brown trout are in the river above Railroad Bridge.

Antelope Lake (10 acres)

This body of water near the Clark Fork River in the eastern Panhandle is stocked with cutthroat and rainbow trout.

Priest Lake (23,360 acres)

Priest and Upper Priest lakes formed after the last ice age and they are connected by a shallow, winding channel called the Thoroughfare; a narrow waterway two-and-a-half miles long. The channel meanders through some of the area's most spectacular forestland. The entire length is protected from human development as it lies within the boundaries of the Upper Priest Lake Scenic Area.

Priest Lake is popular with anglers seeking mackinaw (lake trout) although the average size of the fish is about 20 inches. Its maximum depths is 369 feet with an average depth of 123 feet. It is a cold-water fishery with more than 100 miles of tributary water. Cutthroat trout and kokanee are protected by catch-and-release regulations and some tributary closures. Anglers are encouraged to fish for resident cutthroat stocks above some of the natural barriers (waterfalls) rather than for the more sensitive lake-run fish. The lake-run fish produce future generations for the lake. Bull trout are present and protected and there are resident wild trout in the reaches above the falls. Elev.: 2,434 feet

Upper Priest Lake (1,400 acres)

Upper Priest Lake can only be reached by boat or foot trail. Its maximum depth is about 100 feet. Cutthroat and bull trout and kokanee must be released immediately.

There are more than 50 miles of tributary water in this cold-water fishery. Upper Priest River and its tributary streams, as well as Upper Priest Lake, are managed with catch-and-release regulations to help maintain wild native species. There are kokanee salmon, but not in significant numbers. Lake trout are present and harvest is allowed, but anglers are not allowed to use live bait. Elev.: 2,435 feet.

Priest River

There are more than 120 miles of river, including tributary water. The main river is too warm in the summer to support a good trout fishery, but mountain whitefish are numerous. Many tributary streams are dominated by brook trout. The entire Priest River drainage is managed with a slot limit on cutthroat that limits harvest to two fish, with no cutthroat allowed between eight and 16 inches. Some brown trout are found in the drainage.

Granite, Kalispell, Lion, Two Mouth, Beaver and Indian creeks

All tributaries to Priest Lake are managed to allow harvest of brook trout, but cutthroat trout, bull trout and kokanee are protected from harvest with catch-and-release regulations.

East River, North and Middle Forks East River

A tributary system to the Priest River below Priest Lake that is home to a unique population of bull trout that spend their adult life in Lake

Pend Oreille. Brook trout are present in beaver ponds lower in the drainage, but anglers should be aware that bull trout may be present and no harvest of bull trout is allowed.

Chase Lake (125 acres)

This is a mid-sized, warm-water fishery south of Priest Lake in the Kaniksu National Forest with special largemouth bass regulations. Catch-and-release for bass from January 1 through July 1. After July 1, there is a slot limit where no fish between 12 and 16 inches can be kept. There is a two-fish limit. Perch and pumpkinseed also are present. Elev.: 2,500 feet.

Blue Lake (120 acre)

This Bonner County warm-water lake west of Sandpoint is stocked with tiger muskie. Other species include largemouth bass, northern pike, crappie, perch, bluegill, bullhead catfish and pumpkinseed. Electric motors only. Elev.: 3,414 feet.

Freeman Lake (30 acres)

A mixed fishery with put-and-take rainbow trout and largemouth bass, bullhead and channel catfish, crappie, perch, pumpkinseed and tiger muskie. There is a 40-inch minimum on tiger muskie.

Jewel Lake FFW (35 acre)

This medium sized fishery west of Cocolalla Lake is stocked with channel catfish and catchable rainbow trout and has a naturally reproducing population of yellow perch and bluegill. Elev.: 2,476 feet.

Mirror Lake (90 acres)

This medium-sized lake east of Cocolalla Lake is stocked with rainbow trout and kokanee fry. Elev.: 2,369 feet.

Kelso Lake FFW (60 acres)

A put-and-take, stocked rainbow trout lake west of Bayview near Lake Pend Oreille. Warm-water species include largemouth bass, bluegill, bullhead, black crappie, yellow perch and pumpkinseed. Elev.: 2,152 feet.

Little Round Lake (10 acres)

A warm-water fishery near Kelso Lake with largemouth bass, bluegill, bullhead catfish, crappie, perch and pumpkinseed. Any size may be kept. Electric motors only.

Granite Lake FFW (20 acres)

A small, warm-water fishery managed for largemouth bass, crappie, perch, bluegill and bullhead catfish. Elev.: 2,148 feet.

Round Lake FFW (120 acres)

This Bonner County lake is located in Round Lake State Park. Catchable rainbow trout are stocked, with brook trout present. Other species include crappie, perch, bullhead catfish and pumpkinseed. The state park does not allow motors of any kind. Elev.: 2,123 feet.

Cocolalla Lake (800 acres)

This big Panhandle lake is a mixed fishery with cold-water species that include rainbow, brown and cutthroat trout. Fingerling cutthroat and rainbow trout are stocked. Located just off U.S. Highway 95, about 10 miles south of Sandpoint, it is an easy-to-get-to, year-round fishery. Most access sites are on the northeast shore. Private ownership limits other access.

This lake is unique in that it also holds a wide variety of warm-water fish. Channel catfish are the real prize with very good population developing after a IDF&G stocking program. There are official reports of 11-pound cats with some unofficial reports going even higher. In the winter, perch take center stage as ice fishing becomes the obvious method. According to officials, Cocolalla usually provides a long winter fishery. Check with local sport shops. Other warm-water species include largemouth bass, bullhead, crappie and pumpkinseed. Elev.: 2,198 feet.

Cocolalla Creek

A small, cold-water tributary to Cocolalla Lake with rainbow, brook, brown and cutthroat trout.

Shepherd Lake (120 acres)

This lake southeast of Sagle has largemouth bass, crappie, perch, bluegill, bullhead catfish and pumpkin-seed with a limited trophy tiger muskie population. Elev.: 2,289 feet.

Gamble (Gamlin) Lake (130 acres)

This lake, west of the locale of Glengary, is a warm-water fishery with general fishing regulations for largemouth bass, bullhead catfish, crappie, pumpkin seed and perch. There are no facilities. Elev.: 2,087 feet.

Spirit Lake (1,477 acres)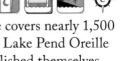

South of Priest Lake in Kootenai County, this lake covers nearly 1,500 acres with a maximum depth of 90 feet. Kokanee from Lake Pend Oreille were planted in the lake in the 1940s and quickly established themselves as the most popular kokanee fishery in Idaho with the largest harvest, per acre, of any lake in the state. The kokanee fishery is maintained with wild shoreline spawners and supplementation with up to 200,000 hatchery fry annually.

Along with high yields of kokanee salmon, Spirit Lake is also stocked with cutthroat trout fingerlings. There are largemouth bass, crappie, perch, bullhead catfish, northern pike, bluegill, pumpkinseed and brook trout. Elev.: 2,448 feet.

Stoneridge (Blanchard) Reservoir (80 acres)

This mid-sized mixed fishery north of Spirit Lake has brook and stocked rainbow trout and bullhead catfish. There are no facilities.

Alpine Lakes

The region's mountain lakes are individually stocked to match the fishing pressure. Westslope cutthroat are the only cutthroat used in the stocking program. Some lakes are reserved for grayling and golden trout. Rainbow and brook trout are also stocked on an as-needed basis. Consult with Fish and Game for information on specific lakes.

The Spokane River Drainage

Lake Coeur d'Alene is the centerpiece of the Spokane River drainage, which draws water from 4,000 square miles of territory at the southern end of the Panhandle Region. Nearly every type of fish available to Idaho anglers can be found here and many of its most popular sites are within short driving distances of the area's larger towns.

Native species in these waters include westslope cutthroat, bull trout and mountain whitefish. Non-native cold-water species thriving here include rainbow trout and kokanee and chinook salmon. Non-native warm-water species include largemouth and smallmouth bass, pumpkinseed, bluegill, sunfish, perch, crappie, bullhead, channel catfish, tiger muskie and northern pike. Many lakes in the drainage area, because of their generally excellent bass populations, are chosen as tournament sites each year.

Like other drainages, the Spokane River has been affected by population expansion and industrial growth. A wide range of developments all have taken a toll, to one degree or another. Cutthroat trout have been the hardest hit, but special regulations throughout the drainage are helping stabilize and improve the situation. Historically, the St. Joe and Coeur d'Alene rivers have been considered to be among the finest trout streams in America.

Rivers, Lakes and other Waters

Lake Coeur d'Alene (31,400 acres)

There are more than 100 miles of tributary streams flowing into Lake Coeur d'Alene, special regulations for the lake and selected streams are improving westslope cutthroat trout populations here.

In the 1960s and 70s, the lake's kokanee salmon population was producing harvests numbering in the hundreds of thousands, topped in 1979 by a count of 600,000 fish. By 1981, kokanee numbers exceeded the lake's carrying capacity and fish size became unacceptably small. Fall chinook salmon were planted in the lake in 1982 to control the kokanee population and the program worked. The chinook are now controlling the kokanee and reproducing there as well. The result: a very popular chinook and kokanee fishery.

The management plan for chinook salmon is geared first and foremost toward maintaining a kokanee yield at a desirable level. Kokanee support the bulk of the fishery in Lake Coeur d'Alene as well as provide the forage to maintain a popular trophy chinook fishery. Kokanee size is directly influenced by their abundance. Chinook management also is geared toward providing more chinook between three and 18 pounds, rather than fish that weigh more than 25 pounds. Chinook anglers enjoy higher catch rates for decent size fish rather than an occasional trophy fish.

Northern pike are managed with liberal seasons and limits to maintain low-density pike populations. Northern pike in the Coeur d'Alene system show some of the higher growth rates of anywhere in the world and six-year-old fish can reach 20 pounds. Low pike populations maintain a desirable growth rate in pike while reducing predation on other important species such as westslope cutthroat trout and largemouth bass.

Other species include bull trout, crappie, perch, bullhead, and pumpkinseed. Smallmouth bass were illegally introduced into the system in the 1990s and are now established throughout the lake. Brook and rainbow trout are insignificant. Elev.: 2,133 feet.

Hayden Lake (3,700 acres)

There are more than 20 miles of closed tributary streams flowing into this quality trout fishery with populations of rainbow, cutthroat trout and splake. Tributary streams are closed to help wild trout re-establish populations in the lake. Hatchery fish are added to supplement the established populations of rainbow and cutthroat trout. Stocked splake are present in low numbers.

Available fish include perch, bullhead, pumpkinseed and northern pike. Hayden Lake is a quality fishery for bass and crappie where anglers can expect to catch larger-than-average fish. It is also a popular ice fishery. Elev.: 2,224 feet.

Upper & Lower Twin Lakes (850 acres)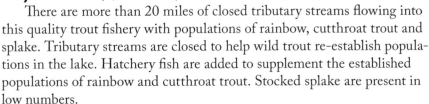

These mixed fisheries are stocked with catchable rainbow trout with cutthroat trout and kokanee in the lower lake. Warm-water species include largemouth bass, crappie, perch, pumpkinseed, sunfish, northern pike and bullhead catfish. Kokanee salmon fry are stocked annually in the lower lake only. Elev.: 2,244 feet

Fernan Lake FFW (300 acres)

Located east of Coeur d'Alene, Fernan Lake is one of the best urban fisheries in the state. Approximately 23,000 fish are harvested each year by shoreline and boat anglers. A mixed fishery, Fernan Lake is stocked with catchable rainbow trout and fingerling cutthroat. Brook trout are present at the mouth of Fernan Creek.

Warm-water species include largemouth and smallmouth bass, northern pike, crappie, perch, pumpkinseed, bullhead and channel catfish. The lake is also an excellent location for ice fishing for perch and trout. Elev.: 2,133 feet.

Hauser Lake (550 acres)

This lake near the Washington border is stocked with catchable rainbow trout, fingerling cutthroat trout as well as kokanee fry. Along with largemouth bass, crappie, perch, pumpkinseed, sunfish, bullhead catfish and northern pike. Stocked channel catfish and tiger muskie are also present. There is a 40-inch size limit on tiger muskie and Hauser Lake had produced all of the state record tiger muskie through 2002. Elev.: 2,195 feet.

Chatcolet Lake (600 acres)

This large, warm-water lake south of Lake Coeur d'Alene has largemouth and smallmouth bass, bullhead, crappie, perch, pumpkinseed and northern pike. Within the Coeur d'Alene Indian Reservation a tribal fishing license is required. Elev.: 2,131 feet.

Benewah Lake (400 acres)

Another warm-water lake in the region south of Coeur d'Alene Lake, with largemouth and smallmouth bass, bullhead catfish, crappie, perch, pumpkinseed and northern pike. Elev.: 2,126 feet.

Round Lake (400 acres)

This warm-water lake in Benewah County lies at the southern end of Coeur d'Alene Lake and has largemouth and smallmouth bass, bullhead catfish, crappie, perch, pumpkinseed and northern pike. Elev.: 2,131 feet.

Coeur d'Alene River

One of America's prime trout waters, the Coeur d'Alene River can be divided into three areas. In the two upper reaches, which include the Little

North Fork above Laverne Creek and the North Fork above Yellow Dog Creek, it is catch-and-release fishing, including the tributary waters. The major species is westslope cutthroat trout.

The rest of the drainage is managed for wild westslope cutthroat trout, but limited harvest is allowed outside the protected slot limit area (see fishing regulations). All hatchery stocking of rainbow trout was discontinued in 2003 to reduce impacts on

native species. Some wild rainbow are still found in the lower section of the North Fork Coeur d'Alene River. Brook trout are found in tributary streams, but they are not numerous or widespread. Mountain whitefish are fairly numerous, especially in the lower portion of the drainage where larger, deeper holes are present.

Harvest fisheries for hatchery rainbow trout are now provided in catch-out ponds located along the river like Steamboat Pond, Clee Creek Pond and Day Rock Pond. Elsie and Glidden lakes are also drive-to mountain lakes that offer harvest fishing for hatchery rainbow trout and wild brook trout. All of these waters are managed as FF waters.

Lateral Lakes:

These lakes are year-round fisheries for warm-water fish. Except for Rose and Bull Run lakes, all the lateral lakes are connected to the Coeur d'Alene River by channels.

Anderson and Blue lakes have restrictive regulations to help the largemouth bass population. Northern pike are managed with liberal limits and a year-round season to keep their numbers low. Low populations of northern pike maintain high pike growth rates and reduce the number of bass and cutthroat trout lost to the pike.

Blue Lake is a trophy bass fishery. Anderson Lake is a quality bass fishery. Rose Lake has bluegill but no northern pike and is stocked with channel catfish. Other species in this chain of lakes include perch, bullhead, crappie and pumpkinseed. Be sure to check the IDF&G Regulations. Average elevation is around 2,129 feet.

Anderson (720 acres)

Thompson (200 acres)

Blue (200 acres)

Swan (200 acres)

Medicine (340 acres)

Cave (700 acres)

Killarney (500 acres)

Black (400 acres)

Rose (300 acres)

Bull Run (100 acres)

Day Rock Pond FFW (one acre)

This small, cold-water pond is stocked with rainbow trout.

Elsie Lake FFW (eight acres)

Another small, drive-to mountain lake, south of Kellogg, with stocked rainbow trout and brook trout. Elev.: 5,096 feet.

St. Joe River

This river is considered to be one of the finest trout streams in America. The slack water area of the St. Joe River, below the town of St. Maries, is a mixed fishery with largemouth bass, crappie, perch, bullhead, channel catfish and cutthroat trout. See *Idaho's Big 10* page 32.

Below Avery, there are 78 miles of cold-water fishery managed for a limited harvest fishery for cutthroat trout with a slot limit. Stocking of hatchery rainbows was discontinued in 2003 and wild rainbow trout are rare. Mountain whitefish are common and anglers may encounter the occasional bull trout which must be released immediately.

Above Avery, the North Fork of the St. Joe and Marble Creek are all managed for wild cutthroat trout. Brook trout are present in a few tributary stream and harvest is allowed on brook trout.

There are about 35 river miles of the St. Joe above Prospector Creek with cutthroat trout and mountain whitefish.

Marble Creek

This is a cold-water tributary to the St. Joe River west of Avery, supporting cutthroat trout. It enters the St. Joe from the south.

Dismal Lake (eight acres)

This small, drive-to mountain lake in the St. Joe National Forest is stocked with catchable rainbow trout and has a developing grayling program. Elev.: 5,343 feet.

Big Creek

A tributary to the St. Joe River west of Marble Creek, with cutthroat trout. It enters the St. Joe River from the north.

St. Maries River

The upper portion of the river supports cutthroat trout and mountain whitefish. The slack water of the river is a mixed fishery with largemouth bass, crappie, perch, bullhead catfish and cutthroat trout. Tributary waters are cold-water fisheries with cutthroat and brook trout.

Spokane River

An urban trout fishery, the Spokane River has only a short run within the state, but it is the only outlet for Lake Coeur d'Alene. From Lake Coeur d'Alene to the Post Falls Dam, there are 10 miles of river that is basically a reservoir with Coeur d'Alene Lake fish present. Common species include cutthroat trout, largemouth bass, crappie, perch, bullhead catfish and pumpkinseed. From the Post Falls Dam downstream to the Washington state line, it's six miles of wild rainbow trout and brown trout water, managed under Wild Trout regulations with a special season. Check your regulations.

Alpine Lakes

There are eight managed alpine lakes in the Spokane drainage that cover more than 140 surface acres of water. The lakes are stocked with trout fry on a two-year rotation. Only westslope cutthroat trout are used in cutthroat lakes. Some lakes are reserved for Arctic grayling and golden trout. Rainbow trout are stocked in some lakes and lakes with reproducing brook trout are not stocked.

Airstrips

Cavanaugh Bay (state)

This public airstrip is located on the eastern side of the southern portion of Priest Lake, about three miles north of the town of Coolin. The airstrip is grass at an elevation of approximately 2,484 feet. There are some obstructions on approach. The airport has a caretaker, usually from May through mid September. No winter maintenance and heavy snowmobile use during the winter. The strip is 3,100 feet long and 120 feet wide.

Magee (state)

Located in the Coeur d'Alene National Forest near the Magee Ranger Station and the Trail Creek Work Center, this public strip is 2,450 feet long and 150 feet wide. Beaver activity sometimes floods the area. Trail Creek and Teepee Creek are nearby.

Priest Lake (state)

This grass airstrip is located two miles west of Kalispell Bay on the west side of Priest Lake. It is 2,950 feet long and 175 feet wide. Camping sites are nearby.

Porthill (state)

The state's northernmost airstrip located east of the Kootenai River is also known as Eckhart International Airport. The strip is 3,650 feet long and 175 feet wide at an elevation of 1,756 feet.

LEARNING TO FISH WITH A FLY

There are as many ways to learn fly fishing as there are anglers on the water. The best way is to get in the water, cast some line, snag a tree branch, impale yourself with a hook, slip on the rocks, fill your waders with water, then try not to repeat your errors.

The ability to read the water or send a size-20 blue-winged olive forty feet to a feeding fish doesn't develop overnight and it doesn't take a lifetime either. It does, however, take a certain mentality.

Writer and artist Russell Chatham wrote in the preface of his book, **Dark Waters**, "With the exception of painting, nothing in my life has held my interest as much as fishing. Fishing with a fly, a bait, a hand line; I don't much care. Fishing, in my estimation, is not a hobby, a diversion, a pastime, a sport, an interest, a challenge or an escape. Like painting, it is a necessary passion."

My father holds such a passion. When I was a boy he put a fly rod in my hand and explained the balance and dynamics that go into casting a fly. My first attempts seemed pitiful and worthless. I gave up too soon and continued to fish with spinners and bait. If I only knew then what I know now.

When I was twenty-four my father and I went to my grandpa's fishing shack on the Au Sable River near Glennie, Michigan. We drove to a favorite fishing spot in the Huron National Forest and started fishing late one soggy afternoon. I worked downstream with some Panther Martin and Mepps spinners while my father worked a few of his favorite holes. As it grew dark I thought of leaving the water.

The sky was thick with fog moving silently and slowly through the treetops. The roiling water took on an oily sheen yet the woods seemed vibrant and alive. I stopped fishing and had the feeling that I should turn around and leave, but I didn't.

At the base of a steep, rock-strewn bank I watched my father weave an intricate pattern of line and fly in the misty air. The sky grew heavy and the pines on the high bank of the far shore faded into one deep mysterious backdrop.

My father stayed at his one position in the stream and worked the hole for half an hour as I sat on the sandy bank fifty yards away, waiting for the serious rain. Watching him cast through the mist, I realized it wasn't just the fly rod, but also a centered and powerful concentration that drove the fly through the air to a gentle landing on the holy waters of the Au Sable.

I watched as he caught three fish. When it grew too dark to even imagine where his fly might be on the water we went back to the shack for some whiskey and burgers.

During the next few years I picked up a fly rod occasionally, but never with the passion it deserved or needed. I became reacquainted with fly fishing on a trip to Livingston, Montana, but my attempts at landing a trout with a fly on the

Yellowstone River were as unproductive as my attempts on the Au Sable had been.

I learned two very important lessons in fly fishing on that trip: Fish with someone who is better than you and don't get discouraged.

Somehow through my travels I landed in Idaho and had the good fortune to meet four anglers who were willing to share some of their secrets. John C. straightened out my cast and bestowed a double haul upon me. "A double haul is a very unnecessary cast," he said on the front lawn of his house during one of our informal casting lessons, "but a one-iron is a very unnecessary golf club and every golfer worth his salt has one in his bag."

Pat R. who works at a local newspaper showed me that fishing is just a matter of driving to a river and getting in. Dan E., a trout bum from the banks of Silver Creek and the Wood River country, grew up in Hailey, Idaho and was chased by a Brahma bull while trespassing on private property at Kilpatrick Bridge. (He made it to the river after a 100-yard sprint while strapped into his float tube. He still carries a few scars but he hasn't trespassed since.) Dan showed me that fishing can be hazardous to your health.

And then there is ol' Doc Peterson. He is in his seventies, blind in one eye, deaf in one ear and beset by an arthritic shoulder that limits his casting. He's hunted and fished most of his life and was a professional guide in Wyoming. He ties his own flies and builds his rods and gets around on a river like a mountain goat on a steep slope. What's more, when the fishing is slow and most people are opting for naps or waiting for the next hatch, he's catching fish.

Together, with my father, these four people have taught me more than any book or video. They took the time to share some of their secrets and opened my eyes to new ideas. They also possess the passion that Chatham deems necessary in such a personal activity. And in fishing, as in any other enterprise in life, there is no substitute for passion.

Joe Evancho

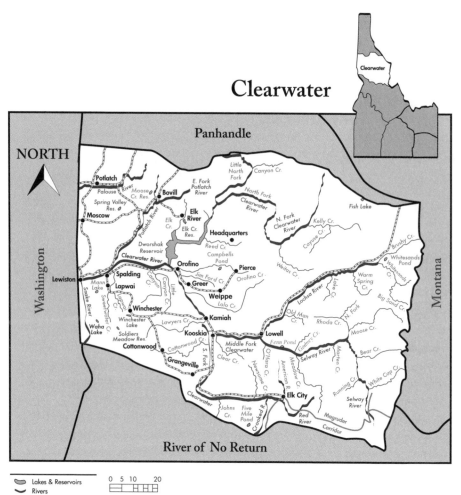

Clearwater

Clearwater

The Clearwater Region is one of the most productive fishing areas in the state, boasting more than a dozen species of game fish. It is also one of the most primitive. Lewis and Clark traveled through this area on their Voyage of Discovery and much of the land remains nearly as primitive today as it was in the early 1800s.

The major drainage is the Clearwater River and it drains an area of 25,000 square miles from the northeast corner of the region, near the Montana border, south to the north side of the Salmon River in the Frank Church River of No Return Wilderness area. The region also includes part of the Snake River downstream of Hells Canyon Dam and the Salmon River downstream of Riggins. For most of the way across the interior of the state, the north shore of the Main Salmon River acts as the region's southern boundary.

There are several world-famous trout streams in the Clearwater Region. North Fork Clearwater, Kelly Creek and the Lochsa and Selway rivers are spread across this wilderness drainage with their headwaters high in the forestlands of the Bitterroot Mountains. These streams alone would make a trip to the region worthwhile.

Part of the Selway, and bits and pieces of the Lochsa and South Fork Clearwater rivers, run through rugged areas. The Lochsa and the Selway meet near Lowell and they form the Middle Fork of the Clearwater River and are part of the National Wild and Scenic River System. There are still some areas here where man has had little impact. Some roadless areas, though exceedingly rugged, are not designated wilderness.

But progress has taken its toll, even in the Clearwater Region. The building of the Dworshak (Northfork Clearwater River) and Hells Canyon (Snake River) dams eliminated natural production of steelhead and salmon above these dams as they have no fish-passage capacity. The Salmon and Snake river sections in the Clearwater Region are migration corridors for chinook salmon and steelhead spawners. Other dams on the Columbia and Snake rivers have had negative impacts on the fishery to the extent that these fisheries are maintained with an aggressive stocking program to supplement returning wild fish. Still, anadromous fisheries in the Clearwater Region will require maintaining naturally spawning fish and preservation of spawning habitat.

Other native species found in this region include rainbow, cutthroat and bull trout and mountain whitefish. There are approximately 708 mountain lakes in the region of which, for a variety of reasons, 452 are fish-less. That leaves 256 mountain lakes with fish. Of these, 172 lakes that have populations of introduced species that are not currently being stocked. These lakes have fish that were planted in 1930s, '40s and '50s. Of these 172 lakes, 129 were stocked with western trout species and 43 were stocked with eastern brook trout. Seventy-three lakes are stocked on a rotating basis (three-year cycle) to maintain fish populations. There are 11 with naturally occurring populations of native species.

So whatever your choice, from spin-casting for bass, dock-fishing for bluegill with a bobber and worm, fly-fishing for trout or salmon, or hiking to a high mountain lake, there is something for you in the Clearwater Region.

The Palouse River Drainage

The Palouse River drainage is the smallest in the state, carrying runoff from mountain woodlands and rolling farm country to the Idaho-Washington border. It drains from elevations of 5,000 feet.

Its upper reaches have been impacted by road building, logging and mining. The lower areas are heavily farmed. The highest quality remaining trout habitat is found near the Palouse River headwaters.

Some trout ponds have been developed in reclaimed mining areas.

Rivers, Lakes and other Waters

The Palouse River FFW

From the Washington border to its headwaters in the St. Joe National Forest, including tributaries, there are 70 miles of Palouse River in the state. Closer to the Washington border, it is a mixed fishery, stocked with catchable rainbow trout. Other species include brook trout and smallmouth bass.

Upstream, the water is prone to low levels late in the season. The upstream waters are also the most pristine in the drainage, with numerous area campsites. Catchable rainbow trout are stocked in the Laird Park area in the spring. Laird Park has large camping (28 sites) and picnic areas and it is located on the upper reaches of the Palouse River.

Clearwater River Drainage

The area along the Clearwater River was originally inhabited by various bands of Nez Perce along the western edge of what is now Clearwater County in central Idaho. Hunting and fishing parties traveled in and out of the area while others would travel to prairies and meadows above the river to gather roots and berries.

From its headwaters in the mountains of the Bitterroot Range on the Idaho-Montana border, the Clearwater River runs west across the state to Lewiston where it joins the Snake River. Starting at an elevation of almost 9,000 feet, the river drops to just more than 700 feet above sea level as it drains an area of approximately 9,640 square miles. Its major tributaries are the Lochsa and Selway rivers and the South and North forks of the Clearwater River.

There are several famous trout streams in the region. The North Fork of the Clearwater River and its main tributary, Kelly Creek, and the Lochsa and Selway rivers flow clean and clear from the eastern region, which is primarily national forestland. Most of the western half of the drainage is private with large corporate timber holdings and agricultural ground. There are 63 miles of the main Clearwater and 11 miles of the South Fork within the boundaries of the Nez Perce Reservation land.

Rivers, Lakes and other Waters

Clearwater River

From its mouth in Lewiston, past the South Fork of the Clearwater at Clear Creek near Kooskia, this 75-mile stretch of river is managed to maintain a variety of fishing opportunities. No fishing is allowed on the perimeter of the Dworshak National Fish Hatchery near Ahsahka.

It is catch-and-release fishing for steelhead from July 1 through the harvest season opener (check IDF&G regulations), after which you can keep hatchery steelhead—returning fish that are missing their adipose fin. From 2001 through 2003 the river saw near record returns of steelhead and chinook salmon.

Other species include rainbow, cutthroat and bull trout, mountain whitefish and smallmouth bass. Be sure to check the most current Idaho Fish and Game regulations for salmon and steelhead restrictions. See *Idaho's Big 10* page 37.

Winchester (Lapwai) Lake (85 acres)

Located southeast of Lewiston this popular local fishery in Winchester Lake State Park is stocked with fingerling and catchable rainbow trout. Other species include largemouth bass (generally five to 12 inches) bullheads and channel catfish, tiger muskie, crappie and yellow perch. This is a very popular fishery for bank anglers, float tubers and ice fishing. Elev.: 3,906 feet.

Spring Valley Reservoir FFW (53 acres)

Three miles east of Troy, this reservoir is stocked with catchable and fingerling rainbow trout. There are also largemouth bass, tiger muskie, crappie and bluegill. This is a family fishing area. Elev.: 2,780 feet.

Mann Lake (145 acres)

This lake on the Nez Perce Reservation is stocked with catchable and fingerling rainbow trout and is managed by the Lewiston Orchards Irrigation District. Other species include rainbow trout, largemouth bass, crappie, channel catfish and bluegill. Elev.: 1,801 feet.

Waha Lake (94 acres)

This mixed fishery located northwest of Soldiers Meadow Reservoir in Nez Perce County is stocked with kokanee and rainbow trout. It also holds smallmouth bass, splake, crappie and perch. Elev.: 3,389 feet.

Soldiers Meadow Reservoir FFW (101 acres)

This reservoir southeast of Waha Lake in Lewis County is stocked with catchable and fingerling rainbow trout and kokanee salmon. This reservoir is the uppermost in the Lewiston Orchards Irrigation District and in the summer low water levels make the boat ramp inaccessible. Elev.: 4,557 feet.

Moose Creek Reservoir (50 acres)

This lowland reservoir west of Bovill is stocked with catchable rainbow trout and managed as a trophy largemouth bass fishery so check current IDF&G regulations for size and bag limits. Other species include bluegill, crappie and pumpkinseed. Elev.: 3,033 feet.

Campbell's Pond FFW (seven acres)

Located approximately six miles west of Pierce, this put-and-take pond is stocked with catchable rainbow trout, bluegill and pumpkinseed.

Robinson's Pond (two acres)

It is catch-and-release for bass from January 1 through July 1. After

July 1 there is a slot limit where no fish between 12 and 16 inches can be kept. There is a two-fish limit.

Fred Warren Pond (quarter acre)

This pond north of Lewiston is designated as a kids' fishing site for kids 14 years old and younger and is wheelchair accessible. This pond is stocked with catchable rainbow trout.

Deer Creek Reservoir (86 acres)

This newly developed reservoir was built on Potlatch land and is located 14 miles from Pierce. It is a day-use fishery and stocked with cutthroat and rainbow trout.

White Sands Pond (three acres)

This pond next to the Lochsa River near the Powell ranger station is stocked with catchable rainbow trout and offers good fishing near Brushy and Crooked Fork creeks. Elev.: 3,420 feet

Potlatch River

The Potlatch has both anadromous and general fish populations with brook and stocked rainbow trout. It is also a warm-water fishery with smallmouth bass and closed to harvest of adult steelhead and salmon.

East Fork Potlatch River

This eighteen-mile stretch of river is a cold-water fishery with a bonus brook trout limit of 25. It is managed as Wild Trout water for steelhead.

Lolo Creek

Stocked with steelhead fry smolts and adult surplus from Dworshak to help sustain populations, this stream is a cold-water fishery with rainbow, cutthroat and brook trout, mountain whitefish, steelhead and chinook salmon. Closed to harvest of adult salmon and steelhead.

Other Main Stem Tributaries

These tributaries are managed to improve present habitat for steelhead and rainbow trout with no stocking. Bull trout are present and protected.

Middle Fork Clearwater River

The Middle Fork of the Clearwater River begins at the Selway/Lochsa confluence, near Lowell.

Harvesting of hatchery steelhead is allowed up to the mouth of Clear Creek near Kooskia. Beyond that there are 23 miles of river up to the confluence of the Lochsa and Selway. Other species include chinook salmon, rainbow, cutthroat and bull trout and mountain whitefish. Bull trout and chinook salmon are protected.

Clear Creek

This creek enters the Middle Fork of the Clearwater River east of Kooskia and is the upstream boundary for steelhead fishing on the Middle Fork of the Clearwater. Species include chinook salmon, steelhead and bull trout which cannot be harvested. Other species include rainbow and cutthroat trout. Chinook and steelhead are released above the Clear Creek weir for natural reproduction so this area is closed to harvest.

Lochsa River

From the mouth of the Lochsa River to Wilderness Gateway bridge, there are 27 miles of river of Quality Trout water, including tributaries. This number can be misleading as many of the tributary streams are too small to fish, yet provide good to excellent habitat for various species.

Upstream from the Wilderness Gateway Bridge, including Crooked Fork Creek above Brushy Fork, it is closed to steelhead harvest and catch-and-release rules apply. Special regulations may apply so check current Fish and Game regulations. Other species include cutthroat, bull and rainbow trout and mountain whitefish. Tributary streams do not open until July 1. See *Idaho's Big 10*, page 35.

Selway River

There is no hatchery release of steelhead in the Selway River to avoid dilution of the native gene pool in this preservation area. Chinook salmon are closed to adult harvest. Other species include rainbow and cutthroat trout and mountain whitefish. Bull trout are present and protected.

It is quality water from Meadow Creek Bridge upstream and managed as catch-and-release trout habitat. Species include cutthroat and rainbow trout and mountain whitefish.

There are special regulations for the Selway River and some tributaries. The season opens July 1, to protect spawning trout and steelhead parr. This wild trout water contains cutthroat and rainbow trout and mountain whitefish. Tributary streams do not open until July 1. See *Idaho's Big 10* page 35.

Fenn Pond FFW (one acre)

Stocked with rainbow trout, this lower Selway area pond is near Lowell.

North Fork Clearwater River (below the dam)

There are less than two miles of river from Dworshak Dam to its mouth. The area is managed to maximize return of hatchery steelhead and spring chinook. Rainbow trout, kokanee and mountain whitefish are present. Bull trout are present and protected.

Dworshak Reservoir (16,000 acres)

At 718 feet, the Dworshak dam is the largest straight axis dam in North America. From the dam at Ahsahka, west of Orofino, to Grandad Bridge, there are 41 miles of tributary water feeding this 53-mile long reservoir. The fishery is open year-round with a 25-kokanee limit per day. Kokanee salmon are the most abundant species here and the reservoir is managed to provide catchable numbers of these fish, though recent changes in water releases have resulted in more though smaller kokanee. Trolling is the most effective fishing method for kokanee here.

Catchable rainbow trout are stocked at the boat docks and shoreline structures located at strategic points in the reservoir. In 1982 a state-record 22-inch smallmouth bass weighing more than 8 pounds was caught in the reservoir. All stocked, catchable fish are sterile.

Upstream from Grandad Bridge to the end of the slack water the river is managed with general season regulations. In the fall cutthroat trout move down from the upper tributaries to spawn. Other species include bull trout, crappie and mountain whitefish.

There are isolated campsites, accessible only by boat, along the 183 miles of shoreline. You can get information on other camping and access sites at the Corps of Engineers visitor center at the dam. Elev.: 1,594 feet.

North Fork Clearwater River (above the reservoir)

Special regulations are enforced on this section of river to protect cut-throat trout. It is managed under Quality Trout rules with a two-fish daily

limit on cutthroat that must be at least 14 inches. You can only fish with artificial flies and lures with barbless hooks. No bait is allowed. Other species include cutthroat, rainbow, bull and brook trout and mountain whitefish.

Elk Creek

On this Dworshak Reservoir tributary, and its other tributary streams, anglers must include brook trout in their daily limit. Special bass limits and seasons apply. Check the current IDF&G regulations.

Elk Creek Reservoir (81 acres)

This reservoir located south of the town of Elk River holds brook and stocked rainbow trout, smallmouth and largemouth bass. Brook trout must be counted in angler's trout limit. Fed by Elk Creek from the north, the reservoir merges with the larger Dworshak Reservoir farther south. Elev.: 2,808 feet

Little North Fork Clearwater

From its mouth to Foehl Creek, this cold-water fishery is currently being managed with general stream seasons. There are about 60 miles of river and tributary streams in this section. Species include bull and rainbow trout and mountain whitefish. Bull trout are protected.

Above Foehl Creek there are wild trout with limited harvest on approximately 55 miles of river and tributaries. Species here include protected bull trout, rainbow and cutthroat trout and mountain whitefish.

Breakfast Creek

A tributary to the Little North Fork of the Clearwater River, this stream has a daily bag limit of two trout. Species present include a healthy bull trout population with westslope cutthroat and a few rainbow trout.

Weitas Creek

A tributary to the North Fork of the Clearwater River this stream has a daily bag limit of two trout. Species present include westslope cutthroat, rainbow and bull trout and mountain whitefish.

Kelly Creek

This is quality trout water managed as catch-and-release. Many areas

are roadless and because of its inaccessibility many sections of the river are of the highest quality. Important species include cutthroat, rainbow and bull trout and mountain whitefish. See *Idaho's Big 10*, page 33.

Cayuse Creek

A major tributary of Kelly Creek, this is catch-and-release water with restricted harvest rules and barbless hooks only. Check IDF&G regulations. Like Kelly Creek, much of the Cayuse Creek area is roadless and many sections of the creek are of the highest quality. Species present include cutthroat, rainbow, brook and bull trout and mountain whitefish.

South Fork of the Clearwater

The American and Red rivers meet to form the South Fork of the Clearwater just outside Elk City in the Nez Perce National Forest. The 65 miles of river from its confluence with the Middle Fork of the Clearwater near Kooskia offers mixed fishing with the primary emphasis on hatchery steelhead. There is also a large stock of mountain whitefish. Important species include steelhead, chinook salmon, rainbow, cutthroat and bull trout.

It is a very popular fishery for native cutthroat trout. General trout limits apply but there is a two-fish limit for cutthroat trout and they must be at least 14 inches. There are some mainstem spring chinook in the river from May through July and some steelhead in March and early April.

Ten Mile Creek

There are 20 miles of wild trout water flowing through roadless areas here. Steelhead and chinook use this creek west of Elk City as a spawning tributary. It is populated with wild rainbow and cutthroat trout and mountain whitefish. There are restricted harvest limits on cutthroat and rainbow trout. Bull trout are present and protected.

Crooked River

This river is a tributary to the South Fork of the Clearwater River southwest of Elk City. It is closed to fishing from the mouth to the fish weir. Five Mile Pond in the Crooked River drainage has a general fishing season. Species present include brook, bull, cutthroat and rainbow trout with steelhead and mountain whitefish.

John's Creek

This tributary to the South Fork of the Clearwater River, west of Ten

Mile Creek, has a two-trout limit. Species present include rainbow, cutthroat and bull trout and mountain whitefish.

Newsome Creek

This is a release point for hatchery steelhead and chinook salmon in the Nez Perce National Forest. Other species include rainbow and cutthroat trout and mountain whitefish. Bull trout are present and protected.

Red and American Rivers

These cold-water systems, near Elk City, have historically held steelhead and chinook salmon. Other species include rainbow, bull, brook and cutthroat trout, as well as mountain whitefish. Bull trout are protected.

Karolyn's Pond (one acre)

This put-and-take fishery is stocked with catchable rainbow trout south of Elk City at the Red River Fish Hatchery.

Other South Fork Tributaries

The Department of Fish and Game releases hatchery chinook and salmon into more than 100 miles of selected South Fork tributaries. Other important species include cutthroat, bull and rainbow trout. Bull trout are protected and be aware of the differences between immature rainbow trout and salmon.

Five Mile Pond (one acre)

This put-and-take fishery is stocked with catchable rainbow trout, five miles upstream on the Crooked River at Five Mile Creek.

....

Alpine Lakes

There are 15 managed lakes in the Little North Fork Drainage of the Clearwater River. Many of these lakes are stocked to handle heavy angling pressure. Westslope cutthroat are stocked in most of the lakes.

Some lakes are reserved for specialty species such as golden trout and Arctic grayling. Other lakes are stocked with kokanee and lake trout to reduce stunted populations of brook trout. Contact the regional Fish and Game field office for more information and to check the current IDF&G regulations.

Snake River Idaho-Washington border to Hells Canyon Dam

The Snake River in the Clearwater Region runs from the Washington-Idaho border at Lewiston (the confluence of the Snake and Clearwater rivers) to the Hells Canyon Dam in the south end of the Clearwater region. It flows through the deepest gorge in the United States in the Hells Canyon National Recreation Area (HCNRA). Yes, it is deeper than the Grand Canyon!

Forty miles of river upstream from the Oregon/Washington line to Big Canyon Creek is designated as a scenic river and the following 32 river miles are designated as wild. There are hundreds of high mountain lakes above the canyon rim on both sides of the river.

The HCNRA has three rivers that are designated as Wild and Scenic. The Inmaha and the Rapid rivers are in Oregon while the section of the Snake River that borders Idaho, Oregon and Washington farther downstream is also listed. The Hells Canyon fishery is unique in that sturgeon, trout, migrating steelhead, salmon and a host of warm-water species share it.

Before the extensive stocking program developed by the IDF&G in cooperation with the Forest Service, most of the mountain lakes in the wilderness were without fish. Now, many of these lakes contain either rainbow or cutthroat trout. Some have two species of trout in them, depending on their size and depth. Access to these lakes is by foot or horseback. The higher elevations remain inaccessible throughout much of the year due to snow. Access roads and trails begin to open in June and remain open through September and October.

The Idaho portion of wilderness has alpine and sub-alpine areas with several lakes. Vegetation is sparse and broken by large areas of rocks. Larch, lodgepole pines and firs make up the mid-region forest base with the lower elevations comprised of mainly rocky barren slopes with a sprinkling of trees, mostly ponderosa pine and Douglas fir. Travel is difficult at best and thorough preparation should be taken to ensure a safe trip into the region.

Both the Oregon and Idaho sides of the river, in the upper portion of the recreation area, are surrounded by wilderness. Legislation passed by Congress in 1989 prevents development of new hydropower projects on the Snake River.

The lower portion of the river is blocked by Lower Granite Dam, which lies 40 miles downstream from Lewiston in Washington State. The reservoir extends above the towns of Lewiston and Clarkston, making the area an inland seaport.

The Snake River is a migration corridor for adult and juvenile anad-

romous fish moving to and from the Salmon and Clearwater river regions upstream from Lewiston. Every spring and fall chinook and sockeye salmon and steelhead pass through this stretch of the river. Fall chinook spawn in the river and other tributaries that are suitable for spawning as well, so be careful not to upset redds.

Hells Canyon Dam creates upstream storage and controls river flow. Vertical water levels can fluctuate three to four feet daily below the dam. The quality of the water passing through the dam has improved greatly thanks to up-river impoundments. These upriver reservoirs act as settling basins that trap sediment. Recreational use of the river from Hells Canyon Dam to Lewiston is very high.

Fishing regulations regarding the fishing season, bag limits and licenses are established by each state and since the Snake forms the boundaries between three states they all are involved. If fishing outside of Idaho, anglers should obtain regulations of the state where they intend to fish. See *On the Border* page 11.

Granite Creek

This tributary to the Snake River in the southern reach of the Clearwater Region has a two-fish limit and is managed under general season regulations. Species present include a few chinook, rainbow trout and steelhead. There are some bull trout also.

Sheep Creek

This tributary to the Snake River in the southern reach of the Clearwater Region has a two-fish limit and is managed under general season regulations. Species present include chinook, rainbow and bull trout and steelhead.

Salmon River Drainage

Some Salmon River tributaries are managed by the Clearwater Region. For clarity we have included these tributaries, and associated waters, in the River of No Return section of this book. These rivers, lakes, and streams are located in the Gospel Hump and Frank Church wilderness areas.

....

Airstrips

Cayuse Creek (backcountry)
This backcountry airstrip is located in the Powell District of the Clearwater National Forest This remote area is accessible by four-wheel drive vehicle. The airstrip is 1,800 feet long and 100 feet wide.

Fish Lake (backcountry)
Located in the Selway-Bitterroot Wilderness at an elevation 5,675 feet this airstrip, as with most in the backcountry, must be approached with great caution. Downdrafts can cause problems over the lake, so early morning and evening flights are highly recommended.

Elk City Airport
This airstrip serves Elk City and Idaho County and is owned by the Elk City Booster Club. The gravel runway extends for 2,600 feet. The facility is at an elevation of 4,097 feet about a mile from Elk City.

Moose Creek (USFS)
This airport serves Moose Creek Ranger Station and Idaho County and is owned by the Forest Service. The airport has two runways. The longest is a turf runway extending 4,100 feet. The facility is at an elevation of 2,454 feet about a mile from Moose Creek Ranger Station.

Shearer (wilderness)
This airstrip in the Selway Bitterroot Wilderness is 2,000 feet long but only 25 feet wide. Its elevation is 2,634 feet. A singularly beautiful area along the banks of the Selway River.

Big Bar (backcountry)
The terrain rises abruptly on all landside quadrants of this airstrip. Recommend landing upstream and takeoff downstream. Stay on center line, because of rocks on either side. Turn around at the higher end by windsock. Use caution when turning. The canyon makes tight turns north of strip.

Clearwater

Notes

_____

_____

_____

_____

_____

_____

_____

_____

_____

_____

_____

_____

_____

_____

_____

_____

_____

_____

_____

_____

_____

_____

_____

_____

_____

_____

_____

_____

_____

River of No Return

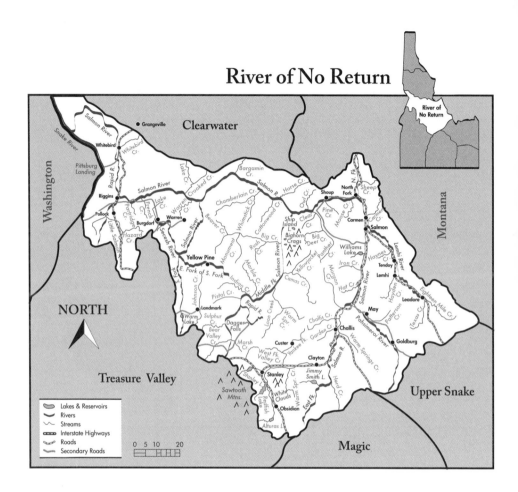

River of No Return

Lewis and Clark were the first non-natives to travel through the Salmon River country and when they saw the frothing white water and impenetrable rapids, they quickly looked for another route to the Columbia River. Before jet boats, only one-way trips down the river were possible.

The River of No Return is the longest free-flowing river entirely in one state. In the midst of this vast expanse lies the Frank Church River of No Return Wilderness Area, an oasis of towering forests, breathtaking high country and pristine waters. The region has been divided into four sections according to its drainages and covers the central section of the state.

From its headwaters above Stanley in the Sawtooth Wilderness to its junction with the Snake south of Lewiston on the Idaho-Oregon border, the river forms a 400-mile arc within the region. Some of its areas are accessible by vehicle and many are not. In this primitive area the Frank Church, Sawtooth, Gospel Hump and Hells Canyon wilderness areas are roadless, but have hundreds of foot trails and numerous mountain airstrips.

In and outside the wilderness areas, alpine lakes dot the region, and some may be accessible by four-wheel drive vehicle, pack animal, foot trails or air. Most are reached only by non-motorized trail systems. Many of the high mountain lakes are either stocked by air or have naturally reproducing populations of cutthroat, rainbow or brook trout. Many are barren of fish and left that way for amphibians and reptiles.

Much of what Lewis and Clark saw in 1805 is what is seen today by those who travel into this rugged, mountainous land. Like other areas, the River of No Return region has also felt the impact of progress and the development of its lands, forests and waters. However, much of its territory is protected by wilderness status and will be into perpetuity.

Main Salmon River Drainage

From its headwaters in the Sawtooth Mountains to its junction with the Snake at the Idaho-Oregon border, the Salmon drains 14,000 square miles of Idaho territory.

For thousands of years, salmon and steelhead have made the incredible journey of more than 800 miles from the Pacific Ocean to the middle of Idaho by way of the Columbia, Snake and Salmon rivers. Each year salmon and steelhead are challenged by man-made changes but many are able to survive the trip that takes them through a series of dams blocking the waterways along the Columbia and Snake rivers. These numbers vary annually but what is consistent is the decline in the number of returning wild salmon and steelhead. It is possible that eventually the wild chinook spawning runs will cease entirely, ending a life cycle that has been in motion for many millennia.

Steelhead numbers are declining as well, but because they are better able to deal with man-caused impediments and with hatchery releases, it is hoped that with holistic management they will continue to provide a harvestable fishery.

The beauty and quality of the Salmon River drainage stems from its isolation in the wilderness areas and its free-flowing status, protected by federal legislation. As such, it will continue to provide outstanding fishing and other recreational opportunities as long as that status is maintained.

To keep things simple, the Main Salmon River has been divided into three sections. The Upper Salmon starts in the headwaters above Stanley in the Sawtooth Mountains and goes north to North Fork, north of the town of Salmon, Idaho. The Middle Salmon begins at North Fork and goes west to Riggins.

The Lower Salmon runs north from Riggins to its junction with the Snake in the northwest corner of the region. Each section and its drainage areas are thoroughly discussed. Don't confuse these sections with the forks because the Middle, South, Yankee and East forks all drain into the Main Salmon.

Upper Salmon

From its headwaters in Blaine County to the town of North Fork, north of the city of Salmon, the Salmon River is 173 miles long and drains approximately 6,000 square miles of Idaho high country. Highways 93 and 75 border the river for nearly its entire length. The headwater area, upstream from Thompson Creek, lies within the Sawtooth National Recreation Area (SNRA). Major tributaries include the Lemhi, Pahsimeroi, East Fork of the Salmon and Yankee Fork rivers.

The drainage area is characterized by mountains sliced by river valleys. Major mountain ranges include the Bitterroot Range along the Idaho-Montana border; the Lemhi Range, southwest of the Lemhi River; the Lost River Range, southwest of the Pahsimeroi River; the White Cloud Peaks, east of the upper Salmon River; and the Sawtooth Range within the Sawtooth National Wilderness, west of the upper Salmon River.

Numerous lakes in the Stanley area are accessible by road, providing good, reachable fishing, hiking and camping opportunities. They include Stanley, Redfish, Little Redfish, Yellowbelly, Petit, Alturas and Perkins lakes. Also, hundreds of lakes within the Sawtooth Wilderness and White Cloud Peak areas provide fishing opportunities in a secluded, wilderness setting for backpackers. Salmon, Stanley and Challis are the only major population centers in the upper Salmon drainage. Logging, mining, ranching and recreation are all major industries in the area.

Because of intense fishing pressure, approximately 75,000 hatchery, catchable rainbow trout are stocked in popular areas of the Upper Salmon drainage each year.

Anadromous management in the Salmon River from North Fork to the headwaters emphasizes maintaining existing natural spawning populations of chinook and steelhead and preserving quality habitat. This section of river is also managed for hatchery steelhead harvest and to produce fishable levels of cutthroat and rainbow trout. Mountain whitefish are also in this area of the river.

From the East Fork of the Salmon to the Yankee Fork, there is good habitat for spawning chinook. Many of the headwater tributaries in the subalpine valley are important spawning and rearing areas for spring chinook.

From the mouth of the East Fork to the Sawtooth Fish Hatchery, it is put-and-take fishing with a rainbow trout stocking operation to offset intensive fishing pressure in the summer months. Species include rainbow, bull and cutthroat trout and mountain whitefish. Wild steelhead, chinook and bull trout are protected.

95

It is put-and-take fishing for rainbow trout from the hatchery to its headwaters, again to offset summer fishing pressure. Only fish with a clipped adipose fin may be kept. This area is also supported by natural reproduction. Major species here are rainbow, cutthroat, brook and bull trout as well as mountain whitefish. Steelhead, chinook salmon and bull trout are protected.

Hundreds of miles of tributary water between North Fork and the headwaters are open during the general fishing season. This figure can be deceiving because some of the tributaries are too small to fish but are important nurseries for young fish. Species present include rainbow, cutthroat, bull and brook trout and mountain whitefish. Steelhead and chinook spawning tributaries are closed to fishing in this area. See regulations for specifics on the water you are looking to fish.

Rivers, Lakes and other Waters

Yankee Fork

The Yankee Fork flows 26 miles from its headwaters to the Salmon River and is fed by another 70 or so miles of tributary water. Because the soils are primarily granite, and not conducive to bug life, many streams are infertile.

Gold was discovered in the drainage in 1873 and mining activity continues today throughout the drainage, particularly along Jordan Creek. Secondary roads border the entire length of Jordan Creek and the Yankee Fork upstream to McKay Creek. The Lower West Fork is accessible by road and the remainder of the stream is bordered by trail. Even with the mining activity the Yankee Fork supports minor runs of chinook and steelhead.

Hatchery steelhead have been planted and resident species include rainbow, cutthroat and bull trout. The dredge ponds in the lower Yankee Fork are stocked with catchable rainbow trout during the summer months and are heavily fished.

East Fork of the Salmon River

The East Fork of the Salmon River flows 33 miles from the confluence of its South and West forks in the Boulder/White Cloud Mountains before entering the Salmon River east of Clayton. Silver was discovered on Kinnikinik Creek near Clayton in the 1880s and the Clayton silver mines are still active. They are some of the oldest mines in Idaho that remain in operation.

The White Cloud Peaks (east) and the Boulder Mountains (south) dominate the drainage. Castle Peak is one of Idaho's tallest at 11,000 feet. Wolves were reintroduced to Idaho in 1995 and at least one pack calls the East Fork region home in 2004. Wildlife includes elk, bighorn sheep, mountain goats, deer, wild horses, bear, coyotes, river otters, blue herons, sandhill cranes, hawks and eagles.

Water supply and quality in the upper drainage is excellent for fish spawning and rearing. In the lower drainage, the river cuts through a zone of volcanic soils that erodes easily. Lack of aquatic vegetation here, plus many human and livestock intrusions cause heavy sedimentation, particularly during spring runoff.

The East Fork drainage supports spring and summer runs of chinook salmon and steelhead and is one of the region's most important spawning and rearing areas. It is managed with catch-and-release regulations for cutthroat trout, and bull trout are protected.

Rainbow trout and mountain whitefish are also present and can be harvested.

Pahsimeroi River

The Pahsimeroi Valley lies between the Lemhi and the Lost River mountain ranges. Counting tributaries, there are more than 225 miles of waterway draining an area of nearly 850 square miles. Many of the tributaries are too small to fish but are important as nurseries. A large portion of the Pahsimeroi Valley is privately owned and heavily irrigated, particularly in the lower drainages. Water supply and quality in the upper drainages is excellent for spawning and rearing. Since most of the water is on private land, access is limited, helping to keep fishing pressure down and populations high.

The Pahsimeroi hatchery, owned by Idaho Power Company and located a few river miles upstream from the river's confluence with the Salmon River at Ellis, is operated by Fish and Game. Salmon and steelhead making their way up the Pahsimeroi to spawn are captured here. Wild fish are allowed to pass upstream while hatchery fish are used to resupply the river population.

Adult steelhead returning to the hatchery are very important in maintaining a strong population of steelhead in the upper Salmon waters. Also, summer chinook eggs are taken to the Sawtooth Hatchery, A-run steelhead are trapped for eggs that are taken to Hagerman Valley hatcheries where they are reared for future plantings and released back into the

Pahsimeroi River or nearby in the Salmon River.

Pahsimeroi resident species include brook, bull trout, cutthroat and rainbow trout, as well as mountain whitefish. The Pahsimeroi is managed under catch-and-release regulations for cutthroat. Six rainbows (none less than 14 inches) may be harvested. Twenty-five brook trout and mountain whitefish can be kept. Important tributaries include Trail, Grouse and Doublespring creeks on the south and Big Creek that enters from the north.

Kids Creek Pond

Located in Salmon, this water is stocked to provide fishing opportunities for kids. Six fish can be kept per day. The season is year-round with no length limits. Gear can be obtained from the library in Salmon.

Big Creek

This is significant water and the main tributary to the Pahsimeroi, populated with cutthroat and protected bull trout and mountain whitefish.

Warm Spring Creek

This is a Clayton-area fishery with rainbow and cutthroat trout that parallels U.S. Route 90. This creek is also an important bull trout stream.

Lemhi River

The Lemhi River flows 56 miles from the confluence of Texas and Eighteen Mile creeks to the Salmon River at the city of Salmon. This is an out-of-the-way Idaho treasure rich in history, natural resources and recreational pursuits. The region is also the gateway to the 2.4-million-acre Frank Church River of No Return Wilderness.

This river drains a broad valley of fertile agricultural and grazing land of approximately 1,290 square miles between the Bitterroot and Lemhi mountain ranges. The valley includes more than 25,000 acres of land irrigated for growing hay and grazing cattle. The most common form of irrigation is flood irrigation, which uses an extensive system of ditches. All the major ditches are designed and built to prevent fish loss. In low-water years, agencies and irrigators work cooperatively to ensure many sections of the river do not run dry in an effort to maintain passage to the mainstream. This effort allows adults to reach the spawning areas upstream.

The drainage supports runs of both salmon and steelhead. The amount of spawning habitat has been reduced by stream alteration but some is still available, particularly in the upper reaches. The mainstream Lemhi

is managed with a six-fish limit with none less than 14 inches for rainbow trout. Brook trout (limit 25) and mountain whitefish (also 25-fish limit) are present and cutthroat and bull trout, steelhead and chinook salmon are closed to harvest.

Many of the Lemhi tributaries are managed as wild fisheries with naturally producing rainbow, brook and cutthroat trout and whitefish. Bull trout and adult steelhead and chinook salmon are closed to harvest. Important tributaries include Kenney, Hayden, Big Eightmile, Big Timber, Texas and Eighteen Mile creeks.

Several meadow lakes in the Lemhi drainage including Iron, Meadow and Wallace lakes are stocked to provide a put-and-take fishery. Many high mountain lakes are stocked with rainbow, cutthroat and golden trout and Arctic grayling on a rotating three-year basis.

Mountain whitefish is the most numerous species, but there are also rainbow, cutthroat, brook and bull trout and cuttbow hybrids. Hayden Creek, a major tributary, supports a spawning population of bull trout as well as small numbers of cutthroat, salmon and steelhead.

Lake Creek

This is a wild rainbow fishery of about five miles that flows into Williams Lake. This lake is closed in the spring (opens July 1) to protect spawning rainbows.

Williams Lake (180 acres)

Located south of the city of Salmon, this lake is populated with rainbow and bull trout. General season regulations apply. Its fish supply is supported by natural reproduction and a stocking program. Elev.: 5,243 feet.

Wallace Lake FFW (10 acres)

This is family fishing water northwest of Salmon stocked with catchable size rainbow trout. There is a six-fish limit with no size restrictions Also a popular ice-fishing area. Elev.: 8,089 feet.

Iron Lake FFW (18 acres)

This is a rainbow trout family fishing water in the Salmon National Forest southeast of Salmon that feeds Iron Creek. Also a popular ice-fishing area. Elev.: 8,808 feet.

Mosquito Flat Reservoir (27 acres)

This is a rainbow trout hatchery-supported fishery that is also a popular ice-fishing area. Located 11 miles west of Challis in the Challis/Salmon National Forest. There are also some brook trout available. Elev.: 6,944 feet.

Bayhorse Lakes FFW (22 acres)

These lakes hold rainbow trout and are popular ice-fishing destinations. Located 12 miles west of Challis, Bayhorse Creek Road goes west to Bayhorse Lake, past several historic mines. The entire area is rich in mining history, and a great place for exploring. There is a foot trail to Little Bayhorse (24 acres, elevation approximately 8,333 feet) which is east of the big lake. Both lakes feed Bayhorse Creek. Elev.: 8,579 feet.

Hawley Creek

This Lemhi tributary is a wild fishery for rainbow and cutthroat trout, with some natural cutthroat production. Hawley Creek also supports bull trout, which are protected. You might have to hike a while to get to the good fishing if the lower sections are dewatered.

Meadow Lake FFW (16 acres)

This lake near the ghost town of Gilmore is stocked with catchable rainbow trout and is managed with family fishing rules that allow 6 fish with no size limit. Elev.: 9,167 feet.

Alpine Lakes

There are more than 400 acres of alpine lakes in the Lemhi drainage and many are stocked to provide a diversity of angling opportunities. Aerial stocking of selected lakes occurs on a three-year rotating basis. Stocked species include Arctic grayling, rainbow, cutthroat and golden trout.

Morgan Creek

This is a wild fishery with natural reproduction for rainbow, cutthroat, brook and bull trout north of Challis.

Valley Creek

From its mouth to its headwaters, this 35-mile stretch of water is a catch-and-release fishery for cutthroat, with some natural reproduction. All of Valley Creek is restricted to the harvest of hatchery rainbow trout (limit six with a clipped adipose fin).

General rules apply to mountain whitefish. Bull trout, steelhead and chinook salmon are protected.

Stanley Lake Creek FFW

Below Stanley Lake, the creek is stocked with catchable-size rainbow trout.

Alturas Lake Creek

This is wild trout water with limited natural reproduction of some species. Species include cutthroat, rainbow, brook and bull trout. Its headwaters begin at nearly 8,900 feet and it feeds and flows out of Alturas Lake.

Stanley Lake (128 acres)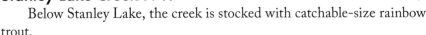

Family fishing water for rainbow, brook and lake trout and kokanee salmon. The rainbow trout are stocked. The lake is located off Highway 21 west of Stanley. Elev.: 6,519 feet.

Little Redfish Lake (65 acres)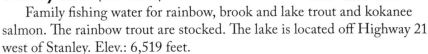

Brook trout and kokanee salmon are present with some natural reproduction. Bull trout are protected. Elev.: 6,483 feet

Redfish Lake (1,502 acres)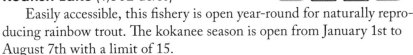

Easily accessible, this fishery is open year-round for naturally reproducing rainbow trout. The kokanee season is open from January 1st to August 7th with a limit of 15.

This is one of a few lakes in the Stanley Basin where sockeye salmon return to spawn. None of Idaho's famous redfish, or sockeye salmon, returned to Redfish Lake in 1997, and only one sockeye, Lonesome Larry, returned in 1998. Only 342 sockeye have returned since 1995. Sockeye used to spawn here by the thousands, giving the lake its name.

In 1991, the Idaho Department of Fish and Game began a program to preserve the existing population and prevent their extinction. The fish are unique because they are the only population of sockeye salmon in the Snake River drainage. They are distinguished by their toughness as well: They travel farther than any other North American sockeye population—more than 900 miles—to reach the ocean; they travel to the highest elevation of 6,545; and they are the most southerly population of sockeye in North America.

In 2000, the program experienced its first significant return of hatchery-produced adults. Two hundred fifty-seven sockeye salmon returned to collection facilities on Redfish Lake Creek and the upper Salmon River at the IDF&G Sawtooth Fish Hatchery, and the majority of those adult returns were released into the system for natural spawning. In 2001, 26 hatchery-produced adults returned to collection facilities in Idaho, in 2002, 21 hatchery-produced adults returned to the Stanley Basin, in 2003, three returned and 27 returned in 2004.

The lake holds bull trout and kokanee. Bull trout are protected. The lake's campgrounds are the Hilton of the camping world with hot showers for a fee, gas, laundromat and pay phones available. Elev.: 6,545 feet.

Yellowbelly Lake (188 acres)

This lake north of Petit Lake is managed as a catch-and-release fishery for rainbow and cutthroat trout. The lake also has a population of fairly large brook trout with a limit of 25. Elev.: 7,076 feet.

Petit Lake (389 acres)

This cold-water fishery is one of a few lakes in the Stanley Basin that has a historical return of sockeye salmon. Today it is managed under general rules to provide a fishery supported by natural production of Kokanee with a limit of 15. Cutthroat trout are present. Adult sockeye salmon are closed to harvest. Bull trout are present and protected. Elev.: 7,002 feet.

Valley Creek Lakes 1 & 2 (20 acres)

These lakes are managed as a trophy cutthroat trout fishery under catch and release rules.

Alturas Lake (838 acres)

One of a few lakes in the Stanley Basin that had a return of sockeye salmon. Kokanee are present with a limit of 15 per day. Adult sockeye and bull trout are protected. Elev.: 7,011 feet.

Perkins Lake (51 acres)
Connected to Alturas Lake by Alturas Lake Creek this lake is managed with general regulations for rainbow trout and kokanee salmon. Adult sockeye and bull trout are closed to harvest. Elev.: 7,011 feet.

Meadow Lake (15 acres)
Located near Leadore, this lake is stocked with catchable rainbow trout. It has a nice camping area.

Iron Creek
This creek has a healthy population of rainbow trout.

Carlson Lake (eight acres)
Brook trout fishing is the reason to go to this serene mountain lake.

Jimmy Smith Lake (50 acres)
This lake is supported by natural production of rainbow trout. It is a popular summer fishery and ice-fishing spot in the Sawtooth National Recreation Area south of Clayton. It feeds Big Lake Creek which is a tributary to the East Fork of the Salmon River. Elev.: 6,322 feet.

Herd Lake (20 acres)
This high mountain lake has a high population of rainbow trout and is a popular ice-fishing spot in the East Fork Salmon River drainage in the Challis/Salmon National Forest. Elev.: 7,174 feet.

....

Alpine Lakes

There are more than 5,000 acres of managed fisheries in the upper region of the Main Salmon River. These high mountain lakes offer diverse fishing opportunities. In some areas, vehicle access is limited so selected lakes are stocked from the air on a three-year rotation.

Species that are stocked include rainbow, cutthroat, golden and brook trout and Arctic grayling fry. Some lakes are not stocked because they are too shallow or some natural reproduction occurs, or some other factor. Other lakes in the basin are not stocked to allow for biodiversity of species.

Lost River Outfitters

Main Salmon River Drainage
The Middle Salmon

The middle run of the Main Salmon stretches from its junction with the North Fork near the town of North Fork to its junction with the Little Salmon near Riggins. It is a distance of 135 miles, most of it roadless, with the river dividing the Frank Church and Gospel Hump wilderness areas. The Middle Fork of the Salmon River is a tributary to this section.

There is a paved road from North Fork to Shoup, a distance of about 15 miles. West of Shoup, an unimproved road follows the river west for 22 miles to the road's end at Corn Creek near the confluence of the Middle Fork of the Salmon. There is a boat ramp at Corn Creek that is heavily used by floaters during the summer and jet boaters during the fall and spring steelhead seasons. From Vinegar Creek, near Riggins upstream to Corn Creek, the river is classified as wild and from Corn Creek to the North Fork it is classified as recreational.

From Corn Creek, it is a downstream hike to Horse Creek, which spills down from high mountain country. This section of water is a wintering spot for juvenile salmon. The area is considered so critical for the sur-

vival of chinook salmon that the river from Horse Creek
to the Little Salmon is closed to salmon fishing. The area
is closely monitored by U.S. Fish and Wildlife personnel.

Wild steelhead also migrate to the Horse Creek area
in the early fall and stay over prior to resuming their
spawning run in the spring. Since wild and hatchery steelhead mingle
here, and wild steelhead are protected, caution is demanded. Only hatchery
steelhead, identified by a clipped or missing adipose fin, can be taken.

There are sturgeon downstream from Horse Creek. Westslope cutthroat trout emigrate from the Middle Fork to winter in the same area.

The section of the Salmon River from North Fork to Horse Creek is
fed by more than 150 miles of tributaries, giving anglers plenty of room to
move. Some tributaries are insignificant. There are wild steelhead, hatchery chinook and steelhead in these waters, so some of the tributaries are
protected. But there are rainbow, cutthroat and brook trout to be taken as
well. The tributaries in this area are managed with general regulations.

From Horse Creek to the Little Salmon River near Riggins the river
is closed to the harvesting of adult non-hatchery steelhead and chinook
salmon. The river is also closed to harvest for cutthroat and bull trout
and white sturgeon. Rainbow trout are managed under wild trout regulations and mountain whitefish, brook trout and smallmouth bass are
managed under general rules. Regulations for specific waters need to be
checked carefully.

The Bargamin Creek watershed, about halfway between Shoup and
Riggins, is also critical steelhead spawning area. Because it is a roadless
area, its seclusion offers added protection for Salmon River steelhead.

Species found in the middle stretch of the Salmon include rainbow,
cutthroat, and bull trout, mountain whitefish and some smallmouth bass.
There are no significant impoundments in the entire Salmon River Drainage. The river is managed to support existing natural spawning populations
of chinook and steelhead, as well as other important and catchable species.

Rivers, Lakes and other Waters

North Fork Salmon River

This river meets the Main Salmon at the town of North Fork in the Salmon National Forest. There are 22 miles of fishable water on the North Fork where cutthroat trout are protected by catch-and-release regulations. The North Fork is closed to fishing for steelhead, chinook salmon and bull trout.

Horse Creek

This creek enters the Salmon River from the north near the border of Lemhi and Idaho counties and covers about 19 miles of river with rainbow, cutthroat, and bull trout, mountain whitefish, steelhead and chinook salmon. The area is managed for wild trout and salmon and steelhead habitat preservation. Hatchery fish are not planted here. This is an important spawning and rearing tributary for A-run steelhead.

Partridge Creek

Entering the Salmon River east of Riggins in the Payette National Forest, this creek is closed to steelhead, chinook salmon and bull trout fishing. It is managed as wild trout water for other species including rainbow, cutthroat, and brook trout. Mountain whitefish are present.

French Creek

Draining an area near Elk Meadows, east of Riggins in the Payette National Forest, the water is closed to steelhead and chinook salmon fishing. It is managed as wild trout water for rainbow and cutthroat trout. Mountain whitefish and brook trout are present. Bull trout are protected.

Panther Creek

Panther Creek flows for 33 miles through the high mountain country dropping more than 5,000 feet from its headwaters before it meets the Main Salmon River about 10 miles southwest of Shoup. This tributary is closed to steelhead and chinook fishing because of its potential to become a spawning and rearing area. There are nearly 100 miles of streams in the Panther Creek drainage with reported runs of chinook and steelhead. This figure is misleading as many tributaries are unfishable. This area is

managed with general fishing rules and is supported by natural reproduction.

Panther Creek Road (FR 055) runs parallel to the stream most of the way to the border of Lemhi and Custer counties at Morgan Creek Summit. On the south side of the summit FR 055's name changes to Morgan Creek Road.

The same rules apply to tributary streams in this reach of the river.

Alpine lakes

There are more that 500 acres of high mountain lakes in this drainage area that are stocked on a rotating basis. Species include rainbow, cutthroat, brook and golden trout, and rainbow and cutthroat trout hybrids (cuttbows). Arctic grayling are present as are protected bull trout.

Main Salmon River Drainage
The Lower Salmon

From Riggins, the Salmon River travels along the edge of the Nez Perce National Forest next to U.S. Highway 95 to near White Bird where it begins a western sweep on down to its junction with the Snake in southwestern Nez Perce County. From its headwaters in the Bitterroot Mountains to its confluence with the Snake River the Salmon River is more than 400 river miles long with a drop in elevation of more than 8,000 feet.

Hatchery steelhead smolt (young fish approximately two years old) are regularly released into the Salmon River from the Little Salmon near Riggins. These plantings help maintain good levels of hatchery steelhead in the downstream areas for future harvest.

About 10 miles downstream from Riggins the river flows through a steep canyon with a number of tributaries that are important producers of wild steelhead. These tributaries, with their good to excellent habitat, successfully support young steelhead waiting to make their way to the ocean. These fish are what scientists are banking on to rejuvenate the wild steelhead population.

The section of river running through the canyon is classified as wild and is a popular spring and fall hatchery steelhead fishing area. Hatchery steelhead are identified by a clipped adipose fin. It is catch-and-release for wild steelhead.

Rapid River and its tributaries are managed for the production of spring chinook salmon, wild trout and steelhead production. There is a 2-trout limit, however no bull trout may be harvested. The area from 50 yards upstream and downstream from the fish trap, and all waters within the posted boundaries of the Idaho Power hatchery, are closed to fishing.

White sturgeon are also found in this stretch of the Salmon River and are managed as a catch-and-release species. Cutthroat and bull trout are found here as well. Bull trout cannot be harvested anywhere. Some tributaries have restricted bag limits for cutthroat trout. There are stocked rainbow trout in this reach of the river as well as smallmouth bass and mountain whitefish.

U.S. Highway 95 flanks the river from Riggins to White Bird. From White Bird to the river mouth, the area is primarily roadless.

Rivers, Lakes and other Waters

Slate Creek

There is about 60 miles of streams in this drainage including tributaries. Steelhead and chinook salmon are present and closed to harvest, as are bull trout. Rainbow and cutthroat trout are managed under wild trout regulations.

White Bird Creek

This creek enters the Main Salmon River southwest of the town of White Bird near the site of the White Bird Battlefield—a point of interest worth the effort to visit. Steelhead and chinook salmon are present and closed to harvest. Rainbow trout are managed under wild trout regulations.

Tolo Lake FFW (40 acres)

This lake is a warm-water fishery near Grangeville. No motors allowed. Bluegill and crappie are present and the lake is stocked with rainbow trout. Elev.: 3,238 feet

Grangeville Pond (five acres)

A cold-water fishery with brook trout and good public access points south of the town of Grangeville.

Alpine Lakes

There are many alpine lakes in the drainage, each
with its individual management plan. Species include
rainbow, cutthroat, brook, and golden trout and Arctic grayling. Cuttbow
hybrids are also stocked in these lakes.

Little Salmon River Drainage

The Little Salmon River, with its headwaters west of the resort town of
McCall, flows through Meadows Valley in Adams County where it meets
the Main Salmon in Riggins. Its major tributaries include Goose, Hazard
and Boulder creeks and Rapid River. Major lakes and reservoirs include
Fish (Mud) Lake, Goose Lake, Brundage Reservoir and the Hazard lakes.

It drains 516 square miles from elevations of 9,000 feet in the Seven
Devils Mountains to 1,760 feet at its mouth. The Seven Devils Mountains
feature high, jagged peaks such as He Devil and She Devil, from the sum-
mits of which you can stare down into Hells Canyon or scan the horizon of
four states—Oregon, Washington, Nevada and Idaho.

The drainage is wild, rugged forestland. The river, from its mouth to
and including Hazard Creek, supports catchable steelhead with rainbow,
cutthroat, brook and bull trout and mountain whitefish.

Waterfalls on the Little Salmon River prevent migrating fish from
going upstream beyond Round Valley Creek. Above the falls, the Little
Salmon is a meandering stream with many steep flowing tributaries.

Rapid River is a significant tributary to the Little Salmon. Upper
Rapid River is classified as a wilderness river and its drainage area provides essential and quality spawning and rearing habitat for steelhead and
salmon. It also supplies catchable spring chinook most years.

Located along the banks of Rapid River near Riggins, the Rapid
River Fish hatchery is the largest collection, spawning and rearing facility
of spring chinook salmon in Idaho. It was constructed in 1964 by Idaho
Power as part of its fish conservation program to maintain runs of spring
chinook salmon in both the Snake and Salmon Rivers with an annual
production of 3 million young salmon as a license requirement.

The majority of these fish are released directly into Rapid River. In
most years between one hundred thousand and a million fish may be transported to the Snake River and released below Hells Canyon Dam to miti-

gate for runs lost to construction of Oxbow, Brownlee and Hells Canyon dams. These dams were built without fish passage facilities and eliminated the runs of steelhead and salmon up the Snake River and its tributaries.

The power company has also constructed a facility at Hells Canyon for trapping adult steelhead and salmon from the Snake River. Salmon from the Hells Canyon trap are transported to Rapid River Hatchery for spawning and rearing.

Adult salmon arrive at the Rapid River trap (located about two miles downstream from the hatchery) from early May through August.

The fish arriving at the Rapid River Hatchery through mid-July are classified as spring chinook and later arrivals are designated summer chinook if they are not marked. These summer chinook are released back into Rapid River to maintain a naturally reproducing population above the hatchery.

Because of the sensitive nature of the chinook and steelhead population, the entire stream is closed when those species are present. For more information on open seasons contact the IDF&G in McCall.

From its mouth near Riggins to its confluence with Round Valley Creek (except the Rapid River) there are about 100 miles of river and tributary water that is managed for sport fishing and the production of steelhead and chinook salmon. When there are enough hatchery fish returning the harvest of the excess hatchery fish is allowed. Bull trout may be found below Round Valley Creek and are protected.

Species that are managed with general fishing rules include rainbow, brook and cutthroat trout and mountain whitefish.

From Round Valley Creek to its headwaters, the Little Salmon holds rainbow, and brook trout and mountain whitefish. Bull trout are present and protected in the entire drainage.

Rapid River

Wild steelhead and chinook salmon spawn above the Rapid River hatchery and they are protected. Upstream from the hatchery the river is open from Memorial Day and has a 2-trout limit. There is bull trout spawning habitat above the hatchery and they are protected.

Fish (Mud) Lake (30 acres)

New regulations allow for the harvesting of cutthroat trout under wild trout regulations on this lake west of McCall. Elev.: 4,658 feet.

Brundage Reservoir (270 acres)

This body of water is managed as a trophy fishery for rainbow and

cutthroat trout. It is located off Goose Lake Road in the Payette National Forest. Elev.: 6,214 feet.

Goose Lake (520 acres)

General fishing rules apply to this popular fishery in the Payette National Forest that has brook and cutthroat trout and is planted with hatchery rainbow trout. Elev.: 6,358 feet.

Hazard Lakes

There are two major Hazard lakes found in the Grass Mountains north of McCall. Both are east of FR 527. The main Hazard lake (65 acres—Elev.: 7,061 feet) has an access road and campsites. It holds brook and rainbow trout. Big Hazard Lake (130 acres—Elev.: 6,969 feet) is a 300-yard walk from the first Hazard Lake and has brook trout. Upper Hazard Lake (37 acres—Elev.: 7,428 feet) is approximately a two-mile hike and it has brook trout.

Lake Serene (10 acres)

Located in the Payette National Forest this trophy fishery's elevation is approximately 7,090 feet. The lake holds brook and rainbow trout. Lake Serene has a 20-inch size minimum and a two-fish limit. Elev.: 7,090 feet

....

Alpine lakes

There are more than 42 alpine lakes in the Little Salmon drainage. The fishable lakes are stocked with fingerlings on a three-year rotational basis to provide species diversity. The lakes are stocked with rainbow, cutthroat, golden and brook trout and Arctic grayling.

South Fork Salmon River Drainage

The South Fork of the Salmon River runs through Valley and Idaho counties in central Idaho and enters the Main Salmon River at Mackay Bar.

Its headwaters are at an elevation of approximately 7,300 feet and the river drops more than 5,000 feet before it enters the Main Salmon. Its topography varies from steep canyons to mountain meadows. The Idaho

Batholith is composed largely of weathered granite that is sensitive to disturbance and has few nutrients. This granite can be as big as a house or as small as sugar granules.

Important tributaries in the drainage include the Secesh River, the East Fork of the South Fork of the Salmon River and Johnson Creek. To the south, Warm Lake is the area's largest lake at 640 acres. The remaining fishable lakes range in size from one to 60 acres.

Resident species include rainbow, cutthroat, brook, lake and bull trout, mountain whitefish, kokanee salmon and numerous non-game species.

The South Fork is one of only a few drainages in Idaho that support populations of wild B-run steelhead. The Clearwater River and Middle Fork Salmon are the others. These are predominately large steelhead that have spent two or three years in the ocean. Several steps have been taken to protect the native gene pool of these fish.

The wild salmonid species present include salmon, steelhead, cutthroat, rainbow and bull trout and mountain whitefish. Stolle Meadows has a salmon observation platform where salmon can be observed on their spawning beds.

Rivers, Lakes and other waters

Secesh River

From its headwaters near Burgdorf, the Secesh River travels through miles of rugged Idaho terrain. It also supports critically important chinook spawning and rearing habitat. Its resident populations also include cutthroat, rainbow and bull trout and mountain whitefish.

There are 93 miles of Secesh River tributaries in this drainage and they are carefully protected against habitat deterioration. The river is managed as wild trout preservation waters with cutthroat, rainbow, brook trout and mountain whitefish in residence. To maintain the native gene pool no hatchery fish are planted in the Secesh River.

East Fork of the South Fork

The East Fork Salmon River drainage area is 540 square miles and includes the White Cloud Peaks to the west and the Boulder Mountains to the south.

The upper drainage is excellent for spawning and rearing while the lower drainage runs through highly erosive volcanic soils. The drainage supports

runs of spring and summer chinook salmon and steelhead trout. The East Fork is one of the most important tributaries for salmon spawning and rearing in the upper Salmon River drainage. Hatchery steelhead in this drainage are B-run fish from Dworshak National Fish Hatchery.

Chinook and steelhead are protected. Cutthroat, rainbow and brook trout are managed as wild. Mountain whitefish are present. Surplus hatchery salmon were planted in the East Fork of the South Fork headwaters in the reclaimed Stibnite Mine area that had a remnant wild population.

Johnson Creek

A tributary to the East Fork of the South Fork of the Salmon River, south of Yellow Pine, this 54-mile stretch of trout water, including tributaries, offers cutthroat, brook and rainbow trout fishing. Bull trout are present and protected. The Nez Perce tribe is developing a summer chinook program on Johnson Creek.

Loon Lake (100 acres)

Accessible only by foot, this lake in the Payette National Forest has been stocked with rainbow trout in the past and more recently with westslope cutthroat trout from the McCall hatchery.

In 1943 a WWII B-23 bomber on a training mission out of Tonopah, Nevada experienced engine trouble and had to make an emergency landing on frozen Loon Lake. The plane slid across the ice before coming to a halt in the forest on the south shore of the lake. All crew members survived. The fuselage can still be visited on the south end of the lake. Elev.: 5,800 feet.

Warm Lake (640 acres)

This large mountain lake is located west of Landmark. It contains rainbow, lake and brook trout and kokanee salmon, and is regularly stocked with catchable-size trout. Elev.: 5,300 feet.

Alpine Lakes

The 36 alpine lakes covering 890 surface acres in the South Fork of the Salmon River drainage are managed to produce catchable to trophy-size fish. Species include rainbow, brook, golden and cutthroat trout as well as Arctic grayling. Most of the lakes are maintained on a three-year fry-stocking rotation.

Middle Fork Salmon River Drainage

Much has been written about Idaho's wild Middle Fork of the Salmon River. It flows through the Frank Church River of No Return Wilderness, the largest wilderness area in the lower 48 states.

The topography of the Middle Fork Drainage is extremely rugged and the region is remote. Road access is limited to a single point on the main river at Dagger Falls, with secondary roads only to the upper ends of a few tributaries. The principal means of access are aircraft, boat and trail. Some tributaries can be reached by vehicle but the upper waters are accessible only by foot trail.

Many backcountry airstrips are found in the drainage, but extreme caution must be taken flying in to any wilderness area. It is highly recommended that pilots new to the area fly in with an experienced pilot on their first visit to these highly technical and dangerous landing sites.

Much of the Middle Fork drainage contains native species. Anadromous species include wild, indigenous spring and summer chinook and steelhead. The Middle Fork is one of only a few drainages in the Columbia River Basin that supports a population of wild, B-run steelhead—predominately large fish that spend two to three years in the ocean.

A permit is required to float this incredible wilderness and there are three ways to get one. The most common is to apply for a permit during the lottery season that runs from June through August. During the pre- and post-season you can call the Middle Fork Ranger station and request a date. Those permits go fast. The third way is to call the station and ask for any available cancelled permits.

Although the Middle Fork supported a major chinook fishery in the late '60s with annual harvests exceeding 2,000 non-treaty fish harvest has not been allowed since 1978. Middle Fork steelhead are sometimes caught in the main stem of the Salmon, which is open to non-native fish harvesting. Native steelhead must be released immediately.

Native resident game fish include cutthroat and bull trout and mountain whitefish. The Middle Fork cutthroat population has been identified as a pure westslope strain, yet is unique from any other westslope strains found in the current range.

There are no major dams in the Middle Fork drainage and many of the streams are in pristine condition. Some tributary streams have been, and are being, altered by livestock and forest management practices. Other tributaries are impacted by natural events, such as forest fires, that cause stream bank erosion and riparian vegetation damage.

So if you are looking for native rainbow or cutthroat trout your best opportunity is from July through September on this classic dry fly water with aggressive fish and beautiful scenery.

Rivers, Lakes and other Waters

Middle Fork Salmon River

From its mouth to Roaring Creek, a distance of four miles, the season is from Memorial Day weekend to September 30 for catch-and-release fishing only to preserve wild stocks of steelhead. No bait may be used and barbless hooks only. Primary species include cutthroat, rainbow and bull trout, steelhead, chinook salmon and mountain whitefish.

From Roaring Creek upstream to the confluence of Marsh and Bear Valley creeks (the beginning of the Middle Fork of the Salmon River) it is catch-and-release regulations for trout. An exception is the area from the observation deck below Dagger Falls to the pack bridge above Dagger Falls which is closed to fishing. Access to this quality fishery is generally limited to foot travel.

On most large tributaries of the Middle Fork the regulations are catch-and-release with barbless hooks and no bait. See *Idaho's Big 10*, page 39.

Big Creek

Located in Valley County east of McCall and north of Yellow Pine, Big Creek is the largest tributary of the Middle Fork and flows due east for more than 30 miles through central Idaho's Frank Church Wilderness before entering the Middle Fork of the Salmon River.

From its mouth to its headwaters, it is catch-and-release for all species except mountain whitefish and brook trout. Other species include cutthroat, rainbow and bull trout. Steelhead, chinook and bull trout are protected.

Camas Creek

It is catch-and-release to protect wild stocks of cutthroat and rainbow trout. Species include rainbow, cutthroat and bull trout, mountain whitefish, steelhead and chinook salmon. No bait and barbless hooks only.

Indian Creek

This creek is catch-and-release for its full nine miles to protect wild trout. No taking of adult chinook and steelhead. Species include rainbow, cutthroat and bull trout, mountain whitefish, steelhead and chinook salmon. No bait and barbless hooks only.

Loon Creek

This creek is also managed as catch-and-release water to protect wild stocks from over-harvest. There is no taking of adult chinook and steelhead to protect wild stocks. It also contains cutthroat, rainbow and bull trout and mountain whitefish. No bait and barbless hooks only.

Marble Creek

It is catch-and-release in its lower 2 miles (to Prospect Creek) to protect wild stocks from over-harvest. Closed to taking of adult chinook salmon and steelhead to protect wild stocks. Other species include cutthroat and bull trout and mountain whitefish. No bait and barbless hooks only.

Pistol Creek

Catch-and-release in lower 3.5 miles (to Forty-five Creek) to protect wild stocks from over-harvest. Closed to taking of adult chinook salmon and steelhead to protect wild stocks. No bait and barbless hooks only.

Sulphur Creek

Catch-and-release for cutthroat and rainbow trout. Closed to harvest of adult chinook and steelhead to protect wild stocks. No bait and barbless hooks only.

Cape Horn, Beaver and Knapp creeks

These are wild trout waters with cutthroat, rainbow and bull trout and mountain whitefish. Regulations call for catch-and-release fishing for all trout except brook trout.

Marsh Creek

From its mouth to Cape Horn Creek, it is catch-and-release for all trout species. Closed to harvest of chinook and steelhead. Trout species include cutthroat, rainbow, bull and brook trout. Heavily fished.

From Cape Horn upstream, this is a naturally supported fishery with catch-and-release regulations with barbless hooks and no bait. Species include cutthroat, rainbow, brook and bull trout as well as mountain whitefish. No bait and barbless hooks only.

Bear Valley Creek

Catch-and-release fishing for cutthroat trout and bull trout. Riverside campsites are available. No bait and barbless hooks only.

Josephus Lake (seven acres)

Stocked with catchable rainbow trout with cutthroat trout present. Elev.: 7,048 feet.

Yellowjacket Lake (six acres)

Stocked with catchable rainbow trout. Elev.: 7,935 feet.

Cape Horn Lakes (44 acres)

Cape Horn #2 (middle lake) is stocked with catchable rainbow trout to provide a fishery for the scout camp. The larger (upper) lake is a brook trout fishery. Elev.: 6,559 feet

Seafoam Lakes

Extremely difficult vehicle access. A four-wheel drive vehicle is suggested to reach this brook trout fishery. There are four lakes ranging from five to 11 acres. The largest lake is at an elevation of approximately 7,777 feet and the highest is at approximately 8,188 feet in the Challis National Forest. They are stocked with Arctic grayling on a three-year rotation.

Elk Creek Lake

This is catch-and-release for trophy trout.

Big Horn Crags Mountain Lakes

This area south of the Main Salmon River and east of the Middle Fork of the Salmon River has many high mountain lakes accessible only by foot or horseback.

Many are stocked on a three-year rotation with either brook, rainbow, cutthroat or golden trout. Arctic grayling are stocked as well. The land is rugged and caution should be taken in the back country.

....

Alpine Lakes

There are more than 2,000 acres of alpine lakes with diversified fishing in this drainage area The stocked species (fry) include cutthroat, rainbow, golden and brook trout, and Arctic grayling. Bull trout are present and protected. *Idaho High Mountain Lakes–First Edition* available spring 2005.

Blue Mountain Ponds

Divide Mountain Lakes

Hayden Ponds FFW

Hyde Pond FFW

Kelly Creek Pond FFW

Lemhi Range Lakes

Sawtooth Mountain Lakes

Squaw Creek Pond

Stanley Basin Mountain Lakes

White Cloud Mountain Lakes

Yankee Fork Ponds FFW

Lake Rock Lake
A trophy alpine lake.

Long Lake
A trophy alpine lake.

Tule Lake
A trophy alpine lake.

Brush Lake
A trophy alpine lake.

Insignificant Bodies of Water

Owl, Pine, Moose and Sheep creeks are tributaries of little significance.

....

Airstrips

Indian Creek (backcountry)

Located in the Frank Church River of No Return Wilderness, this popular airstrip is the longest in the wilderness at 4,650 feet long and 40 feet wide. Its elevation is 4,701 feet.

Johnson Creek (backcountry)

A popular airstrip south of Yellowpine on Johnson Creek. The strip is 3,400 feet long and 150 feet wide with an elevation of 4,923 feet. A caretaker grooms the strip and keeps the area's amenities—toilets, showers and bunkhouse—clean. Phone service is available as is a freezer for making ice.

Krassel (backcountry)

This dirt airstrip is located on the South Fork of the Salmon River and is a major jumping off point for firefighters in the backcountry. Krassel Forest Service airport serves McCall and Valley County. The turf runway extends for 1,500 feet. The facility is at an elevation of 3,982 feet and about 17 miles from McCall. No camping facilities.

Bernard (backcountry)

Located 28 miles upstream for the confluence of the Main and Middle forks of the Salmon River. There is one pit toilet at the campground. There are a few trees in the narrow canyon. The elevation is 3,636 feet.

Big Creek (backcountry)

Big Creek Airport serves Big Creek and Valley County and is owned by the Idaho Division of Aeronautics. The turf runway is 3,550 feet long. The facility is at an elevation of 5,743 feet and about a mile from Big Creek.

Bruce Meadows (backcountry)

Bruce Meadows Airport serves Stanley and Valley County and is owned by the Idaho Division of Aeronautics. The turf runway is 5,000 feet long. The facility is at an elevation of 6,370 feet and about 20 miles from Stanley.

Cabin Creek (backcountry)

This airstrip serves Big Creek Ranger Station and Valley County and is owned by the Forest Service. The turf runway is 1,750 feet long. The facility is at an elevation of 4,289 feet and about 17 miles from Big Creek Ranger Station.

Chamberlain (backcountry)

This USFS airstrip serves Chamberlain Guard Station and Idaho County. The airport has more than one runway. The longest is a turf runway 4,100 feet long at an elevation of 5,765 feet about a mile from the Chamberlain Guard Station.

Cold Meadows (backcountry)

Similar in terrain to Bruce Meadows, located near the headwaters of Disappointment Creek, a tributary to the Salmon River. Access is by foot, hoof or wing.

Dewey Moore (backcountry)

This is a difficult airstrip and should not be taken lightly. Elevation is 4,494 feet. The strip is located on the north side of Big Creek, about 19 miles west of the junction of Big Creek and the Middle Fork of the Salmon River.

Dixie Town (backcountry)

Located parallel to Main Street in Dixie this airstrip is 4,500 feet long and 100 feet wide. The elevation is 6,250 feet.

Dixie USFS (backcountry)

Located about three miles southwest of Dixie this airstrip's elevation is 5,135 feet. The airstrip is grass and 4,500 feet long and 100 feet wide. Pit toilets are available but no campsites.

Mackay Bar (backcountry)

This airstrip is located at the confluence of the South Fork of the Salmon and the Main Salmon in the Payette National Forest at a private guest ranch. The dirt airstrip is 1,900 feet long and 75 feet wide. Its elevation is 2,045 feet.

Slate Creek (backcountry)

The only public airstrip on the Salmon River, about 20 miles south of Riggins. No camping at the airport. Historical area with a museum is located along U.S. Highway 95 between Riggins and White Bird. This dirt runway is at 1,660 feet, is 2,600 feet long and 165 feet wide.

Upper Loon Creek (backcountry)

This airstrip serves Challis and Custer County and is owned by USFS. The gravel runway is 2,500 feet long. The facility is at an elevation of 5,500 feet and about 26 miles from Challis.

Flying B (backcountry)

Breakfast is only one reason to fly into this backcountry airstrip located along the Middle Fork of the Salmon River. The private guest ranch has a grass airstrip at an elevation of 3,647 feet, is 2,100 feet long and 50 feet wide.

Soldier Bar

Located by Big Creek, this airstrip is one of the most difficult strips on the drainage. It is used by hunting parties more than anglers because of the thousand-foot descent to the creek below the landing field.

Warren (backcountry)

Warren /USFS airport serves Warren and Idaho County and is owned by the Forest Service. The dirt runway extends for 2,765 feet. The facility is at an elevation of 5,896 feet and a mile or less from Warren.

Sulphur Creek (backcountry)

Located four miles from the Middle Fork this is a private guest ranch where high mountain lakes are accessible by foot or horseback. Breakfast is one reason to make the trip but the fishing may be the real star. The strip is at 5,860 feet, is 3,100 feet long and 50 feet wide. (backcountry)

Landmark (backcountry)

Located about two miles east of the Landmark Ranger Station, this strip is not as easy as it appears. There are lodges nearby (12 miles west of the airstrip) at Warm Lake with cabins and campsites. Its elevation is 6,680 feet.

Mahoney Creek (backcountry)

Located 350 feet above the Middle Fork of the Salmon River. There are no facilities and the camping is rustic. The dirt airstrip is at 4,618 feet, is 2,150 feet long and 30 feet wide.

Orogrande (backcountry)

Uncertain if this strip is being used. It is at 4,400 feet and is 2,800 feet long and 50 feet wide.

Smiley Creek (state)

Smiley Creek Airport serves Galena and Blaine County and is owned by the Idaho Department of Aeronautics. The turf runway is 4,900 feet long. The facility is at an elevation of 7,160 feet and about 6 miles from Galena. At 7,160 feet it is one of the highest airstrips in the state.

River of No Return

Notes

CHOOSING AN OUTFITTER

The River of No Return Wilderness is truly a fly-fisherman's paradise with beautiful streams and pristine high mountain lakes that set the stage for a true wilderness adventure. Many of these lakes and streams are rarely visited and untouched by human intrusion. Guided horse pack and backpacking trips are great ways to experience this country and all the fantastic fishing it has to offer. No one knows the River of No Return Wilderness like the outfitters and guides that reside in this beautiful country.

Finding an outfitter is your first step. An **outfitter** is someone who offers guided trips for compensation and generally has been fishing the region and has firsthand knowledge of the area. To operate legally in Idaho, outfitters must be licensed with the state Outfitters and Guides Licensing Board. A **guide** is an outfitter's employee. Guides must be certified in first aid, must train with a licensed outfitter, and must be licensed with the state board.

Guided Pack trips

Imagine riding through a canyon on horseback along Loon Creek, a crystal-clear ribbon of wilderness water in the heart of the backcountry. Once you ascend the narrow trails and reach base camp at one of the many hot springs or meadows, you can fill your days with as much fishing for all the rainbow, cutthroat and bull trout you want. On most trips, professional and experienced guides can show anglers the best holes and what flies the fish are rising to, while providing all the necessary equipment. Most wilderness guides have spent many seasons in the backcountry and are more than willing to share some of their outdoor lore with clients.

Chasing trout all day can wear a body down. On fly-fishing pack trips, anglers return to base camp ready for a warm, delicious meal. Relaxing by the campfire, enjoying a good dinner and conversation is a perfect prelude to falling asleep to the soothing sound of the river, and dreaming of the next day's adventure.

Guided Backpacking trips

Guided backpacking trips to high mountain lakes are sometimes the only way these hidden lakes can be reached. The Mystery lakes are a perfect example. Because the terrain is extremely rocky and difficult on horseback, they can only be reached by foot, and it is a two-and-a-half hour trip—mostly up!

It is a difficult hike and not well marked but well worth the effort. Tents and supplies can be carried and set up right at the lake. Once arriving at the selected lakes, anglers will be delighted to find beautiful golden, cutthroat and rainbow trout. The Mystery lakes, in the heart of the Frank Church Wilderness are stocked with golden trout. These special fish rarely see an artificial fly and take them eagerly. The lower Mystery lake is a crystal-clear alpine lake as blue as a robin's egg.

The upper Mystery lake sits approximately 1,500 feet above the lower lake and is known for containing the larger and feistier fish, primarily bull trout. Guides can assist you in your navigation to the lakes, setting up camp, cooking, casting, fly-tying and even setting up your equipment and materials for you. High mountain lake fishing is truly an adventure you will always remember!

This ProTip is brought to you by the
Diamond D Ranch
for more information call **800.222.1269**
e-mail **diadlld@aol.com**
or visit **www.diamonddranch-idaho.com**

See advertisement on page 241.

Treasure Valley

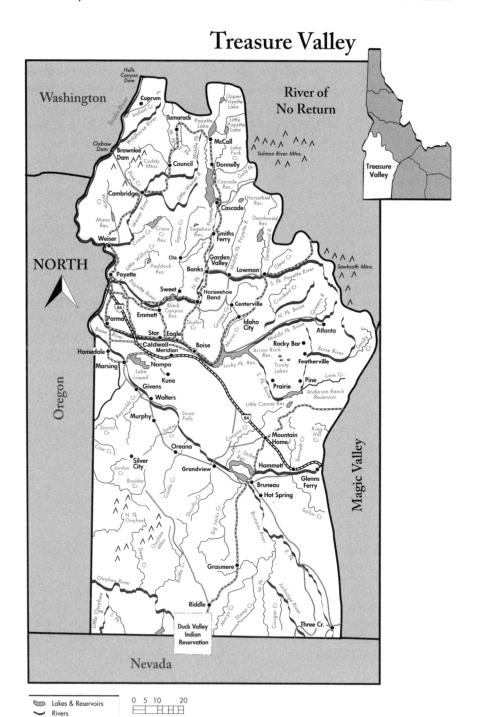

Drainages:
Weiser
Payette
Boise
Owyhee/Bruneau
Snake

Treasure Valley

The diversity of the Treasure Valley region is part of its treasure. From the fertile reaches of the Snake River Plain to its isolated and arid land of southern Owyhee country, visitors can choose desert solitude, alpine lake serenity or a variety of options in between. Warm-water and cold-water fisheries abound throughout the region and the choice of fishing is varied indeed—from channel cats to rainbow trout and from flat, still waters to rushing mountain streams.

In 1862 a group of miners found gold near Idaho City, about 25 miles northeast of Boise. Shortly after the strike the boomtown was the largest in the Northwest with a population of nearly 15,000. Today the region is lined with placer mine tailings as a reminder of its mining past. With fishable water ranging from the Sawtooth Mountains on the east to the Oregon border to the west, and from the Salmon to the north, to the Owyhee Mountains to the south, the Treasure Valley offers a wide and exciting variety of fishing opportunities.

As it is throughout most of the state, the Snake River is the major waterway as it flows from C.J. Strike Reservoir to Hells Canyon Dam. Six major waterways join the Snake as it moves across the Snake River plain in the region—the Weiser, Payette, Boise, Owyhee and Bruneau rivers in Idaho and Oregon's Malheur River.

Smaller tributaries flow out of the mountain ranges flanking the river: the Seven Devils, Cuddy, Hitt and Owyhee ranges.

Where tributaries drain high, mountainous terrain there are typically steep, boulder-strewn streams with deep pools. Most of these streams that can successfully support fish are populated with native rainbow trout.

In the northern section of the region, the McCall area has more than 300 lakes and several major river drainages within 20 miles of the city limits making this area very popular with anglers. There are fish for every season, both warm-water and cold-water species. The view of the mountains is spectacular and wildlife makes this a great destination for a memorable fishing vacation.

Snake River Drainage

From Hells Canyon to C.J. Strike

Archeologists have been able to trace the history of the Snake River as a fishing spot back to 5,000 BC with the discovery of salmon traps in Hells Canyon. Steelhead bones found in the Owyhee uplands appear to be at least 3,000 years old. Throughout the centuries much has changed, of course, as water from the Snake has been impounded and diverted to produce electrical power, irrigate land and provide water for livestock.

The river, between the backwaters of C.J. Strike Reservoir south of Mountain Home and Hells Canyon has been greatly altered by the construction of five major hydroelectric dams. As a result there are 111 miles of impoundments of river now covering 27,000 surface acres.

From C.J. Strike Reservoir to Brownlee Reservoir, the water is flat and quiet with few rapids or riffles. Large islands provide good fishing for smallmouth bass, largemouth bass, channel catfish, crappie, bluegill, sunfish, white sturgeon and flathead catfish. In C.J. Strike Reservoir you can find an appealing assortment of cold- and warm-water fish. Upstream to Swan Falls, it is mainly smallmouth bass, channel catfish and white sturgeon. In the stretch near Walters Ferry it is good fishing for crappie, channel catfish and smallmouth bass.

....

Rivers Lakes and other Waters

Hells Canyon Reservoir (2,500 acres)

Hells Canyon Reservoir is 26 miles long and contains both warm-water and cold-water fish including wild and stocked rainbow trout, smallmouth bass and crappie. Less common are largemouth bass, bluegill, perch and channel and bullhead catfish. Kokanee are also present and managed under general fishing regulations. Sturgeon are present and must be released immediately.

When it is cold, rainbow trout are the most popular species and it's crappie and smallmouth bass when it is warmer. Elev.: 1,750 feet.

Oxbow Reservoir (1,500 acres)

This is a 12-mile long impoundment of the Snake River between

Oxbow and Brownlee dams. Oxbow's important species include rainbow trout, smallmouth bass and crappie with largemouth bass, bluegill, perch and channel catfish also present.

During the cold-weather months, rainbow trout are most sought-after. During warm weather it's crappie and smallmouth bass. This is a quality fishery for smallmouth bass; season opens July 1. From January 1 through the end of June it is catch-and-release only. There's a two-fish limit for the rest of the year and all bass between 12 and 16 inches must be released. Elev.:1,840 feet.

Brownlee Reservoir (15,000 acres)

Brownlee Reservoir is the largest of three Hells Canyon complex reservoirs on the Snake River and it is one of the most-fished bodies of water in Idaho.

It is located on the Idaho/Oregon border about 80 miles northwest of Boise and provides 55 miles of high-quality smallmouth and crappie fishing. Other species include bluegill, largemouth bass, crappie, perch, bullhead, channel catfish and white sturgeon.

There are also stocked and wild rainbow trout in this section. Sturgeon must be released immediately. Elev.: 2,077 feet. See *On the Border*, page 11.

Wildhorse River & Indian Creek

These tributaries of the Snake River are managed as wild trout water for natural reproduction of rainbow, bull and brook trout. Indian Creek enters the Snake River below Oxbow Dam and Wildhorse River enters the river below Brownlee Dam.

Halverson Lake

This is a largemouth bass, bluegill and crappie lake along the Snake River south of the town of Melba. Elev.: 2,355 feet.

Reynolds Creek

Native rainbow trout are the primary species in this wild trout tributary south of Givens in Owyhee County.

Swan Falls Reservoir (900 acres)

Located south of Kuna and adjacent to the National Birds of Prey area, this impoundment holds smallmouth bass, channel catfish, bluegill, bullhead and perch. Below the dam there is good fly-fishing for very large carp. The National Birds of Prey area has dozens of rare and exotic falcons, eagles and hawks as seasonal visitors. Elev.: 2,303 feet.

C.J. Strike Reservoir (7,500 acres)

About thirty miles upstream from Swan Falls near Mountain Home, this reservoir is managed under general fishing regulations for a vast array of fish that includes smallmouth and largemouth bass, flathead, channel and bullhead catfish, black and white crappie, bluegill, pumpkinseed, perch, rainbow trout, mountain whitefish and sturgeon. Smallmouth bass dominate the fishery and sturgeon must be released immediately.

The reservoir is also used for sailing and waterskiing and there are picnic areas with tables and barbecue grills. Boat ramps, rest rooms, and unimproved free camping areas for overnight stays are also available. This is also a favorite recreation spot for servicemen and women stationed at nearby Mountain Home Air Force Base.

Petroglyphs, prehistoric markings left behind by ancient Native American tribes can be found at the north shore picnic area along with an explanation of what some of the symbols mean. Elev.: 2,455 feet.

Crane Falls (84 acres)

This lake rubs shoulders with the mighty Snake River south of Mountain Home and holds trophy largemouth bass populations. It is managed under general regulations for bluegill, pumpkinseed, bullhead and crappie. The lake is also stocked with rainbow trout.

The lake is a very rich and productive seep lake, separated from C.J. Strike Reservoir by a thin stretch of land. It is popular with float tubers as there is limited bank fishing because of high weeds. Elev.: 2,460 feet.

Cove Arm (76 acres)

This fishery is adjacent to Crane Falls and is primarily inhabited by warm-water fish including largemouth and smallmouth bass, bluegill, yellow perch, pumpkinseed, crappie, channel and bullhead catfish. The stocking of rainbow trout in this riverside impoundment has been discontinued. Elev.: 2,461 feet.

Snake River from C.J. Strike to Castle Creek

Managed to maintain a high catch rate of smallmouth bass, this 55-mile stretch of river also includes largemouth bass, channel catfish, crappie, bluegill, pumpkinseed, perch, rainbow trout, mountain whitefish and sturgeon. Castle Creek enters the River east of Murphy.

Weiser River Drainage

The Weiser River basin in southwestern Idaho drains the Seven Devils Mountains to the north and west, the Cuddy Mountains to the west and the West Mountains to the east. It flows in a southwesterly direction until it empties into the Snake River south of Weiser.

The river starts at 8,000 feet in the mountains and falls nearly 6,000 feet at Weiser and the drainage covers more than 1,600 square miles of low rolling foothills cut by the river and many small streams. Following runoff in the spring, the river almost always experiences extremely low flows during the remainder of the year.

The Weiser River has no main stem storage reservoirs. Private irrigation districts have built four reservoirs on tributary streams: Lost Valley,

C. Ben Ross, Crane Creek and Mann Creek. All were constructed for irrigation and typically fill during the high spring runoff, only to become extremely low in the late summer and early fall. In very dry years all but Mann Creek Reservoir have gone dry.

Crane Creek Reservoir contains healthy numbers of crappie. From the mouth of the Weiser River upstream to Galloway Dam, low summer flows and poor water quality limit populations of smallmouth bass, channel catfish and mountain whitefish. Few trout are present.

Upstream, in the cooler water and tributary streams, species include rainbow, brook and bull trout, smallmouth and largemouth bass and mountain whitefish. The smallmouth bass go up as far as Goodrich Creek. Beyond that point water temperature limits most of the bass movement in the river.

Rivers, Lakes and other Waters

Little Weiser River
There are naturally produced trout populations in this tributary river. Species include rainbow, brook and bull trout and mountain whitefish. Bull trout are protected.

Middle Fork Weiser River
There is limited planting of rainbow trout near campgrounds on the Middle Fork. Other fish found in this stretch are brook and rainbow trout and mountain whitefish.

West Fork Weiser River
This stretch of river is populated with rainbow and brook trout and mountain whitefish.

Mann Creek Reservoir (281 acres)
This impoundment north of Weiser holds largemouth bass, bluegill, crappie, mountain whitefish and hatchery rainbow trout. Some wild rainbow trout are present. It is the only one of the four major reservoirs in the region that does not go dry during low water years. Elev.: 2,887 feet.

Crane Creek Reservoir (2,200 acres)

Largemouth bass, bullhead and crappie are found in this reservoir located east of Weiser. Elev.: 3,196 feet.

Ben Ross Reservoir (1,353 acres)

Located north of Crane Creek Reservoir this is a significant bluegill fishery with good populations of largemouth bass, bullhead, bluegill, crappie and rainbow trout. Quality bass regulations are in effect starting July 1. Regulations allow two bass only—none between 12 and 16 inches. Elev.: 3,153 feet.

Lost Valley Reservoir (1,633 acres)

This reservoir west of New Meadows features 10- to 16-inch rainbow trout from annual fingerling and catchable-rainbow plants. Brook trout are available. Perch stunt every few years requiring IDF&G to treat the lake and start over with hatchery catchables. Elev.: 4,760.

Payette River Drainage

Upper Payette Lake is fed by the North Fork of the Payette River that begins at about 6,073 feet where Cloochman and Trail creeks meet. The South Fork of the Payette begins at more than 8,000 feet in the Sawtooth Mountains and the Middle Fork of the Payette begins at nearly 6,300 feet in the Boise National Forest.

The main stem, flowing southwesterly for more than 175 miles, empties into the Snake River near Payette at an elevation of 2,125 feet. The Payette River Basin drains 3,240 square miles.

The North Fork drains 950 square miles and the South Fork 1,200 square miles. The drainage is comprised of granite soils that erode easily and are low in nutrients.

Due to its wide range in elevations, the Payette River has a wide variety of fish and fish habitats excluding salmon and steelhead that were shut out of the drainage by the Black Canyon Dam. There are many high mountain lakes that are stocked on a three-year rotation with a variety of trout and char. There are five major impoundments in the Payette Basin: Black Canyon, Sagehen, Paddock, Cascade and Deadwood reservoirs. There are several other smaller impoundments and larger, natural lakes, such as Payette Lake. Paddock Reservoir, on Little Willow Creek, has one of the state's better populations of crappie and is also a good fishery for largemouth bass.

Rivers Lakes and other Waters

Payette River

From its confluence with the Snake River at the city of Payette to the Black Canyon Dam near Emmett (about 45 river miles), water levels are controlled by the Black Canyon Dam. Many boaters and skiers also use the resource. Directly below Black Canyon Dam fishing is put-and-take with catchable rainbow trout and steelhead (when available). Other fish species include smallmouth and largemouth bass, channel catfish, mountain whitefish, black crappie, flathead catfish, bullhead, bluegill, yellow perch and pumpkinseed.

This stretch is well known for its smallmouth bass fishing. From Black Canyon Reservoir to the confluence of the North and South forks at Banks, the character of the river changes. Farther upstream the river has some of the most famous white-water rafting water in the U.S. The slope of the river increases, producing a buildup of cold-water species such as native rainbow trout, mountain whitefish and a few bull trout. Most of the fish in this section are wild.

Black Canyon Reservoir (1,000 acres)

The most common species here are warm-water fish: largemouth bass, crappie, bullhead, bluegill and channel catfish. There are three day-use parks below the dam and many areas accessible to bank anglers. Elev.: 2,503 feet.

Sawyer Ponds

This ponds hold largemouth bass, bluegill, crappie, pumpkinseed and stocked trout.

Emmett Airport and Star Road ponds FFW (four acres)

These are family fishing waters located within the Emmett city limits. General rules apply and these ponds have largemouth bass, bullhead, bluegill, pumpkinseed and channel catfish. Elev.: 2,345 feet.

Paddock Reservoir (1,302 acres)

Managed as a warm-water fishery, this reservoir's species include largemouth bass, crappie, bullhead catfish and bluegill. Elev.: 3,215 feet.

Horseshoe Bend Mill Pond (12 acres)

This small pond outside the town of Horseshoe Bend holds largemouth bass, pumpkinseed and bluegill. It is also stocked with catchable rainbow trout. Elev.: 2,600 feet.

Squaw, Willow and Little Willow creeks

These waters offer wild trout fishing for rainbows. There is a remnant population of bull trout in Squaw Creek and they are closed to harvest.

Sagehen Reservoir (180 acres)

This cold-water reservoir is a put-and-take fishery for catchable rainbow trout. Very popular—located in a heavily timbered area with trails. Elev.: 4,925 feet.

North Fork Payette River

From Banks to Smiths Ferry, this section of river, including tributaries, is managed for wild trout, primarily rainbow trout and mountain whitefish.

The Cabarton reach is roadless and produces wild trout in the area south of the Cascade Reservoir. The stretch from Smiths Ferry to the dam at Cascade, including tributaries, is also wild trout habitat. Its important species include rainbow trout and mountain whitefish. From Tamarack Falls Bridge to Lardo Dam, IDF&G is establishing naturally reproducing trout populations. The species in this section of river include rainbow and brook trout, mountain whitefish and kokanee salmon.

Cascade Reservoir on the North Fork is another heavily fished area in the state. Anglers have the opportunity to harvest perch and rainbow trout.

From Payette Lake to the headwaters at Fisher Creek, and other tributaries, it is a heavily fished put-and-take trout fishery for rainbow trout with brook trout and mountain whitefish. It has been stocked with cutthroat in an attempt to establish a self-sustaining population. It is closed to kokanee salmon fishing.

Gold Fork Creek

There are supplemental plantings in heavily fished areas. Species in this river, and tributary water, are put-and-take rainbow trout with brook trout, kokanee and bull trout. Bull trout are protected.

Lake Fork Creek

This stretch of wild trout waters, including tributaries, is populated by rainbow, brook and bull trout.

Above Little Payette Lake to Brown's Pond, it's trophy water with special regulations to encourage natural reproduction of rainbow trout and kokanee salmon.

From Brown's Pond to the headwaters, the creek is supplemented with hatchery trout in the higher-use areas. There are mountain whitefish, brook trout and stocked, catchable rainbow trout.

Boulder Creek

This stretch of river, northwest of McCall, holds rainbow and brook trout with supplemental stocking of hatchery trout in higher-use areas.

Valley County Ponds

There are more than 1,000 acres of rainbow and cutthroat trout water in the Valley County ponds. Three ponds below the Cascade Reservoir offer fine fishing for anyone looking for a fishing experience but not a wilderness adventure.

Browns Pond, south of the airport below Cascade Reservoir, is heavily fished water and Rowland's Pond, also known as Scouts Pond, has a high catch rate. Poor Man's Pond, on Boulder Creek Road, is another popular urban fishery. These are designated family fishing waters.

These ponds, with their ease of access, are important because they offer fishing opportunities to individuals who cannot, or do not care to, go into the more rugged regions to fish. They are excellent classrooms for beginners as well.

Horsethief Reservoir (1,270 acres)

This fishery offers good fishing and easy access. Fishing is open year round and the reservoir is stocked with catchable fish. The reservoir contains rainbow, brook, and brown trout and cuttbow hybrids and splake. Yellow perch are also present. Elev.: 5,050 feet

Brush Lake

Trophy trout waters for rainbow, cutthroat and cuttbow hybrids. Elev.: 7,092 feet.

Louie Lake
Trophy waters for cutthroat trout. Elev.: 7,000 feet.

Cascade Reservoir (28,300 acres)
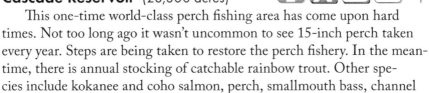
This one-time world-class perch fishing area has come upon hard times. Not too long ago it wasn't uncommon to see 15-inch perch taken every year. Steps are being taken to restore the perch fishery. In the meantime, there is annual stocking of catchable rainbow trout. Other species include kokanee and coho salmon, perch, smallmouth bass, channel catfish, crappie and tiger muskie. Elevation: 4,836 feet.

Corral Creek Reservoir (40 acres)

A very good fishery near Cascade and south of Horsethief Reservoir stocked with rainbow trout. Elev.: 5,250 feet.

Herrick Reservoir (30 acres)

A very good rainbow trout fishery near Cascade south of Corral Creek Reservoir with bullhead catfish. Elev.: 4,872 feet.

Payette Lake Complex
There are three Payette Lakes. The biggest one, usually just called Payette Lake, is actually Lower Payette Lake. Upper Payette Lake is a small lake 19 miles north of McCall and drains into Lower Payette Lake. Little Payette Lake is east of McCall.

Little Payette Lake (1,450 acres)
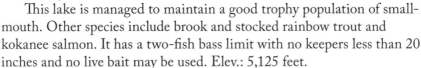
This lake is managed to maintain a good trophy population of smallmouth. Other species include brook and stocked rainbow trout and kokanee salmon. It has a two-fish bass limit with no keepers less than 20 inches and no live bait may be used. Elev.: 5,125 feet.

Upper Payette Lake (400 acres)

This is a hatchery-supported system with splake, brook trout and stocked rainbow trout in the Payette National Forest north of Payette Lake. Elev.: 5,515 feet.

Payette Lake (5,337 acres)

General fish management regulations apply to stocked west-slope cutthroat and rainbow trout. Hatchery rainbow are used to supplement heavily fished areas.

The lake trout are old-growth fish planted in the 1950s and, according to Fish and Game, there are some lakers weighing more than 30 pounds. All lake trout (mackinaw) must be released. Elev.: 4,993 feet.

Middle Fork Payette River

North of Crouch to Silver Creek Plunge Bridge, it's put-and-take fishing with catchable rainbow trout. Other species include cutthroat trout, mountain whitefish, brook, rainbow and bull trout.

Above Silver Creek Plunge Bridge, no fish are stocked in order to retain the area as a native fishery. The area is under wild trout management rules and species present include rainbow, cutthroat, brook and bull trout and mountain whitefish.

Granite Lake (300 acres)

North of Brundage Reservoir. Stocked with rainbow trout. Elevation: 6,742 feet.

South Fork Payette River

The South Fork of the Payette River supports good populations of wild rainbow trout and is one of the most popular recreation areas in the region. From its mouth to the Deadwood River it is wild trout water with rainbow trout and an occasional bull trout. No stocking.

From Helende to the headwaters in the Sawtooth Mountains there is no stocking, and the river is managed as a wild trout area. Important species include cutthroat and brook trout, mountain whitefish and bull trout. Rainbow trout are the dominant species.

Below Lowman, anglers share the river with white-water rafters and kayakers for space on the river. Primarily a rafting river during warm weather.

Deadwood Reservoir (3,000 acres)

This impoundment in the Boise National Forest is managed as a kokanee salmon fishery. It is also managed to maintain a self-sustaining population of westslope cutthroat trout. A thirteen-pound Atlantic salmon was caught in 1995 from a stocking program of a few years earlier.

Other species include rainbow, brook and bull trout, landlocked chinook salmon and mountain whitefish. Bull trout are protected. Elev.: 5,315 feet.

Deadwood River

From its mouth to the Deadwood Dam, including tributaries, there are 30 miles of water maintained as a wild trout fishery. The important species in this roadless area include rainbow and bull trout and mountain whitefish.

Clear Creek

This tributary to the South Fork of the Payette near Lowman is a wild trout fishery with rainbow and bull trout and mountain whitefish.

Canyon Creek

This creek enters the South Fork downstream from Grandjean then can be accessed from the highway to the Stanley Basin before Banner Summit. Cutthroat and rainbow trout are the primary species.

Bull Trout Lake (90 acres)

Brook trout provide the majority of the fishing in this lake a few miles off the highway between Lowman and Stanley. Martin Lake is west of Bull Trout Lake and is accessed by a foot trail. The area is managed to provide fishing in an attractive, forest setting. Bull Trout Lake is stocked with hatchery rainbow. Elev.: 6,936 feet.

Warm Spring Creek

From its confluence with the South Fork Payette to Bull Trout Lake, including tributaries, there are 30 miles of water maintained as a wild trout fishery. The important species in this roadless area include rainbow and bull trout and mountain whitefish.

Alpine Lakes

About half of the alpine lakes within the Payette River drainage are stocked to provide anglers with a variety of fishing opportunities for rainbow and westslope cutthroat trout and cuttbow trout hybrids and Arctic grayling. Some of the lakes have self-sustaining trout populations. Brook trout are present in many alpine lakes.

Boise River Drainage

With its headwaters in the Sawtooth Mountains, the Boise river flows through some of the most spectacular scenery in the state. From above Atlanta to its confluence with the Snake River near Parma the basin drains approximately 4,100 square miles in southwest Idaho. Over its course it drops almost 8,000 feet in elevation and flows for 200 miles.

The North Fork headwaters are above 8,000 feet in the Sawtooth Wilderness National Recreation Area and the river drains more than 300 square miles before it meets the Middle Fork above Twin Springs.

The Middle Fork begins in a high mountain lake above Atlanta and flows south and west where it meets the South Fork of the Boise River to form the backwater of Arrowrock Dam.

The South Fork, the most famous and heavily fished of the three forks, begins at the confluence of the Ross Fork and Johnson Creek. The basin drains about 1,300 square miles in the Boise Mountains.

Of the three major impoundments, Anderson Ranch, Arrowrock and Lucky Peak. Anderson Ranch on the South Fork provides the most diverse cold-water fishery with a variety of trout and kokanee salmon.

From the wild lands of the Boise and Sawtooth Mountains the main stem of the river is impounded by Arrowrock and Lucky Peak dams. Upstream of the impoundments the rivers and streams contain populations of native rainbow trout, mountain whitefish and bull trout. Brook trout, rainbow and some cutthroat trout are found in tributary streams.

Passing through Arrowrock the river changes again as it passes through downtown Boise and the Boise State University campus and along the paved riverside path known as the Greenbelt where the river is stocked with fingerling brown and rainbow trout and adult steelhead seasonally.

The river is stocked with catchable size rainbow trout year-round and managed for heavy fishing pressure. Brood stock steelhead are planted

when available. This section through town is heavily fished, and one of the most productive urban fisheries in a major metropolitan area in America.

From the west end of Ada County the river is a mixed fishery supporting numerous warm-water species including largemouth and smallmouth bass, channel catfish, crappie and mountain whitefish with some rainbow trout.

Throughout the lower region mountain whitefish make up the bulk of the game fish population with hatchery-reared, put-and-take rainbow trout, wild rainbow trout and brown trout also present. See *Idaho's Big 10* page 40.

....

Rivers, Lakes and other Waters

Park Center Pond and Veterans Park Pond

General regulations apply on these public waters managed to maximize local fishing in Boise. Species of importance include largemouth bass, bluegill, pumpkinseed, smallmouth bass, bullhead and channel catfish, crappie and rainbow trout. Elev.: 2,716 feet.

Beach's Pond (five acres)

This small urban pond holds smallmouth bass and bullhead catfish. No camping.

Caldwell Ponds FFW (nine acres)

This urban fishery is stocked with hatchery trout and it also contains largemouth bass, bluegill, bullhead and channel catfish, crappie and pumpkinseed.

Wilson Springs Ponds FFW (11 acres)

There are several ponds here. Some are fly-fishing only for trout and some have smallmouth and largemouth bass.

Duff Lane Pond (2 acres)

These ponds off State Highway 44 east of Middleton have channel catfish, largemouth bass, bluegill and crappie.

Lake Lowell (10,000 acres)

This man-made lake is managed by both the Bureau of Reclamation and the U.S. Fish and Wildlife Service. Fish species include rainbow trout, largemouth bass, smallmouth bass, crappie, yellow perch, pumpkinseed, bluegill, bullhead and channel catfish and rainbow and cutthroat trout.

Both species of bass are managed by quality regulations while the other species are managed by general regulations. Open year-round. Elev.: 2,523 feet.

Logger Creek

This is a quality fishery with a high volume of catchable fish of minimal size. Species include rainbow and brown trout and mountain whitefish. Brood stock steelhead are planted when available.

Grimes and Mores Creek

Placer mining tailings from the gold rush days of Idaho City can still be seen throughout the area. Both streams have brook and hatchery rainbow trout and mountain whitefish.

North Fork Boise River

From its mouth to Rabbit Creek it is managed as a wild fishery for rainbow trout with mountain whitefish present. Bull trout are protected.

From Rabbit Creek to Deer Park (Hunter Creek). It is a put-and-take rainbow trout fishery and from Deer Park to the headwaters general management rules apply. Brook and cutthroat trout are also present. See *Idaho's Big 10* page 40.

Middle Fork Boise River

This stream is often overlooked in favor of the South Fork. It is an excellent late-season fishery with many wadeable sections. From Arrowrock to its confluence with the North Fork of the Boise River (11 miles) the river is stocked with catchable rainbow trout after high water through Labor Day.

The run from the North Fork confluence upstream to the Atlanta Power Dam is a quality, wild trout fishery with low fishing pressure. Important species include rainbow, bull, cutthroat and brook trout and mountain whitefish. From the Atlanta Dam to the Sawtooth Wilderness boundary, it's a put-and-take fishery with catchable rainbow trout stocked

after high water periods until Labor Day.

The section upstream from the Sawtooth Wilderness boundary, including all tributaries, is managed as a wild fishery and has low angler densities. Bull trout are protected. See *Idaho's Big 10* page 40.

South Fork Boise River

From Arrowrock Reservoir to Neil Bridge, the South Fork is general regulation water. Species present are rainbow trout and mountain whitefish. Bull trout are protected. From Neil Bridge to Anderson Ranch Dam the river is managed as trophy water with a two-fish limit and no bait and barbless hook restrictions. All fish less than 20 inches must be released.

From Anderson Ranch Dam Reservoir to Beaver Creek, it is a put-and -take fishery for rainbow trout with general regulations for kokanee and mountain whitefish.

From Beaver Creek to Big Smoky Creek the river is managed as a quality fishery with general regulations for kokanee and mountain whitefish. From Big Smoky Creek to the headwaters it's a put-and-take fishery with quality trout water. Easy access and numerous campgrounds make it a popular area. Its species include rainbow and bull trout, mountain whitefish and kokanee salmon. See *Idaho's Big 10* page 40.

Indian Creek Reservoir (221 acres)

When water is available largemouth bass and bluegill are stocked in this body of water that can be seen from I-84 near the Boise Stage Stop truck stop (exit 71).

Big Smoky Creek

From its mouth to Calf Creek, this river is a put-and-take rainbow trout fishery with quality trout habitat. Easily accessible with mountain whitefish and kokanee salmon.

From Calf Creek to the headwaters, it's 15 miles of wild trout fishery with a self-sustaining rainbow trout population along with mountain whitefish and protected bull trout.

Little Smoky Creek

This is a 20-mile long put-and-take rainbow trout fishery with general season regulations applying.

Other tributary streams

There are 277 miles of tributaries that drain into the Boise River above Anderson Ranch Reservoir. These waters hold rainbow and bull trout and mountain whitefish. Some are insignificant as fisheries.

Lucky Peak Reservoir (2,850 acres)

Lucky Peak Reservoir's elevation is about 3,000 feet. The reservoir is created by Lucky Peak Dam and it stores water used for farms in the surrounding area. It's a popular site for boating and fishing enthusiasts.

This reservoir, about 16 miles southeast of Boise, is a rainbow trout fishery with planted fish making up the majority of the catch. The reservoir is stocked with kokanee salmon on a regular basis. Other species include smallmouth bass, perch, sturgeon, chinook salmon and bull trout.

Lucky Peak reservoir provides a two-story fishery with smallmouth bass occupying the warm inshore waters and rainbow trout and kokanee residing in the deeper cold-water areas. Kokanee and bull trout are protected.

Arrowrock Reservoir (4,000 acres)

This impoundment northeast of Lucky Peak, fed by the South Fork of the Boise River, includes smallmouth bass, perch, rainbow and bull trout and mountain whitefish. It is also stocked with kokanee salmon and fingerling rainbow trout. Elev.: 3,222 feet.

Anderson Ranch Reservoir (4,740 acres)

This reservoir is formed by Anderson Ranch Dam and covers seven and a half square miles. It is managed by the Boise National Forest and is approximately 14 miles long and a mile wide, with depths to 315 feet and 50 miles of shoreline. Located southeast of Boise, hiking, boating, waterskiing and fishing are its major recreation activities. Fish species are kokanee, rainbow trout, smallmouth bass, yellow perch and bull trout. Season open year-round

Located in the center of Elmore County, on the South Fork of the Boise River, this reservoir is popular for its kokanee salmon. Other species in this impoundment include bull trout, perch, fall chinook salmon, smallmouth bass and mountain whitefish.

Good spawning conditions in its tributary streams provide a continuous supply of kokanee. This is one of the more popular kokanee fisheries in southern Idaho. Elev.: 4,202 feet.

Mountain Home Reservoir

This reservoir off Interstate 84 is stocked with rainbow trout and has largemouth bass and bluegill.

Little Camas Reservoir (1,455 acres)

During normal to high-water years this reservoir is very productive and holds good-sized rainbow trout and smallmouth bass. Located about 10 miles from Anderson Ranch Dam, is regularly stocked with hatchery fish. Low-water years are another story. Elev.: 4,924 feet.

Featherville Dredge ponds (three acres)

Put-and-take fishing for rainbow trout in the old gold mining district. Elev.: 4,519 feet.

Big Trinity Lake (25 acres)

Accessible by road, this put-and-take fishery is planted with rainbow and cutthroat trout fingerlings each fall. Elev.: 7,733 feet.

Little Trinity Lake (three acres)

Stocked with rainbow and cutthroat trout this put-and-take fishery is accessible by road and is north of Big Trinity Lake. Elev.: 7,777 feet.

Alpine Lakes

There are 224 alpine lakes in the Boise Drainage. Most are too small to support a fishery, so Fish and Game currently stocks only 68. Those that are stocked provide anglers with a broad variety of fishing opportunities. Rainbow, cutthroat and brook trout are abundant with lesser numbers of golden trout and Arctic grayling.

The Owyhee River and Bruneau River Drainages

The canyon lands of the Owyhee and Bruneau rivers offer some of the most spectacular scenery in the state. Located in Idaho's southwestern corner, Owyhee County is Idaho's second largest county by area. It is bordered by Nevada on the south, Oregon on the west, Canyon, Ada and Elmore counties on the north and Twin Falls County on the east.

The name, Owyhee, comes from early fur trappers. In 1819, three Hawaiian trappers, part of Donald McKenzie's fur-trapping expedition, were sent to trap a large stream that emptied into the Snake River. When they did not return, McKenzie investigated and found one man murdered in camp and no sign of the others. The stream was named Owyhee in their honor and is an early spelling for the word Hawaii. "Bruneau" is French for "brown water", probably indicating the river color after rainstorms.

The Owyhee and Bruneau rivers are located in southwestern Idaho, southeastern Oregon and northern Nevada in an area that thousands of years ago was once Lake Idaho, a massive body of water covering the entire region. A small tributary to the Salmon, draining the lake, eroded toward its headwaters until it reached the lake, creating a gigantic outlet that would eventually scour out Hells Canyon. The huge lake emptied, leaving, among other things, the Owyhee and Bruneau drainages.

Today, the basin encompasses approximately 11,340 square miles of semiarid high desert country, with 8,000 square miles in Idaho. In the higher bench lands, the Bruneau and Owyhee rivers have scoured out beautiful desert canyons. This magnificently lonely area is one of the most remote and sparsely populated in the nation.

Owyhee River Drainage

Elevations in the Owyhee drainage range from 8,100 feet in the Owyhee mountains to 2,400 feet at the Snake River.

There are 239 miles of river, including tributaries, downstream from the South Fork. The waters are managed to maintain high catch rates for smallmouth bass and rainbow trout.

The North Fork is a cold-water fishery, managed for wild trout with

rainbow trout as the major species.

The South Fork of the Owyhee River, including its tributaries, is managed for high catch rates of smallmouth bass and rainbow trout. The 12-mile section from the confluence of the Main and South Fork to the Nevada border has smallmouth bass and a rainbow trout population that varies from year to year.

Populations of native rainbow trout are found throughout most of the Owyhee River drainage. A Bureau of Land Management resource inventory identified rainbow trout in 23 of 27 perennial streams and seven of 15 intermittent streams in the drainage. Due to the unique qualities of this fishery and the inaccessibility of the Owyhee region, this entire drainage is managed for species preservation. Lahontan cutthroat trout have been introduced into several reservoirs near Riddle.

Bruneau River Drainage

Elevations in the Bruneau drainage range from more than 10,000 feet in the Jarbidge Mountains to 2,455 feet at its mouth. There are no cutthroat trout in the Bruneau River drainage, but rainbow trout are found in good numbers and there are some bull trout. Native rainbow trout are also found in some tributaries (above the mouth of the Jarbidge River), including Big Jacks and Little Jacks Creek.

From the mouth of the Bruneau River upstream to the Bruneau Hot Springs, the water is ideal for smallmouth bass and channel catfish. There are some rainbow trout here. There's significant fishing pressure on the more accessible streams of the Bruneau River Drainage, but pressure is extremely light on the inaccessible waters, for obvious reasons.

The Bruneau and the main stem of the Jarbidge, downstream from its confluence with the Bruneau River, are popular floating and rafting waters. From the upper diversion dam to the West Fork, including tributaries, it is managed as wild trout water with rainbow and bull trout and mountain whitefish. Access is limited to this deeply incised river canyon.

The East Fork, including Clover Creek and its tributaries, is a cold-water fishery, managed as wild trout water with rainbow, bull and brook trout, as well as mountain whitefish. Access is limited to this reach by deep canyons.

The Bruneau River from the upper diversion dam to the West Fork is also a cold-water fishery managed for wild trout. The river contains populations of rainbow trout and mountain whitefish as the predominant species. Bull trout are present and protected.

The Bruneau River, West Fork, lower East Fork, lower Sheep Creek and the Jarbidge River have been recommended for National Wild River status.

Grazing on some of the tributary streams has detrimentally affected fish habitat.

Lakes, Rivers and other Waters

Deep Creek
This cold-water fishery and its tributaries have native rainbow trout.

Battle Creek
Native rainbow trout are the main species in this desert river.

Blue Creek
This river is a cold-water fishery with rainbow and cutthroat trout. Managed as a wild trout fishery, though an insignificant one.

Juniper Basin Reservoir (200 acres)
This is a warm-water reservoir with crappie as the primary species. It's an insignificant fishery that can dry up late in the season.

Riddle Lakes Reservoir Complex
These are desert reservoirs that are maintained as fisheries when water is available. The roads are rough so four-wheel drive vehicles are recommended. None of the roads, except for perhaps the main Riddle Road, is suitable for RVs or trailers.

Leave gates as you found them. May and June, then again in September, are the best times to visit the area. The constant winds can keep the water murky and make casting a fly a chore.

Blue Creek Reservoir (131 acres)
This reservoir is stocked with rainbow trout after low-water years and it is managed for native rainbow trout preservation. Fishing can be tough

due to difficult access and cloudy water. Elev.: 5,410 feet.

Little Blue Creek Reservoir (188 acres)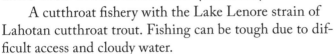

A cutthroat fishery with the Lake Lenore strain of Lahotan cutthroat trout. Fishing can be tough due to difficult access and cloudy water.

Grasmere Reservoir (213 acres)

This reservoir in the Owyhee Desert is stocked with rainbow and cutthroat trout. Elev.: 5,217 feet.

Mary's Creek Reservoir (120 acre)

Stocked with rainbow trout, this reservoir also contains shiners and freshwater shrimp.

Shoofly Reservoir (85 acres) Bybee Reservoir (70 acres)

These reservoirs are stocked annually with trout. Bybee's elevation is 5,434 feet.

Payne Creek Reservoir (70 acres)

This reservoir in the Owyhee Desert is stocked with cutthroat trout.

Squaw Creek Reservoir (80 acres)

Rainbow trout are found in this impoundment that has both warm-water and cold-water species. It's insignificant as far as fishing goes.

Sand Dunes Lakes

Located in Bruneau Sand Dunes State Park near Mountain Home, these lakes cover approximately 100 acres of fishable water. The small lakes at the foot of the dunes provide an excellent bass and bluegill fishery. Fishing from non-motorized boats, canoes, rubber rafts and float tubes is the most common method. Elev.: 2,484 feet.

Sheep Creek

This stretch of water, including Mary's Creek, is a cold-water fishery managed as wild trout water for rainbow trout.

Jarbidge River

"Jarbidge" is a Shoshone Indian word for "monster". The river and tributaries are managed as wild trout waters. Species include bull and rainbow trout and mountain whitefish. Access from the Murphy Hot Springs area may require a hike up a steep canyon. Bull trout are protected.

Big Jack Creek

This is a desert stream managed for wild rainbow.

Jordan Creek

High drainage with a good population of rainbow trout.

Big Boulder Creek

Wild rainbow water.

....

Airstrips

Atlanta (state)

This old mining town still has many year-round residents even though it is a long haul and a dusty road that takes you there. Located on the western edge of the Sawtooth mountain range. Atlanta Airport serves Atlanta and Elmore County and is owned by the State of Idaho Division of Aeronautics. The dirt runway extends for 2,650 feet. The facility is at an elevation of 5,500 feet and about one mile from Atlanta.

Deadwood (backcountry)

This is another tricky one on a hill next to Deadwood Reservoir. There are no tie-downs, and at the top (east end) of the runway a road crosses so watch out for earth-bound vehicles. Its elevation is 5,400 feet.

Garden Valley (state)

Garden Valley Airport serves Garden Valley and Boise County and is owned by the State of Idaho Division of Aeronautics. The turf runway extends for 3,850 feet. The facility is at an elevation of 3,177 feet about two miles from Garden Valley.

Graham (backcountry)

A very backcountry strip on the North Fork of the Boise River. Located east of the river the strip is 2,900 feet long and 50 feet wide at an elevation of 5,726 feet.

Grasmere (desert)

Grasmere Airport serves Grasmere and Owyhee County and is owned by the State of Idaho Transportation Department's Aeronautics Division. The turf runway extends for 2,750 feet. The facility is at an elevation of 5,134 feet and about a mile or less from Grasmere.

Murphy Hot Springs (backcountry/state)

Murphy Hot Springs Airport serves Three Creek and Owyhee County and is owned by the State of Idaho Transportation Department's Aeronautics Division. The turf runway extends for 5,250 feet. The facility is at an elevation of 5,829 feet and about 9 miles from Three Creek.

Smith's Prairie (state)

If you are willing to hitch a ride down to the South Fork of the Boise River from the Prairie Store (about 10 miles) you will find good water from Danskin Bridge upstream to Anderson Dam. Downstream will take you through a narrow canyon with limited access for about 15 miles. The Smith's Prairie strip is located on the high ranchland above the South Fork of the Boise River valley at an elevation of 4,958 feet and it is 5,400 feet long and 175 feet wide.

Simonds (backcountry)

This is a short (900 feet), difficult airstrip on Monumental Creek. Flying in with an experienced pilot is necessary. The strip's elevation is 5,243 feet and it's about 40 feet wide.

Warm Springs (state)

Warm Springs Creek Airport serves Lowman and Boise County and is owned by the State of Idaho Transportation Department's Aeronautics Division. The turf runway extends for 2,850 feet. The facility is at an elevation of 4,831 feet at a distance of about 13 miles from Lowman. Hot springs are available in the area.

Weatherby (backcountry)

Just down-stream from Atlanta on the north side of the Middle Fork of the Boise River. The airstrip's elevation is 4,494 feet and it is 2,260 feet long and 60 feet wide.

ACCESSORIZE

In the words of Somerset Maughn, "You never step in the same river twice." Every angling experience is a new adventure and every adventure requires adaptability, and the ability to adapt may require special tools.

Preparation is the key to a successful fishing trip. Just as it is important to have the right fly or lure for the situation, it is also important to accessorize properly. **Loon Outdoors** product experts have provided brief summaries regarding a few accessories. Some of these may be known to readers while some are new to the fishing industry.

Zingers.   A zinger is an elastic retrievable cord that can attach to your vest or chest pack. Zingers with a stainless steel housing and clip will not corrode, and a wire, retractable cord will last longer than a fabric cord. Zingers help keep your snips, forceps, fly floatant, hook hone, or leader straightener ready for action.

Nippers.   These tools are glorified fingernail clippers that provide anglers the razor sharpness needed to slice through a 25-lb. test monofilament, as well as the precision to trim a piece of 8X tippet from a size 26 midge.

Chest Packs.   A fishing chest pack should be comfortable and compact, yet big enough to hold everything an angler needs. Some packs are designed to hinge outward when opened, allowing instant access and creating a stable, working platform. Some pack designs incorporate inside storage for forceps, thermometers, pliers, etc. with an extra larger pocket. Outside flap covers can hold four tippet sizes, and most packs have a storage pocket for miscellaneous gear in back.

Vests.   Anglers who prefer traditional vests can choose features including shoulder support, padded collars and nylon mesh backs. Choose a pocket configuration matching the gear you carry and a length that keeps lower pockets dry when wading.

Wader Repair Kit.   Leaking waders can ruin your day. Make sure you have a wader patch kit along for minor rips and tears. One of the newer items in the fishing accessory market is the sunlight activated patch kit. Simply smear a drop or two on the tear or pin hole, let dry in direct sunlight and you're ready to get back in the water.

Cleaners & Lubricants.   Fishing line, especially fly lines, perform at their best when they are clean and dirt free. Cleaners and lubricants are solutions that remove slime or some other impurity that might cause a floating line to sink or make a sinking line react in a way it was not designed to react. These accessories are often applied with a cloth and can block damaging UV rays while filling in imperfections in the line. Treated lines cast farther and last longer.

Floatants.   In the course of casting a dry fly, it may become saturated for a variety of reasons, ranging from being dragged underwater by a fighting fish to simply sinking beneath the water. Desiccants (dry floatants) usually come in a plastic or tin container. To dry a saturated fly simply place the fly, with tippet attached, into the container and shake. This removes water and coats the fly with powder floatant in one easy step. For best results coat your fresh, dry fly once with a gel floatant before dipping it into the desiccant before you begin to fish.

If you prefer a gel use one that will not leave a slick on still waters or spring creeks. If you fish the hatches of large flies, such as stone flies, or fish dries for steelhead, before you even get your fly wet work the floatant into the hair and hackle with your fingers and then watch it float high cast after cast. When you need to float a fly in swirling pocket water for hours at a time, gel might give you a longer float.

Sinks.   These putty-like substances are formulated for application to nymphs and sub-surface flies to help them break surface tension and sink rapidly. Sinks can also allow wet flies to absorb water allowing the fly to roll along the bottom as naturally as a dislodged nymph. They can also help sink leaders and reduce leader flash.

There are also biodegradable, pliable, putty-like non-lead sinks on the market. On hot days you can place the product container into the stream to "firm up" to a desirable consistency. On cold days you can keep the container close to your body so it can remain pliable. Place at the head of dry flies or nymphs to sink and attract.

Indicators.   There are natural wool yarns coated with watershed water-proofing treatment on the market today that floats better than nylon or poly yarns. They come in a variety of colors including orange, white and yellow. For best results tie a bit of indicator above a knot allowing the wet fly to float through the water table at the desired depth. Try several colors in series for best visibility, and remember—bigger yarn for bigger flies or weaker eyes.

Biodegradable, high-float strike indicator putty can be used with wets or small dry flies. For best results, wet fingers before handling the putty. Form a football shape piece on a preferred section of leader on a leader knot. This will increase your wet fly hook ups and help you follow dry flies as well. Try a series of different colors to help visibility in varying light conditions.

For more information on fishing accessories call

Loon Outdoors at **208.362.4437**

or visit **www.loonoutdoors.com**

See Sponsor Page in the Sponsor Index p. 242.

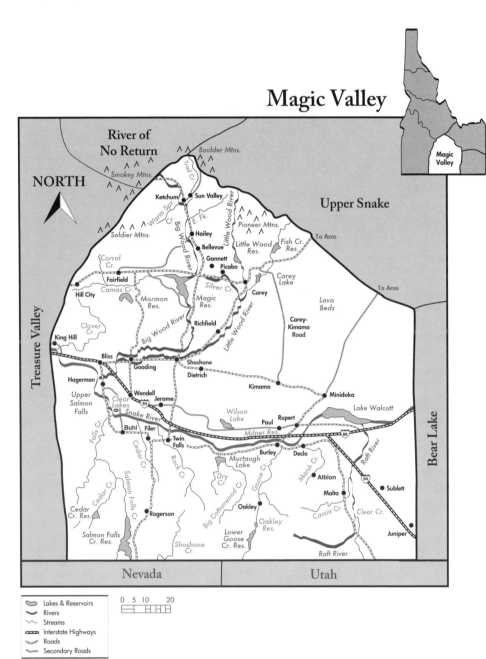

Magic Valley

River of
No Return

NORTH

Boulder Mtns.

Smokey Mtns.

Trail Cr.

Magic
Valley

Upper Snake

Ketchum
Sun Valley

Warm Spr. Cr.

E. Fk.

Big Wood River

Little Wood River

Pioneer Mtns.

To Arco

Soldier Mtns.
Hailey

Bellevue

Little Wood
Res.

Fish Cr.
Res.

Corral
Cr.

Gannett

Picabo

Fairfield

Silver Cr.

Carey
Lake

To Arco

Hill City

Camas Cr.

Mormon
Res.

Magic
Res.

Carey

Lava
Beds

Treasure Valley

Clover
Cr.

King Hill

Big Wood River

Richfield

Little Wood River

Carey-
Kimama
Road

Bliss

Gooding

Shoshone

Dietrich

Hagerman

Kimama

Minidoka

Upper
Salmon
Falls

Clear
Lakes

Wendell
Jerome

84

Snake River

Wilson
Lake

Paul

Rupert

Lake Walcott

86

Bear Lake

Falls Cr.

Buhl
Filer

Cedar Cr.

Twin
Falls

Milner Res.

Burley

Declo

Raft River

Murtaugh
Lake

Dry
Cr.

Goose Cr.

Rock Cr.

March Cr.

Albion

84

Sublett

Malta

Salmon Falls Cr.

Cedar Cr.

Cedar
Cr. Res.

Rogerson

Big Cottonwood Cr.

Oakley

Cassia Cr.

Clear Cr.

Juniper

Salmon Falls
Cr. Res.

Shoshone
Cr.

Lower
Goose
Cr. Res.

Oakley
Res.

Raft River

Nevada

Utah

Lakes & Reservoirs
Rivers
Streams
Interstate Highways
Roads
Secondary Roads

0 5 10   20

Magic Valley

The Magic Region is certain to stir your imagination. From the snowcapped mountain peaks that rise above the Wood River Valley, south to the Snake River, fishing opportunities abound. On its southern edge, the fortune seekers that traveled the Oregon Trail left their marks along the way and the lakes, streams and reservoirs hold a variety of game fish. This region has something for everyone.

You can fish for nine-foot sturgeon in the deep, dark pools of the Snake River, or present tiny dry flies to rainbow trout that leave a faint, shadowy trace as the they sip size 22 mayflies on world famous Silver Creek at the foot of the Picabo Hills. If you are after something less mysterious, though no less challenging, you can toss a flashing spinner to a big bass lurking along the shore of the region's large reservoirs.

There are four major drainages southeast of the Snake River between C. J. Strike Reservoir and Massacre Rocks with a combined area of more than 6,870 square miles: Raft River, Goose Creek, Rock Creek and Salmon Falls Creek. There are three major reservoirs: Oakley, Salmon Falls Creek and Roseworth; and one minor reservoir, Sublett. These reservoirs all support trout fisheries varying from fair to excellent. Sublett has excellent reproduction in its tributary streams, and the region boasts two of the three major walleye fisheries in the state.

As in most of the southern portion of the state, the Snake River plays an important part in the land use and the lives of the people here. It not only provides water for electrical power generation and the irrigation of thousands and thousands of acres of what otherwise would be arid land, but it is an amazingly productive fishery as well.

The Magic Region has more trout farms than any other area of the country, shipping millions of pounds of fish-farmed rainbow trout to every corner of the nation. Freshwater springs flowing from the Snake River Aquifer are the key to the trout farm industry.

Trout habitat in the main Snake River has diminished recently between C. J. Strike and Lake Walcott in Cassia County.

The best area on this stretch is between King Hill and Shoshone Falls where many clean springs enter the river rising from the Snake River Aquifer. These springs include 11 of the 65 springs in the U.S. with an average discharge rate of 100 cubic feet per second or more and the water quality of these springs is excellent.

Water from melting snow in the Lost River Range seeps into the lava flows near the Craters of the Moon National Monument and Preserve on the edge of the Arco Desert. Two hundred years later the water emerges at Thousand Springs on the north bank of the Snake River in the Hagerman Valley.

However, the combination of agricultural, commercial and industrial use of the aquifer has increased the level of nutrients entering the system below the springs.

Still, trophy size trout are taken in some areas of the Snake River. Many of the minor tributaries feeding the Snake are also very good trout waters, supporting fine populations of wild trout, primarily rainbow trout. Some of the streams, especially those that are spring-fed, are used by spawning trout in the stretches of the Snake below the Minidoka Dam. Rod-bending rainbow, brown and cutthroat trout and cuttbow hybrids are all there waiting.

The best trout fishing in the Snake River is usually found near the mouths of springs where cool, clean water enters. There is also good trout fishing in Lake Walcott above Minidoka Dam. Most of those trout are hatchery fish that were stocked as fingerlings. A plentiful food supply means good growth rates resulting in numerous fish in the 14- to 20-inch size class being caught.

Since it is part of the Minidoka Wildlife Refuge, boating access on Lake Walcott is restricted by the U.S. Fish and Wildlife Service. You may fish from a boat from April 1 through September 30 within areas designated by the Fish and Wildlife Service. This includes an area from the dam up the reservoir approximately four miles to a buoy line west of Bird Island in Cassia County.

There are also two smaller boat fishing lanes at Smith Springs and at Gifford Springs east of Lake Walcott. Smallmouth bass are also present in good numbers in Lake Walcott, especially within the upper reaches.

Milner Reservoir also provides excellent smallmouth bass fishing. There are some rainbow trout, yellow perch and channel catfish but most of the action is for smallmouth bass.

Downstream of Milner Reservoir, dam irrigation and industrial use essentially dewater segments of the river channel until it picks up significant spring flows nearer Twin Falls. Access is difficult throughout this segment of the canyon reach, but smallmouth bass are present in some areas. Further downstream, within the Thousand Springs reach, there is more spring influence and that is where you will find rainbow trout. Other species pres-

ent include yellow perch, bluegill, largemouth bass, white sturgeon and numerous species of nongame fish.

There are essentially no brown trout in the main stem of the Snake River. There are, however, brown trout in lower Rock and Billingsley creeks and the lower Malad River.

Warm-water fisheries are also numerous in the main stem Snake River in the Magic region and its impoundments. There is good fishing for largemouth and smallmouth bass, bluegill, bullhead, channel catfish and perch.

Throughout most of the free-flowing reaches of the Snake between Lake Walcott and C. J. Strike Reservoir trout habitat is good and the river contains seven reservoirs suitable for trout. They are Bliss, Upper and Lower Salmon Falls, Shoshone Falls, Twin Falls and Milner reservoirs and Lake Walcott. The Lower Salmon Falls Reservoir trout population is supported by hatchery rainbow trout. Lower Salmon Falls Creek Reservoir in the southern reach of the region is one of three major walleye fisheries in the state.

Many of the smaller lakes, ponds, and reservoirs close to the Snake River have excellent conditions for rainbow trout. White sturgeon, some growing to more than nine feet, are found in the free-flowing region of the Snake River below Shoshone Falls near Twin Falls to C. J. Strike Reservoir.

Not many areas of the world offer the majestic scenery, world-class skiing, fishing, hunting, and celebrity-sighting opportunities available in the Magic Region that includes Sun Valley, Silver Creek and the Wood River Valley. In fact, this is probably the most famous section of Idaho. Even so, there is still plenty of exciting fishing available throughout the rest of the region. That is part of the magic.

Snake River Drainage

From Loveridge Bridge (Highway 51, south of Mountain Home) to the Bliss Dam (47.3 miles), the general fish population consists of rainbow trout, mountain whitefish, channel catfish, smallmouth and largemouth bass, yellow perch and white sturgeon.

The best sturgeon water in this region is the free-flowing river section between C. J. Strike Reservoir and Shoshone Falls east of the city of Twin Falls where sturgeon are successfully reproducing. Sturgeon grow at a rapid rate in this area. Some fish, perhaps holdovers from the TBD (Time Before the Dams) reach lengths of more than nine feet. Angler interest in this species is high, even though it is catch-and-release fishing.

The Bliss Reservoir is five miles long and covers 625 surface acres. Its fish population consists mainly of warm-water species.

In the eight miles of backwaters from the Bliss Pool to Lower Salmon Falls Dam it is catch-and-release for sturgeon. There are also rainbow trout, mountain whitefish, smallmouth and largemouth bass and yellow perch.

Lower Salmon Falls Reservoir, a popular bass fishing area, covers 420 surface acres. It is stocked with rainbow trout at Bell Rapids and holds largemouth bass and bluegill. Boat access is at Bell Rapids and the Lower Salmon Falls Dam. There is no camping, but Idaho Power has picnic areas available.

The Lower Salmon Falls area is a higher-quality summer fishery than the Upper Salmon and a popular wintertime fishery with lots of hatchery rainbows. It is catch-and-release from January through the end of June.

Upper Salmon Falls Reservoir is five miles long with more than 800 surface acres of water. Its rainbow trout, largemouth and smallmouth bass get a lot of attention. Boat access is at Owsley Bridge from Highway 30.

From the backwater of the Upper Salmon Falls Reservoir to Shoshone Falls, there is a collection of mixed fisheries. Habitat for sturgeon is good here. Fishing for these big fish is on a catch-and-release basis only. Dolman Rapids is known for large rainbow trout. This stretch also includes largemouth and smallmouth bass, mountain whitefish and perch.

Anglers often boat up to Pillar Falls from Centennial Park near the city of Twin Falls to fish for rainbow trout and white sturgeon. The fish are stocked at Centennial Park on the south side of Perrine Bridge.

Shoshone Falls Reservoir is a little more than one mile long with a good population of rainbow trout and smallmouth bass.

Twin Falls Reservoir is a cold-water fishery, also one mile long, and it covers 96 acres. It is a mixed fishery with rainbow and cutthroat trout and cuttbow hybrids. The backwaters of the Twin Falls Reservoir to Murtaugh Bridge are managed under general regulations and species include cutthroat and rainbow trout, cuttbows and smallmouth bass.

Murtaugh Bridge to Milner Dam is a little more than eight miles with cutthroat and rainbow trout and smallmouth bass. Cutthroat trout and cuttbows are found mainly between Twin Falls and Milner Dam. Historically, some of these hybrids have reached weights of more than six pounds but recent drought conditions have taken their toll on the fishery.

Milner Reservoir has 3,000 acres of warm-water fish with smallmouth bass, some largemouth bass, perch and channel catfish. This reservoir has become one of the region's most popular destinations for bass tournaments. From the backwaters of Milner Reservoir to Minidoka Dam, there

is good cutthroat and rainbow trout, smallmouth bass and perch fishing.

Lake Walcott (Minidoka Reservoir) near Rupert covers 11,850 surface acres. It is a mixed fishery of stocked rainbow trout, cutthroat trout, perch, bullhead catfish, largemouth and smallmouth bass. These fish grow exceedingly fast but, because of the large area, catch rates are relatively low. Sturgeon that were stocked below American Falls Dam have been caught in the lake. Catfish are no longer stocked by Fish and Game from C.J. Strike to Lake Walcott, but Idaho Power does have a stocking program for Milner Reservoir.

Rivers, Lakes, and other Waters

Billingsley Creek

From its mouth to the Tupper Grade Crossing (5.5 miles) Billingsley Creek rules vary, depending on the section. From its mouth upstream to the old railroad grade upstream of the Billingsley Creek Wildlife Management Area, fishing is allowed under the general statewide rules for seasons, methods and limits.

From the old railroad grade upstream to Tupper Grade it is a two-trout limit with methods restricted to artificial flies and lures only and no trout less than 20 inches are allowed to be kept.

From Tupper Grade upstream to Vader Grade only fly-fishing is allowed. This rule was implemented several years ago under an agreement with the landowner who allows free public access to the segment just downstream of Vader Grade.

Young sturgeon can sometimes be seen swimming among the schooling fish in some of the deeper holes. From Vader Grade to the headwaters, it is wild rainbow trout water.

Malad River

The Malad River originates at the confluence of the Big Wood and the Little Wood rivers about four miles west of Gooding. Rainbow trout can be found in the lower portion of the Malad downstream of Interstate 84. Access to the lower Malad is from Highway 30 north of the town of Hagerman.

There is a two-trout limit to protect the wild trout population. It is an excellent place to try your luck on a good population of wild trout. It is also a good cure for cabin fever on a warm winter day with a fishing season that extends from Saturday of Memorial Day weekend through March 31.

Riley Creek
This two-and-a-half-mile, spring-fed creek has primarily rainbow trout fishing. Some fish are escapees from the National Fish Hatchery and some are catchable-size, stocked rainbow trout. There is early season (March-May) fly-fishing with good hatches of caddis and mayflies. Poison ivy is prevalent in the area.

Bliss Reservoir (254 acres)
Located downstream from Bliss, this body of water is a mixed fishery with rainbow trout and sturgeon with largemouth and smallmouth bass and yellow perch. Elev.: 2,675 feet.

Deep Creek
From its mouth through the Highline Canal south of Castleford, this 16-mile-long river is an insignificant fishery located on mainly private land. It has rainbow trout, most of which are hatchery escapees.

Mud Creek
This creek enters the Snake River from the south above Deep Creek It is an insignificant fishery on mostly private land.

Cedar Draw Creek
This creek enters the Snake River from the south across from Niagara Springs. From its mouth to the Twin Falls Highline Canal, the river is managed with general rules for rainbow trout.

Blair Trail Diversion Reservoir (15 acres)
This impoundment north of Glenns Ferry is stocked with catchable rainbow trout. Bluegill and bullhead catfish are also present. Elev.: 3,478 feet.

Morrow Reservoir (60 acres)
This impoundment north of Glenns Ferry holds largemouth bass and bluegill. General regulations apply and bullhead and black crappie are present. Elev.: 2,815 feet.

Pioneer (Clover Creek) Reservoir (220 acres)
A warm-water fishery east of Glenns Ferry with largemouth bass, bluegill and bullhead. Elev.: 3,087 feet.

Bray Lake (204 acres)
An insignificant fishery north of Bliss that goes dry intermittently.
Elev.: 3,727 feet.

Hagerman Wildlife Management Area
This is a very popular and productive site for anglers with major attractions for other visitors as well. It is managed for put-and-take rainbow
trout fishing with seasons that vary. Largemouth bass and bluegill are also
important species.

The Hagerman State Fish Hatchery is one of the largest in Idaho and
raises approximately 800,000 catchable rainbow trout and 2 million to 4
million rainbow fingerlings for stocking. Water from the springs provides
excellent growing conditions for these fish. Because all fish that are stocked
here have been sterilized they grow at a more rapid rate because they are
not conserving energy for spawning.

There are close to six miles of hiking trails just a short distance from
the National Fish Hatchery. They are open to the public with visitor blinds
along the way that offer an up-close look at waterfowl. This is more than
just a good fishery. There are hiking, wildlife viewing and photo opportunities here as well.

Fishing seasons vary according to waterfowl needs, so check the current regulations for specific seasons.

Frank Oster Lakes
These ponds on the Hagerman Wildlife Management Area include
the Riley Creek impoundments and, though primarily rainbow trout fisheries, they also support largemouth bass and bluegill. Fishing is put-and-
take with no motors allowed. The lakes are managed under general rules.
Though the fishing seasons are established around waterfowl needs, these
lakes offer early season (March-May) action.

Many of the other lakes and ponds in the management area are
stocked with rainbow trout. Largemouth bass, bluegill and channel catfish
are also present.

Niagara Springs Wildlife Management Area Ponds
Located in Niagara Springs State Park these are wild waters with rainbow trout. The springs are part of the world-famous Thousand Springs Complex along the Snake River. Niagara Springs Creek is stocked with rainbow trout downstream of the hatchery diversion providing a put-and-take fishery.

Crystal Lake (eight acres)
Put-and-take fishery near Niagara Springs, stocked with catchable rainbow trout.

Scott Pond (one acre)
Put-and-take rainbow trout fishery. Access by way of a steep, narrow canyon road is fairly difficult, though it can be worth the effort. No trailers.

Dierkes Lake (100 acres)
This is a put-and-take rainbow trout lake near Twin Falls with large-mouth bass, bluegill and channel catfish. A fee is charged to enter the park but that allows you access to the Shoshone Falls viewing area. The lake is being managed as a trophy bass fishery so all fish less than 20 inches must be released. Elev.: 3,559 feet.

Murtaugh Reservoir (827 acres)
This is a significant bullhead and perch fishery east of Twin Falls. Attempts have been made to introduce smallmouth and largemouth bass but its potential as a bass fishery has been limited by low winter pools. Elev.: 3,134 feet.

Wilson Lake (484 acres)
This body of water east of Twin Falls is managed under general regulations primarily for bullhead catfish. Yellow perch, channel catfish and largemouth bass are also present. Elev.: 4,016 feet.

Rock Creek FFW
This creek's headwaters are in the Sawtooth National Forest in western Cassia County. It flows northwest approximately 42 miles through Twin Falls County to its Snake River confluence, north of the city of Twin Falls.

It is a put-and-take fishery for rainbow trout and with brown trout stocked only in the Twin Falls area providing good city-fishing year-round. Above Twin Falls to its headwaters there are put-and-take rainbow trout, brook and brown trout.

Emerald Lake (30 acres)
This lake due north of Burley—visible from I-84— features a good mix of stocked hatchery rainbow trout plus channel catfish, largemouth bass and bluegill.

Freedom Park Pond (one acre)
A cold-water pond stocked with hatchery rainbow trout.

Box Canyon Springs
This is a uniquely aesthetic stream with good aquatic life and riparian habitat, dense rainbow trout population and a two-trout limit. Managed as wild rainbow trout water. Access here is difficult. A species of concern, the Shoshone sculpin, is present.

Banbury Springs
Though not a significant fishery, this cold-water spring in the Thousand Springs area is managed to preserve its unique aesthetic qualities.

Clear Lake
This is a pay-to-fish, fly-fishing only pond located on the Clear Lake Country Club grounds north of Buhl where no Idaho fishing license is required. You can cast to cruising rainbows in the morning and play 18 holes in the afternoon. Primarily float-tube water.

Many fish congregate near the water plumes that come out of the hatchery. Some of the channels offer excellent opportunities to practice stalking and sight casting to large fish. You'll have to leave your tube for the stalking.

The fish are released periodically throughout the year. They are pellet-fed so they will take almost anything shortly after being released. But once they have tasted a hook or two they become wily and worthy game fish. Fish 18 to 20 inches, and larger, are not uncommon. Call the country club clubhouse to see when the last release was made. Elev.: 3,028 feet.

Devils Corral Spring

This stream, east of Twin Falls, is managed as wild trout water for rainbow trout while preserving its unique aesthetic qualities.

Vinyard Creek

This creek, an aquifer spring entering the Snake River on the north side just above Twin Falls, is a major spawning area for cutthroat and cuttbow hybrids.

Half-a-mile long, it is managed to preserve its aesthetic qualities and unique population of cutthroat hybrid trout that spawn and grow in the spring. In the lower reach there are populations of smallmouth and large-mouth bass.

Big Wood River Drainage

The Big Wood is named for the cottonwood trees that line its banks. These trees provide food and shelter for wildlife in Central Idaho's sage-brush desert. The cottonwood forests also protect the river's water quality providing shade that keeps water temperatures low while trapping sediment with an elaborate root system that filters runoff.

This river boasts a healthy population of wild rainbow trout and most of the main stem is not dependant on stocking. Winding its way from its headwaters in the Boulder Mountains through the famous ski resorts of Sun Valley, south past Hailey and Bellevue and into agricultural lowlands, it joins the Little Wood River to become the Malad River before entering the Snake River in the Hagerman Valley.

From its headwaters downstream to Magic Reservoir it supports a population of healthy rainbow, brook and brown trout. The basin drains an area of more than 2,900 square miles with the Big Wood and Little Wood rivers being the major drainages. Water-flow in the Wood River drainage is managed for irrigation and flood control by three major reservoirs: Magic—the largest body of water in the drainage—Little Wood, and Mormon.

This drainage contains the most productive trout streams, lakes, and reservoir habitat in the Magic Region. Nearly all of its major rivers, streams, lakes, reservoirs and ponds are suitable for trout. Rainbow trout are the most important game fish in the drainage, but the lower Little Wood River and Silver Creek support brown trout populations, and portions of the drainage sustain healthy populations of brook trout.

Significant and steadily increasing numbers of brown trout are now found in Magic Reservoir, its backwaters and in the Big Wood River upstream to near Stanton Crossing. No significant numbers of wild trout are found in any of the other major reservoirs in the drainage. Fish populations in the reservoirs are largely dependent on annual plantings of hatchery fish. Trout fisheries in the larger reservoirs are maintained by fingerling plantings, but they occasionally receive catchable trout.

Wild trout populations varying from fair to excellent are found in most of the streams in the drainage. Trophy rainbow trout are found in the Big Wood River between Magic Dam and the Richfield Canal and in Silver Creek and its tributaries. During good water years, trophy rainbow are produced in the Richfield Canal. The Big Wood River from Hailey to Ketchum also produces trophy rainbow trout.

Brown trout reach trophy size in the lower Little Wood River. Wild trout populations are supplemented with catchable rainbow trout in portions of several heavily fished streams.

Silver Creek is not stocked. Stocking takes place only in the Little Wood, downstream of Silver Falls, which is downstream of the Highway 93 bridge south of Carey.

Fishing pressure is very high in portions of the drainage. One of the most heavily fished sections is the Big Wood River between Hailey and the mouth of Prairie Creek at the Prairie Creek campground. Increased demand by anglers for more trophy waters has led to the establishment of stricter regulations on the Big Wood and Silver Creek.

There are 16 fishable alpine lakes in the drainage. All are relatively productive and most support high-quality rainbow and cutthroat trout angling. The lakes are normally stocked by airdrops on a three-year rotation basis through a cooperative agreement between the Idaho Department of Fish and Game and the U.S. Forest Service. Experimental grayling plants made in one alpine lake have done well.

Rivers, Lakes and other Waters

Big Wood River

The lower end of the Big Wood River is known as the Malad River, and should not be confused with the Malad Drainage in the Bear Lake Region. From its mouth to the I-84 bridge the river is mostly a cold-water trout stream with rainbow and brown trout and large suckers. Smallmouth bass are found closer to the mouth.

The 60 miles from the I-84 bridge to the Richfield canal offer an assortment of natural warm- and cold-water species along with planted rainbow trout. Rainbow populations fluctuate with water levels, usually improving after a few good water years. There are also some smallmouth bass.

From the Richfield Canal diversion to the dam at Magic Reservoir, it is a cold-water fishery with primarily rainbow and brown trout and many fish from the reservoir move into this stretch of the river.

It is rainbow and brook trout territory from the Magic Reservoir upstream to the Glendale Diversion (14 miles) with some browns. General fishing rules are in effect.

From the Glendale Diversion, three miles below Bellevue, upstream to the mile marker 122 bridge on Highway 75, the river is managed with quality regulations for rainbow trout with mountain whitefish and brook trout.

From the mile 122 bridge, upstream to the mouth of the North Fork, rainbow trout are managed with trophy regulations (catch-and-release). This section has a maturing population of fish. Species found here include rainbow and brook trout and mountain whitefish. This part of the Wood River contains wild trout as there is no stocking in the Big Wood between Magic Reservoir and the North Fork.

From the mouth of the North Fork to its headwaters it is put-and-take for rainbow trout with brook trout and mountain whitefish present.

Trail Creek

Trail Creek enters the Wood River below Ketchum. From its mouth to Wilson Creek, it is nine miles of rainbow and brook trout water. This area is stocked with catchable rainbow trout.

Warm Springs Creek

Warm Springs Creek enters the Wood River west of Ketchum. From its mouth to Rooks Creek campground, this 11-mile waterway is stocked with catchable rainbow trout. Brook trout and mountain whitefish are present.

Richfield Canal

This fishable canal flows out of Magic Reservoir and is stocked with catchable trout. The canal goes dry some years.

Magic Reservoir FFW (3,776 acres)

This is a major rainbow trout fishery located about midway between Ketchum and Twin Falls. When at capacity, the reservoir is five miles long and a mile-and-a-half wide with a maximum depth of 120 feet.

It is stocked annually with fingerling and catchable rainbow trout. When there is water the fish grow very well and rainbows between four and five pounds can be found there.

Boating is the fishing method of choice at Magic. Bait and bobbers produce good results for hatchery trout and perch. Trolling allows anglers to cover a lot of water as well as reach some of those out-of-the-way inlets. Float tubing is popular and a lot of anglers are fishing with wet flies and sinking lines to get deep to the big fish.

Brown trout populations are growing and in high water years the perch population supports a very active fishery.

This is also a popular ice-fishing area for brown and rainbow trout and perch. Irrigation use can cause water levels to fluctuate. Elev.: 4,801 feet.

Little Wood River

From its mouth east of Gooding to Shoshone, this 18-mile stretch is smallmouth bass water with general rules.

From Shoshone to the Dietrich Diversion Dam (10 miles), water temperatures drop and the bass are replaced by stocked put-and-take rainbow trout with brown trout also present. High impact areas are stocked frequently. From the diversion dam to the downstream boundary of Bear Track Williams State Recreation Area it is a cold-water fishery with brown and rainbow trout managed with general regulations.

Upstream at the boundary of Taylor "Bear Track" Williams State Recreation Area (three miles) it is a flies-only, catch-and-release, cold-water fishery for planted-as-needed brown and rainbow trout. From the state park to the mouth of Silver Creek, it's a brown and rainbow trout fishery.

Irrigation needs can remove all the water from the mouth of Silver Creek to the diversions north of Carey during high-use periods and from

the canal diversion to the dam, so this area of the river is not stocked.

From the Little Wood Reservoir upstream to the second bridge, it is put-and-take for rainbow trout with regularly scheduled stocking in heavily fished areas. The next 20 miles to the headwaters is a wild trout management area with rainbow and brook trout.

Little Wood Reservoir (575 acres)

This is a cold-water impoundment north of Carey stocked with fingerling and catchable rainbow trout. Brook trout are present. Located far from population centers, this reservoir is a popular destination for fishing and camping. There is a small campground, picnic area and boat ramp. Elev.: 5,230 feet.

Fish Creek Reservoir (516 acres)

Water levels have been insufficient to stock since 2002. Things may change in the future so contact Fish & Game for the latest information. Elev.: 5,295 feet.

Carey Lake (200 acre)

Northeast of Carey, this mid-sized lake has large-mouth bass, bluegill, perch, bullhead and channel catfish. Elev.: 4,769 feet.

Lava Lake (20 acre)

A cold-water fishery stocked with catchable rainbow trout near Craters of the Moon National Monument and Preserve. Elev.: 5,177 feet.

Silver Creek

At Silver Creek anglers will find big rainbow and brown trout. The most famous waters of Silver Creek lie within the borders of the Nature Conservancy's Silver Creek Preserve at the base of the Picabo Hills south of Sun Valley. Brook trout are present.

This gin-clear spring creek not only tests anglers' fishing ability but fly tiers know that if one of their patterns is successful on Silver Creek they probably have the know-how to tie for nearly any other river. One of the best trout habitats in the state, this system supports large browns and rainbow trout that will bend your rod to its limit.

This spring creek has a very high carrying capacity of trout due to many factors that make for a recipe for success; one factor being the incredible amount aquatic life in the stream. See *Idaho's Big 10*, page 42.

Stalker Creek

This tributary to Silver Creek has wild rainbow, brook and brown trout.

Loving Creek

From the Nature Conservancy boundary, upstream to its headwaters, except Hayspur Hatchery, this three-mile tributary to Silver Creek is populated by rainbow, brook and brown trout.

At the Hayspur Hatchery grounds, the stream has been diverted into its historic channel below the brood pond and developed as a trophy fishery.

Gravers Lagoon (one acre)

This impoundment is stocked with catchable rainbow trout and occasionally brood stock.

Grove Creek
Five miles of wild rainbow, brook and brown trout water.

Camas Creek
This creek enters Magic Reservoir at its northwestern-most reach. General fishing regulations apply to this cold-water fishery where the most important species is rainbow trout. Most of the land associated with Camas Creek is private. During the summer the water is too warm for trout and some segments are dewatered. The best fishing is in June and July.

Mormon Reservoir (2,700 acres)
This mixed fishery south of Fairfield is biologically rich and grows large rainbow trout and perch. Elev.: 5,046 feet.

Thorn Creek Reservoir (126 acres)
Also a biologically rich cold-water reservoir southeast of Fairfield with good rainbow trout fishing. Popular with float tube anglers. Elev.: 5,510 feet.

Irving Reservoir (Dog Creek) (95 acres)
Located north-northeast of Gooding, this mixed impoundment has largemouth bass, bluegill, channel catfish, tiger muskie and put-and-take rainbow trout.

Other streams in the Big Wood River Drainage
There are more than 265 miles of other streams and creeks in the drainage. Most are wild rainbow and brown trout water with some brook trout present. Some are insignificant.

Alpine lakes

There are 12 alpine lakes in the Big Wood River drainages that are stocked on a three-year rotating basis with cutthroat, rainbow and brook trout and Arctic grayling.

Baker Lake (10 acres)
Baker Lake, in the Sawtooth National Forest, is planted with golden

trout and managed as a catch-and-release fishery.
Fishing rules allow the harvest of two trout, none less
than 20 inches. Species present include cutthroat,
rainbow, golden and brown trout. Bait is not allowed.
Elev.: 8,789 feet.

Lower Box Canyon Lake (5 acres)

This lake is stocked with fingerling trout every three years but may
lose the fish during the winter. Elev.: 8,829 feet.

Salmon Falls Creek Drainage

The largest body of water in this drainage is Salmon Falls Creek
Reservoir, and streams that feed the reservoir support good wild trout
populations. Rainbow, cutthroat, brown and brook trout are found in various locations throughout Goose, Marsh and Salmon Falls creeks and Raft
River drainages.

In drainages upstream of Shoshone Falls native cutthroat populations
have been declining in some areas because of human intrusion and the
introduction of other fish, particularly rainbow trout. In drainages downstream rainbow trout is the common species.

Fishing pressure varies and changes with the terrain. It is high on
Roseworth, Sublett, and Salmon Falls Creek reservoirs, but is relatively
light on streams in the Salmon Falls Creek and Raft River drainages.
Easily accessible streams in the Goose and Rock creeks drainages are
heavily fished.

There are four alpine lakes supporting game fish in the Raft River
drainage: the three Independence Lakes on Independence Mountain near
Oakley and Lake Cleveland on Mount Harrison.

Rivers, Lakes and other Waters

Salmon Falls Creek

This creek has its headwaters in the Humboldt National Forest in
Nevada and enters the Snake River downstream from Thousand Springs
in the Hagerman Valley. From its mouth to Balanced Rock Park, Salmon

Falls Creek is 26 miles long and stocked with catchable rainbow trout at the park with smallmouth bass also in the river.

From the Balanced Rock Park upstream to Salmon Falls Creek Dam there is about 18 miles of river with a mixed fishery that is maintained as wild trout water with rainbow trout. Brook trout and smallmouth bass are also present.

From the backwaters of Salmon Falls Creek Reservoir to the Nevada border there are about 10 miles of river with rainbow and brown trout, smallmouth bass and walleye.

From the mouth of Big Creek, there are a few rainbow and brown trout and lots of non-game fish.

Shoshone Creek

This is troubled water. This is highly degraded water with some trout. Fire and man's intrusion have damaged fish habitat in this desert stream.

Raft River

The Raft River begins at the Utah border near the City of Rocks National Reserve. It flows counterclockwise around the Jim Sage Mountains before it turns north, heading for the Snake River. Populations of cutthroat are found in the Raft River drainages where beaver ponds provide valuable habitat.

Goose Creek

This creek near Oakley has a population of native cutthroat and beaver ponds provide valuable habitat here as well. A species of concern, the leatherside chub, is also found in the drainage.

From Oakley Reservoir to its headwaters (within Idaho) the river is wild rainbow and cutthroat trout water.

Other streams in the Salmon Falls Creek Drainage

There are more than 57 miles of streams and tributaries in the rest of the drainage and most are managed as wild trout water but are insignificant as fisheries. The predominant species is rainbow trout.

Salmon Falls Creek Reservoir (3,400 acres)

The greatest diversity of fish in the area can be found here including kokanee salmon and catchable rainbow trout.

Game species include perch, crappie, smallmouth bass and walleye.

Rainbow trout are stocked and walleye, the most recent addition to the system, are present.

Walleye fishing in Salmon Falls Creek Reservoir is getting the attention of anglers from across the West. IDF&G planted more than a million and a half walleye in the reservoir in 1974 and they have maintained an active stocking program since then.

A 16-pound, two-ounce walleye was caught in the reservoir in 1996. Kokanee and rainbow trout are planted and the reservoir also offers smallmouth bass, crappie and yellow perch. Elev.: 5,009 feet.

Roseworth (Cedar Creek) Reservoir FFW (1,500 acres)

This impoundment is good rainbow trout water, offering excellent float tube angling in the spring and early summer. Elev.: 5,223 feet.

Big Cottonwood Creek

From the Big Cottonwood Wildlife Management Area to its headwaters this creek is managed as a wild cutthroat stream. This creek is west of Goose Creek.

Oakley (Lower Goose) Reservoir (1,350 acres)

Following the successful introduction of walleye in Salmon Falls Creek Reservoir IDF&G began an active walleye stocking program here in 1989. General fishing rules apply for walleye, rainbow and cutthroat trout and yellow perch. Elev.: 4,711 feet.

Sublett Reservoir (133 acres)

This reservoir, and its tributary streams, are biologically rich bodies of water that grow large trout. There are about 30 miles of tributary streams that are managed under wild regulations for cutthroat, rainbow and brown trout.

It is best fished in the spring and fall and is also stocked with fingerling cutthroat trout. Other species include stocked rainbow trout and kokanee and brown and cutthroat trout. Annual irrigation demands draw this reservoir down to low levels every year. Elev.: 5,338 feet.

Stone (Curlew Valley) Reservoir (30 acres)

This mixed fishery is located in the Curlew National Grassland west of Malad City and holds rainbow trout, crappie, and largemouth bass. Elev.: 4,600 feet.

Cassia Creek
From south of Conner to the Sawtooth National Forest border there are five miles of put-and-take rainbow and brook trout water. Its tributary, Clyde Creek, is also put-and-take for rainbow trout. Other species include brook and cutthroat trout.

Independence Lakes (24 acres)
These lakes are managed with special programs for each lake. They are numbered one through four as you move down the drainage.
　　Lake #1 is not stocked as it has a self-sustaining rainbow trout population. (Four acres Elev.: 9,170 feet.)
　　Lake #2 is stocked with Arctic grayling fry when available. (Five acres Elev.: 9,107 feet.)
　　Lake #3 has cutthroat trout and Arctic grayling. This is a non-motorized access area and it's a three-mile hike to the lakes from the trailhead. (15 acres Elev.: 9,049 feet.)
　　Lake #4 is self sustaining.

Lake Cleveland (25 acres)
There is an access road to this high-mountain lake, which is stocked annually with rainbow and cutthroat trout fingerlings. Elev.: 8,261 feet.

....

Airstrips

Magic Reservoir (state)
Magic Reservoir Airport serves Hailey and Camas County and is owned by the Idaho Division of Aeronautics. The airport has more than one runway. The longest is a turf runway extending 4,000 feet. The facility is at an elevation of 4,844 feet and about 15 air miles from Hailey.

Twin Bridges (backcountry)
Twin Bridges Airport serves Ketchum and Custer County and is owned by the Idaho Division of Aeronautics. The turf runway extends for 4,450 feet. The facility is at an elevation of 6,893 feet and about 22 air miles from Ketchum.

Magic Valley

Notes

APPROACH

How many times have you stepped off a bank into the river to spook the largest trout you have seen all summer? Have you ever walked through the mangroves gazing fifty yards out on a bonefish flat, only to have the first fish of the day bolt from under your feet in four inches of water? Have you started in what looked like a prime piece of steelhead water, swinging through what you thought was the bucket, when the guy who walked into the riffle water above you is into a leaping hen fish on the third cast, in water you thought too swift?

It seems like many fishermen approach the water like they work at the office. Make the phone call; get a "yes sir" on the other end, and the product is delivered the next day.

Stop, look, and listen is a grade school lesson that applies to fishing. I have not yet seen a heron make a hundred-yard dash to catch his dinner. I have seen fishermen do that.

I was guiding an older couple on one of our Central Idaho rivers during the green drake hatch a few years ago. We had walked downriver about a quarter of a mile to a long riffle, intending to fish upstream to a deep pool where we would finish. Three gentlemen stepped out of the cottonwoods above us and walked right through the water that we were going to fish, heading for the soft water above. My clients were irate. The hatch had not started yet. I tried to assure them that it would work, and we sat for a half hour waiting for the water to settle and the hatch to begin. We crept through the riffle water and the river edge for two hours and spanked nice rising rainbows. The three anglers above us landed one trout.

Lost River Outfitters

One of my good friends, Marc Bale, spent an entire fishing day on a high bank of one of our Idaho tailwater fisheries reading Dame Julia's book, **A Treatise On Fly Fishing**, and watching a half dozen large rainbows jockey for the prime feeding position during a pale morning dun hatch. The rest of the group caught a bunch of trout. Marc said it was one of the best days he had spent on the river, and I am he sure learned more than the rest of us did.

So take your time. Don't disturb the water. Watch the water first. You might see them rise. You may see the largest fish rise. You may spot a large fish under the water. You might see where the pod is feeding. You should be able to see what they are feeding on, and make a better fly choice. When I do this, it is not about catching the most fish, or sometimes even the largest fish, but about catching the fish that I was trying to catch. That's a nice reward.

Lost River Outfitters

For more tips on fishing techniques call
Lost River Outfitters at **208-726-1706**
or visit us on the web at **www.lostriveroutfitters.com**.
See Sponsor Page in the Sponsor Index p. 242.

Bear Lake

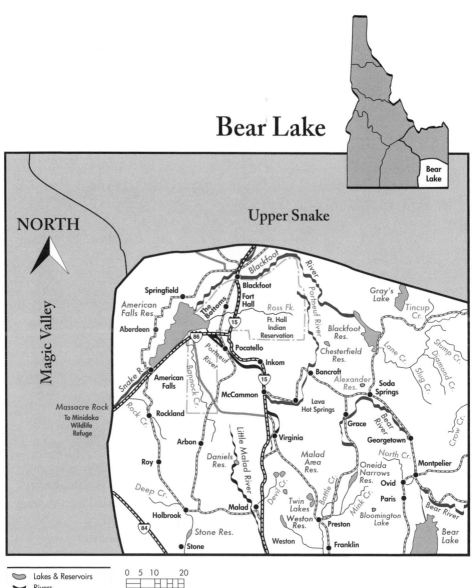

An Angler's Guide

Drainages:
Snake
Portneuf
Blackfoot
Bear
Malad

Bear Lake

Known as the Caribbean of the Rockies because of its distinct water color, this large natural lake in the southeast corner of the state is shared by Idaho and Utah. Its elevation is more than 5,900 feet and it's 20 miles long and eight miles across.

The Bear River and its four major tributaries include more than 500 miles of rivers and streams with several large reservoirs in the region. Although some of the rivers, streams and lakes have been degraded the area still offers some excellent fishing.

With the largest reservoir in the state, American Falls Reservoir, this region offers an amazing diversity of cold- and warm-water fishing. There are wild and planted trout in its lakes, ponds and reservoirs that also offer excellent fishing for bass and other warm-water species. It is also a place to take time out from fishing to enjoy its historical character as well.

The Flood

Approximately 15,000 years ago, Lake Bonneville, the precursor of the Great Salt Lake, broke free of its shore at the north at Red Rock Pass. The draining and subsequent flood is believed to have been caused by sudden erosion of loose material on the shoreline at Red Rock Pass. The water flowed north and covered the area of the Snake River Plain and generally followed the path of the present Snake River.

Thousands of years later, this area of Idaho was the gateway to California and Oregon for early pioneers traveling the Oregon Trail. Weary travelers replenished their supplies at trading posts and rested before moving on farther west. Vestiges of the old trail remain and modern highways follow part of the route.

Like the state's other regions, the Bear Lake region has a character all its own, and its fishing potential is as great as its history.

Snake River Drainage

Lake Walcott to Blackfoot

For the eight miles from the eastern boundary of the Minidoka Wildlife Refuge to Eagle Rock, the Snake is a cold-water fishery for rainbow and brown trout. Channel catfish and smallmouth bass were planted at Massacre Rocks by IDF&G in 1993. Bass are now abundant in this reach of the river.

The six miles upstream from Eagle Rock to the American Falls Dam has some of the finest trout water in the area. It's also known for trophy trout with numerous fish taken in the five-pound class with occasional fish of ten pounds being taken. Most are taken in early summer by boat anglers. Fishing season begins with the general opener on Memorial Day weekend.

American Falls Reservoir, the largest in Idaho, covers 56,000 surface acres. The reservoir is stocked with catchable trout in the early spring and they grow quickly. Many of these hatchery trout caught exceed two pounds. The reservoir also contains a dense population of nongame fish, such as suckers, carp and chubs.

In midsummer, some of the trout planted in American Falls Reservoir migrate downstream as reservoir releases decrease volume and increase water velocity above the dam. When water temperatures become uncomfortably warm and oxygen levels become low. It appears to the biologists that some of the trout tend to move above the reservoir into the Snake and Portneuf rivers as conditions in the reservoir deteriorate.

In the 1980s smallmouth bass were stocked in Ririe Reservoir and in 1991 in Gem Lake, both upriver of American Falls Reservoir. Some of these bass moved downriver and found a good home in American Falls Reservoir. The first bass tournament on American Falls was held in 1999.

The 20 miles from the backwater of American Falls Reservoir upstream to Tilden Bridge is also very good trout water. The river in this area is inaccessible by land because of private ownership on the west side of the river and the Fort Hall Indian Reservation on the east. However, the area is popular with boaters and there are boat ramps available.

There are numerous springs near the upper end of American Falls Reservoir and between the Portneuf River and the Snake River in the area known as the Fort Hall Bottoms. These springs produce approximately 1.8 million acre feet of water annually, more than enough to fill the American Falls Reservoir. However, because irrigation withdrawls occur from April through October the reservoir does not necessarily fill every year.

The two best-known springs in the area are Clear Creek and Spring Creek. Both are good streams and contain native Yellowstone cutthroat, rainbow and brown trout, cuttbows and mountain whitefish. Check with Fort Hall reservation officials for access possibilities.

The 37 miles from Tilden Bridge upstream to the Gem State Power Plant, near Shelley, is best described as having low unstable banks of small river rock. During the irrigation season the river is low in the lower end of this reach as water is progressively diverted at numerous points.

Hatchery rainbows are the main target, but large wild rainbow, brown and cutthroat trout and mountain whitefish are there as well. Most of the land along this stretch is privately owned, so most access is by boat.

From the American Falls Reservoir to the Gem State Dam hatchery, rainbow trout are the most common fish in the system. Other important species include perch and bullhead catfish.

···

Rivers, Lakes and other Waters

American Falls Reservoir (56,000 acres)

This reservoir is the major facility on the Minidoka Project—a water storage reservoir for irrigation, power and flood control. The reservoir also supports boating, canoeing, swimming, wildlife viewing, picnicking, jet boating, water skiing and wind surfing.

Hatchery rainbow trout are the most common fish in the system. Other important species include perch, crappie and bullhead catfish. The season is open year-round although the fishery is dependent on water availability to maintain the minimum pool to carry fish over year to year.

Rock Creek

If you include the tributaries there are more than 50 miles of streams in this drainage that are managed with both quality water (cutthroat trout) and general regulations (rainbow trout).

Springfield Lake (66 acres)

This is a moderate-size reservoir operated primarily for irrigation diversion north of American Falls. Because of excessive predation by cormorants and pelicans, special management and regulations are in place. Rainbow trout are stocked once a year near the end of October after most of the fish-eating birds have migrated south for the winter. These trout are about 17 inches long, thus reducing the chance they will be eaten by birds.

Trophy trout regulations are in place so that the stocked fish are protected from harvest until they reach 20 inches. Artificial flies and lures are required to reduce hooking mortality on trout that are caught and released. This reservoir rarely freezes over, making it a popular cabin-fever remedy in the winter. Elev.: 4,396 feet.

McTucker Ponds (10 acres)

Eight small gravel pits covering 25 surface acres, located between the upper end of American Falls Reservoir and Springfield Reservoir. The two easterly ponds are stocked with catchable size trout at two-week intervals except when frozen over in the winter. Five of them contain largemouth bass, bluegill and channel catfish. An eighth pond seasonally connects with McTucker Creek and is not stocked.

Rose Pond (five acres)

Rose Pond is located north of Blackfoot and contains rainbow trout, perch, bluegill, and largemouth bass. This pond rises and falls with ground water levels as impacted by irrigation and the nearby Snake River water level and it is much larger in the summer than in the winter.

American Falls Reservoir up to Gem State Dam

There are 57 river miles in this cold-water fishery managed as quality water, wild trout water and general fishing water. Cutthroat trout harvest is restricted. This stretch also contains brown trout and small numbers of smallmouth bass immediately below Gem State Dam. Other species include rainbow trout and mountain whitefish.

Portneuf River Drainage

The Portneuf River is a tributary of the Snake River and begins and ends on the Fort Hall Indian Reservation. It is approximately 96 miles long and drains ranches and farms, primarily in Caribou and Bannock counties.

Even though the route was not a part of the Oregon Trail, the Portneuf River was an important element of the development of Pocatello and southeast Idaho. From 1862 to 1878 the route along the river was used by stagecoaches and freighters ferrying people and packages to and from Pocatello.

The Portneuf River drainage and its tributaries total 297 miles of streams and drain nearly 1,300 square miles. The upper reaches are relatively undisturbed. Four irrigation storage reservoirs in the drainages cover more than 1,700 acres.

Upstream of the Chesterfield Reservoir the river is small, has significant beaver activity, and is heavily impacted by cattle. From Chesterfield Reservoir to Kelly-Toponce Road Bridge the river is channelized.

From Pocatello downriver to American Falls Reservoir, the river receives lots of spring water and holds wild rainbow and brown trout.

Rivers, Lakes and other Waters

Portneuf River

Beginning above Chesterfield Reservoir in the Caribou/Targee National Forest, the river travels a circuitous course and enters the American Falls Reservoir on the Fort Hall Reservation northwest of Pocatello. During its flow to the reservoir the river changes characteristics dramatically.

Above the reservoir, the river produces little water and is affected by significant beaver activity, but there are some cutthroat trout. Below the reservoir to Kelly/Toponce Road the river has been severely affected by stream channel alterations throughsome habitat improvements have been implemented.

Between Kelly/Toponce Rd. and Lava Hot Springs there once was a popular fishery which was degraded by a variety of agriculture factors. This river's reach has been restored to a great extent during the past decade and is again a popular fishery for rainbow and cutthroat trout

The section from Broxon Road to Lava Hot Springs is a cold-water fishery managed as put-and-take for rainbow trout. From Lava Hot Springs to Marsh Valley Canal it is put-and-take for rainbow trout with some naturally producing brown and cutthroat.

From the Marsh Valley Canal diversion brown trout are present and rainbows are stocked at a few public access points.

From Marsh Creek to American Falls Reservoir, where quality water is available, the river is stocked with catchable-size rainbow trout. Brown and cutthroat trout are present.

Marsh Creek

Water quality and quantity severely limit the fishery here. The occasional trout, generally cutthroat or brown, are usually found near springs.

Hawkins Reservoir

(40 acres)

This cold-water fishery is located 10-miles northwest of Downey and annually stocked in April with catchable-size rainbow trout. During low water years the reservoir is drained for irrigation by mid- to late-summer. Elev.: 5,135 feet.

Wiregrass Reservoir (Six acres)

This cold-water reservoir west of Downey is stocked annually in March or April. It generally becomes too low to support fish by mid to late summer. Get there early. Elev.: 4,739 feet.

Rapid Creek

This is a cold-water fishery, managed for native cutthroat trout.

Chesterfield Reservoir (1,600 acres)

This cold-water fishery lies partly on the Fort Hall Reservation and is managed with a two-trout limit and is stocked with a variety of fish that include cutthroat, rainbow and brown trout and cuttbow hybrids. In drought years it is drained for irrigation. Elev.: 5,394 feet.

Pebble Creek

A ten-mile-long, cold-water fishery with wild cutthroat and put-and-take rainbow trout.

Toponce Creek

A 12-mile long cold-water fishery with wild cutthroat and put-and-take rainbow trout.

24-Mile Reservoir (44 acres)

This cold-water fishery located east of Chesterfield Reservoir is stocked with mostly hatchery rainbow trout and sometimes with cutthroat trout. It is managed with a two-trout limit and no fish less than 20-inches. Elev.: 5,905 feet.

The Blackfoot River Drainage

From its confluence at Lanes and Diamond creeks the Blackfoot River flows approximately 35 miles to the Blackfoot Reservoir. When full, the reservoir covers more than 19,000 surface acres and holds more than 350,000 acre-feet of water.

The upper reaches of the Blackfoot River are important spawning areas for cutthroat trout. Mature cutthroat leave the reservoir in the late spring to move to the river and spawn in the early summer. Most of the young fish will remain in the rivers and tributaries for a year or two before migrating to the reservoir. They will remain in the reservoir until they are ready to spawn.

Almost all the fish caught in the reservoir are hatchery rainbows. Wild cutthroat must be released. Below the reservoir there is good habitat for trout though mountain whitefish dominate. Low water flows in winter during drought years may limit the population of native cutthroat.

One of the largest phosphate ore reserves in the United States is located in this drainage. Environmental problems associated with phosphate mining are a matter of some discussion. Some believe that the effects have been minimal while others do not share that opinion.

A major management plan was initiated in 1989 for the entire Upper Blackfoot System. Wild cutthroat caught in the reservoir and upper river tributaries must be released. No bait fishing is allowed in the river upstream from the reservoir.

Computer modeling in the late 1980s predicted that it would take 15 to 20 years to restore the wild cutthroat fishery to historical levels. Drought conditions and predation by pelicans and cormorants in recent years have slowed the recovery as well.

Rivers, Lakes and other Waters

Blackfoot River

The upper reaches of the Blackfoot River have important spawning and rearing areas. From the Government Dam to Cutthroat Trout Campground the river is a put-and-take fishery for rainbow trout. Cutthroat trout are managed with quality regulations. From the campground to Rawlins Creek general rules apply for rainbow and quality rules apply to cutthroat trout. From Rawlins to where the Blackfoot enters the Snake

River on the Fort Hall reservation mountain whitefish are present.

Other Blackfoot River tributaries from the river's mouth to Government Dam contain brook and cutthroat trout. Rainbow trout are stocked only in Brush Creek and its tributary, Rawlins Creek.

In the upper reach, above the reservoir, it is a cold-water fishery, mainly for wild cutthroat trout with some brook trout in some of the tributaries. Rainbow trout have recently formed a population in the upper river.

Blackfoot Reservoir (19,000 acres)

This impoundment contains rainbow and Yellowstone cutthroat trout. There is a general limit on rainbow trout and all cutthroat trout must be released. Yellow perch were recently discovered in the reservoir and as of 2004, few perch of harvestable size have been reported. Elev.: 6,125 feet.

Rawlins, Brush and Wolverine creeks

These streams have rainbow, brook and cutthroat trout.

Corral Creek

Brook trout are the major species with cutthroat present.

Dike Lake (35 acres)

This man-made lake was created by building a dike across one of the bays of the Blackfoot Reservoir to prevent a seepage water loss. It is extremely productive when the Blackfoot reservoir is full and its stocked trout can grow rapidly. During drought years there is no fishery in Dike Lake. Elev.: 6,119 feet.

Diamond Creek

Cutthroat and brook trout are found in this important tributary that comes from the headwaters of the Blackfoot River and it is an important cutthroat trout nursery.

Lanes Creek

Cutthroat trout are found in this important tributary that comes from the headwaters of the Blackfoot River and it is an important cutthroat trout nursery.

Bear River Drainage

The Bear River is the longest river in North America that does not drain into an ocean, it drains into the Great Salt Lake. It starts and ends in Utah and circles through Wyoming and Idaho on its way. It enters Bear Lake Valley north of Bear Lake and is diverted at Stewart Dam and flows down Rainbow Canal into Bear Lake. Located on the Idaho-Utah border, it is the largest lake in the drainage, covering 70,000 surface acres, with 32,000 in Idaho.

Trout habitat in Bear River is limited because of low flows in the winter (all the Upper Bear River is stored in Bear Lake during winter) and poor water quality during the season of higher flow. Eroding stream banks keep the river very turbid during the summer. Power facilities have not helped the fishing because the area reservoirs have rapid turnovers with severely fluctuating water levels. Some power plants, such as Utah Power and Light's Soda Point and the Oneida Narrows facilities, affect the river downstream.

The river receives its heaviest fishing pressure in the tailwaters immediately below Alexander and Oneida dams and in the Black Canyon area below Grace Dam. Flows in Black Canyon benefit from numerous springs. Harvest in these areas is primarily hatchery rainbow and brown trout.

Main tributaries to the Bear River include the Cub River, Thomas Fork, Bloomington, Paris, Montpelier, Georgetown, Eight-Mile, Williams, Cottonwood and Mink creeks.

Several irrigation reservoirs support game fish populations in the Bear River Drainage. If year-to-year levels are sufficient, the reservoirs are stocked with hatchery rainbow. In addition, most of the Franklin County reservoirs contain warm-water game fish such as bluegill, perch, largemouth bass and walleye. Collectively, these reservoirs provide a significant amount of regional fishing opportunity.

Rivers, Lakes and other Waters

Bear River

From the Utah state line to near U.S. Highway 91, Bear River is a mixed fishery containing mountain whitefish, channel catfish, rainbow and brown trout, some wild cutthroat trout, walleye and smallmouth bass managed with general regulations.

From U.S. 91 to the Oneida Dam, it is a cold-water fishery for about 12 miles. It is managed as a quality fishery for rainbow, brown and cutthroat trout. At the Oneida Narrows Reservoir, the impoundment holds 500 surface acres of water and is managed for hydropower. Walleye is the major game fish, with some yellow perch and smallmouth bass. From the reservoir headwaters to Cove Dam it is a mixed fishery with rainbow trout and walleye. There are some wild cutthroat trout in here.

The 11 miles from Black Canyon to Soda Point Dam (Alexander Reservoir) is a mixed fishery, managed differently on various sections of the river. Be sure to check your IDF&G regulations. Important species include rainbow, brown and cutthroat trout and mountain whitefish. Below Soda Point it is put-and-take for rainbow trout.

From Soda Point Dam to Bear Lake (79 miles), this cold-water system is managed as a put-and-take fishery for rainbow trout. Quality rules apply to cutthroat trout, and general fishing rules for mountain whitefish and brown trout. Alexander Reservoir has cutthroat trout, channel catfish and perch. The Bear River has 44 miles of tributary waters that are primarily cold-water fisheries with rainbow, cutthroat and brown trout and mountain whitefish. Getting to the water can be difficult as much of the river runs through private land.

Condie Reservoir (117 acres)

Located southeast of Strongarm Reservoir, this mixed fishery holds stocked rainbow trout, largemouth bass, perch, bluegill and tiger muskie. Elev.: 4,890 feet.

Foster Reservoir (146 acres)

Located west of Glendale Reservoir this mixed fishery holds hatchery rainbow trout, bluegill, yellow perch and largemouth bass. Elev.: 4,859 feet.

Glendale Reservoir (230 acres)

This reservoir is located northeast of Preston and contains rainbow trout, cutthroat trout, bluegill, largemouth bass and crappie.

Johnson Reservoir (50 acres)

This reservoir sits due east of Lamont Reservoir east of Preston. You'll find put-and-take rainbow trout, yellow perch, bluegill, largemouth bass and tiger muskie. Elev.: 4,882 feet.

Lamont Reservoir (92 acres)

Sitting beside Johnson Reservoir, this mixed fishery holds put-and-take rainbow trout, largemouth bass, bluegill, yellow perch and tiger muskie. Elev.: 4,875 feet.

Oxford Reservoir (20 acres)

This warm-water fishery southwest of Swan Lake holds largemouth bass and bluegill. Elev.: 4,916 feet.

Treasureton (Strongarm) Reservoir (143 acres)

This reservoir is referred to as Strongarm Reservoir on some maps. Battle Creek feeds and empties this rainbow trout fishery. Elev.: 4,960 feet.

Twin Lakes Reservoir (446 acres)

These two bodies of water are connected by a narrow waterway west of Winder Reservoir. It is managed for put-and-take rainbow trout with general rules applying to largemouth bass, bluegill and yellow perch. A new population of crappie has been developing since 2004. Elev.: 4,770 feet.

Winder Reservoir (446 acres)

This mixed fishery south of Condie Reservoir is managed for put-and-take rainbow trout fishing with largemouth bass, bluegill and yellow perch. Due to recent frequent draining for irrigation, the fishery is mainly a put-and-take rainbow trout fishery. Elev.: 4,880 feet.

Montpelier Reservoir (120 acres)

This cold-water fishery, located east of Montpelier, is a put-and-take fishery for rainbow and cutthroat trout and yellow perch. Elev.: 6,507 feet.

Bloomington Lake (10 acres)

This cold-water, high mountain fishery west of Bear Lake holds primarily cutthroat and rainbow trout. Elev.: 8.166 feet.

Little Valley Reservoir (60 acres)

This impoundment, southwest of Montpelier, is a cold-water fishery for hatchery rainbow and cutthroat trout. It is frequently drained in low-water years. Elev.: 6,545 feet.

Bear Lake Tributaries

Most tributaries to the Bear River support populations of wild trout—either rainbow, cutthroat, brown or brook trout. Highest concentrations of trout are found in the middle and upstream sections. Trout in the lower sections are affected by low summer flows caused by irrigation demands.

Catchable rainbow trout are planted in accessible streams where historically demand is high and water conditions can support fish. Bear River tributaries stocked with rainbow trout in 2004 were Paris, Bloomington, Montpelier, Georgetown, 8-Mile, Whiskey and Trout creeks and the Cub River.

There are 206 miles of cold-water tributary streams that are being managed to rebuild wild cutthroat populations. Other important species include rainbow and brook trout and mountain whitefish. Some of the accessible tributaries are Thomas Fork with cutthroat trout; St. Charles Creek, an important spawning stream for cutthroat; and the upper 10 miles of Cub River which has wild cutthroat and is a popular fishery. Special regulations apply to many of these streams and creeks.

Other creeks of note: Georgetown, Paris and Bloomington creeks.

Bear Lake (79,000 acres)

Bear Lake previously contained populations of sizable cutthroat trout. Due to over-fishing, irrigation diversion and other factors, the natural spawning population has shrunk.

The Utah Department of Natural Resources takes eggs from mature fish that move up Swan Creek. The young are kept at hatcheries for one year, then released back into Bear Lake.

In addition, Bear Lake contains four other species of endemic fish: Bear Lake sculpin, Bear Lake whitefish, Bonneville whitefish and Bonneville cisco. This is a cold-water fishery for Bear Lake cutthroats, stocked lake trout, cisco and Bonneville whitefish.

The largest lake in the region, it offers many other recreational opportunities besides fishing. Elev.: 5,928 feet.

Thomas Fork River

This cold-water, cutthroat trout fishery enters the Bear River in Thomas Fork Valley near the Wyoming border.

Cub River

This is a cold-water fishery with cutthroat, rainbow and brook trout southeast of Preston.

Montpelier Creek

A major Bear Lake tributary that holds brown, brook and cutthroat trout, this creek is also stocked with rainbow trout.

Preuss, Dry and Giraffe creeks

These waters are managed as preserves for cutthroat trout. The fishing season begins July 1 to protect spawners and anglers must release all cutthroat trout.

Malad River Drainage

The Malad once flowed into ancient Lake Bonneville, but it does not connect to the Bear River. Streams in the Malad River drainage total 65 miles. The river is characterized by high silt, high water temperatures and poor trout populations.

Reservoirs in the drainage are used for irrigation water storage. They are drawn down during the irrigation season and refilled in the winter and spring. Two reservoirs, Daniels and Devils Creek, have minimum pools for fish. The reservoirs are planted annually with hatchery rainbow trout.

....

Rivers, Lakes and other Waters

Malad River

From the Utah border to Malad City it is a warm-water fishery with brown bullhead and channel catfish and green sunfish. In some of the upper reaches of the Malad's tributaries there are cutthroat trout.

There are 55 miles of tributaries and all are cold-water fisheries with rainbow and cutthroat trout.

Daniels Reservoir (375 acres)

A cold-water fishery with hatchery rainbow and occasionally cutthroat trout. It is also artificial lures only, with barbless hooks. Only one line is allowed when ice fishing. Following treatments for Utah suckers, Daniels Reservoir was stocked with rainbow-cutthroat hybrids and cutthroat trout. Trophy regulations are now in effect on cutthroat trout. Elev.: 5,166 feet.

Deep Creek Reservoir (174 acres)

This reservoir is located in the western reaches of the region and is a mixed fishery with hatchery rainbow trout and cutthroat trout. Prior to being drained in 2003 it contained largemouth bass and the status of that population in undetermined. Elev.: 4,679 feet.

Devils Creek Reservoir (148 acres)

This cold-water, put-and-take fishery north of Malad City is stocked with hatchery rainbow trout and hatchery kokanee salmon. Native cutthroat trout are also present. Elev.: 5,157 feet.

Pleasantview Reservoir (39 acres)

There are two reservoirs west of Malad City—Upper Pleasantview and Lower Pleasantview. The upper reservoir is stocked with hatchery rainbow. Elev.: 4,709 feet.

Crowthers Reservoir (40 acres)

This cold-water fishery north of Malad City is stocked with hatchery rainbow trout. Elev.: 4,688 feet.

Weston Reservoir (82 acres)

Located northeast of Malad City this is a mixed fishery with hatchery rainbow trout, largemouth bass and yellow perch. Elev.: 5,522 feet.

Upper Snake River

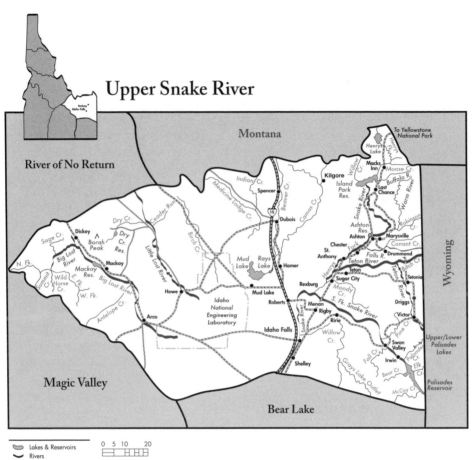

An Angler's Guide

Drainages:
Henery's Fork of the Snake
South Fork of the Snake
Teton
Sinks

Upper Snake

In the eastern region of this incredibly diverse state, both the Henry's and South forks of the Snake River are living and dynamic examples of what makes this area one of America's crown jewels of angling. The region is nestled into the eastern corner of Idaho where spectacular mountains rise and wild rivers run.

The South Fork begins in Yellowstone National Park and flows south through Teton National Park in Wyoming. When it enters Idaho above Palisades Dam it flows in a generally northwest direction until it meets with the Henry's Fork to form the Snake River southeast of the Menan Buttes.

The Henry's Fork begins near Henry's Lake at Big Springs in the Targhee National Forest where 250 cfs of pure spring water flows right out of the ground. The river then moves south across a great caldera covered by a forest of pines with a sprinkling of aspen.

This region is a sightseeing wonder as well as a fishing paradise. Besides the Henry's Fork and the South Fork of the Snake River, two of the most famous fishing areas in the world, the region also boasts the Lost River Range on its western edge (with Idaho's highest mountain, Mt. Borah), the Grand Tetons to the east, and the eerie, lava-strewn landscape of the Craters of the Moon National Monument in between.

South Fork of the Snake River Drainage

The U.S. Fish and Wildlife Service considers this river section to be a unique fish and wildlife habitat. The South Fork drainage area contains the largest continuous cottonwood ecosystem in North America and provides summer habitat for nesting bald eagles and up to 100 species of wintering birds.

Wild Yellowstone cutthroat trout represent more than 50 percent of the catch in the South Fork and tributaries below Palisades Dam. Brown trout are present but make up a much lower percentage. However, what they lack in number they more than make up for in size. The present state record of more than 26 pounds was caught in the river below the dam.

Special regulations instituted in the 1980s restricting cutthroat limits in the upper reaches successfully increased cutthroat numbers and fish size. Based on that success, a restricted cutthroat trout harvest was enacted for the lower South Fork and all tributaries in 1990. Today catch-and-release regulations apply to cutthroat trout. The limit has been removed for rainbow trout and hybrids in an attempt to preserve the Yellowstone cutthroat trout.

Mountain whitefish are the most abundant, but not necessarily the most popular, game fish in the drainage. Whitefish can grow to three pounds or more and can be very exciting on a fly rod or light spinning tackle. Mountain whitefish, like trout, are members of the salmonid family. Though the shape of their mouth differs from that of trout, they are a true salmonid.

Palisades Reservoir's main fish is the fine-spotted Snake River cutthroat trout, with Jackson National Fish Hatchery in Wyoming providing most of those fish. The reservoir also provides a great opportunity for bank, boat and ice anglers. Lake trout and kokanee have been planted but the results of these stockings is not yet known.

....

Rivers, Lakes and other Waters

South Fork of the Snake

From the mouth of the South Fork to Heise it is 23 miles. There are various restrictions on the major species along this stretch, so check your current regulations. It's 40 more miles from Heise to Palisades Dam. Cutthroat trout fishing is strictly catch-and-release on the South Fork. Brown trout are managed with a limit of two fish per day and none under 16 inches can be kept. See *Idaho's Big 10*, page 45.

Dry Bed Canal

This rainbow trout fishery above Lewisville was stocked at one time but now is managed as a wild fishery for cutthroat and brown trout. The waterway is 32 miles long with cutthroat, rainbow, brown trout and mountain whitefish. This canal is sometimes dewatered in the spring for headgate maintenance and a salvage season applies.

Burns, Pine, Rainey, Pritchard and Palisades creeks

These creeks provide 38 miles of catch-and-release water for cutthroat trout with a July 1 opener.

McCoy Creek

This creek enters Palisades Reservoir from the south where there are thirty-five miles of quality cutthroat trout water, including tributaries and general rules for brown trout. Cutthroat trout harvest is limited and the creek has a late season opener.

Tincup, Stump, Crow and Jackknife creeks

These creeks, and their tributaries, flow from southeast Idaho into the Salt River that feeds Palisades Reservoir from Wyoming. Cutthroat, brown and brook trout are present and managed with various regulations. Check the IDF&G regulations for special rules.

Palisades Reservoir (16,150 acres)

The largest impoundment in the region, this reservoir is a put-and-grow fishery for cutthroat trout. Brown trout are all wild fish.

Other important species include lake trout and kokanee salmon.

Palisades Reservoir is open year-round for bank, boat and ice fishing. Brown trout are only a small percentage of the catch in the reservoir, but they do provide the opportunity to catch trophy-size fish. Lake trout and kokanee salmon have been introduced, but only small, natural populations have developed. Elev.: 5,627 feet.

Upper and Lower Palisades lakes (16 acres)

These alpine lakes are cutthroat trout fisheries under wild trout regulations. You have to hike into these lakes that join the Snake River below Palisades dam from the north. Lower Palisades elev.: 6,124 feet. Upper Palisades elev.: 6,627 feet.

Willow Creek

The 20 miles of Willow Creek below Ririe Dam are regulated for irrigation and flood control. The 95 miles of streams in the Willow Creek drainage above Ririe Reservoir run mainly through narrow canyons are well-populated with cutthroat trout.

Water flows vary from extremes of several thousand feet per second during runoff to a few feet per second in late summer and winter.

Because of intense agricultural pressure the fishery has suffered and this drainage has been identified as one of the ten worst soil-erosion areas in the U.S. Water quality improvement programs have been initiated but it will take years for the creek to return to health. Because of its isolation it holds one of the most important populations of Yellowstone cutthroat in the state toward its headwaters.

Ririe Reservoir (1,470 acres)

Ririe Dam was built for flood control and irrigation, and is a put-and-take fishery east of Idaho Falls that is managed to maintain a viable, catchable population of kokanee salmon. Other species include rainbow, cutthroat and brown trout and smallmouth bass.

The reservoir has developed into a very popular fishery. It is one of the most heavily fished trout areas in Idaho. It is primarily supported by hatchery releases of cutthroat trout and kokanee salmon.

Smallmouth bass were planted from 1984 to 1986 and a reproducing population has developed so that smallmouth bass numbers have expanded into an abundant population. A short growing season limits their size. Elev.: 5,111 feet.

Henry's Fork Drainage

The Henry's Fork of the Snake River is one of the most popular rainbow trout fisheries in North America. It's fed by other quality rivers that include the Teton, Fall, Warm and Buffalo rivers.

The river's headwaters are atop the caldera of an ancient volcano that stretches into Montana. It flows south for more than 75 river miles to the Ashton Reservoir near the town of Ashton, the first city south of the caldera on Highway 20. All along the river you will see scene after scene of natural beauty and wildlife ranging from open meadows and pine forests with deer, elk, sandhill cranes, eagles and osprey. It is not uncommon to see moose feeding on the lush vegetation in the shallows in many areas along the watercourse.

From beautiful Henry's Lake at the north reach of the drainage to Island Park Reservoir, the Henry's Fork provides good fishing supported by natural production and supplemented by hatchery rainbow trout.

The area below Island Park Reservoir is world famous and attracts anglers from across the globe. Wild rainbow trout make up the majority of the catch, with brook trout accounting for the rest. Native cutthroat trout were reported as only a small percentage of the fish caught with cuttbow hybrids and mountain whitefish present.

From Island Park Dam to the lowland near St. Anthony, below the Ashton Reservoir, there are natural populations with no hatchery plantings. The area from Island Park Reservoir to Riverside Campground is the world-famous rainbow trout fishery. This is a trophy section. Strictly catch-and-release regulations. The area beneath the caldera near Ashton and St. Anthony is more agricultural than the higher elevations near Last Chance or Island Park and produces good numbers of wild rainbows and some brown and cutthroat trout.

When the Teton Dam failed in 1976, the river below the confluence of the Teton River was severely degraded. Restricted harvest regulations have increased survival and movement of wild cutthroat from the Teton River into this portion of the Henry's Fork, making this section of river a viable fishery once again. It is all natural reproduction here and in good water years the population can build, but years of successive drought take their toll because of high water temperatures and low flows.

Rivers, Lakes and other Waters

Henry's Fork of the Snake River
The two-mile stretch from Big Springs to Henry's Lake Outlet is closed to fishing because of its importance as a spawning, rearing and fish observation area. Historically this area held some very large trout. For more information about the area contact local fly shops. See *Idaho's Big 10*, page 43.

Henry's Lake (6,500 acre)
Henry's Lake is a shallow, highly productive man-made lake located near the headwaters of the Henry's Fork atop the Continental Divide. Since 1924, hatchery operations at the lake have provided cutthroat trout eggs for fisheries throughout the state, including the lake itself.

Water from the lake is used for irrigation near St. Anthony and this stretch of river has been managed as trophy water since 1976 for cuttbow hybrids. It also produces large brook trout, including the state record of more than seven pounds. Cutthroat trout provide the majority of the fish caught in the lake.

Since 1981, cooperative agreements between the Department of Fish and Game, the Henry's Lake Foundation and area ranchers have improved in-stream spawning and rearing habitat through protective fencing of Henry's Lake spawning tributaries. Fish losses to irrigation ditches have also been reduced by cooperative diversion screening projects.

From 1981 through 1984, the department released approximately 2 million cutthroat fry annually. By 1984, cutthroat populations had increased dramatically and this increase posed the potential problem of threatening the trophy management goals of Henry's Lake. Beginning in 1985, cutthroat stocking was reduced to 1 million per year with increased stocking of hybrids and brook trout.

Since then, it has been adjusted to where approximately 1.3 million cutthroat, 200,000 sterile hybrid trout and 100,000 sterile brook trout are stocked annually.

Resident species include cutthroat, brook and cuttbow hybrids. There is good to excellent fishing for trophy cutthroat trout, hybrid trout and brook trout with seasonal limitations and some restricted water. Check regulations. Elev.: 6,480 feet.

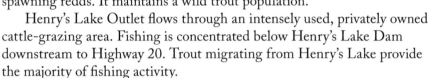

Henry's Lake Outlet

This is a 12-mile section of mostly cutthroat and brook trout that is closed below the dam to protect spawning redds. It maintains a wild trout population.

Henry's Lake Outlet flows through an intensely used, privately owned cattle-grazing area. Fishing is concentrated below Henry's Lake Dam downstream to Highway 20. Trout migrating from Henry's Lake provide the majority of fishing activity.

The Nature Conservancy has purchased a large section of land along the outlet, known as the Flat Ranch, helping to preserve the area for angling and other uses. Moose, pronghorn antelope and sandhill cranes can be seen throughout the preserve. Long-billed curlews and trumpeter swans visit the area during their migrations. The wild trout that inhabit the area include the Yellowstone cutthroat. In the early summer, camas and other wildflowers bloom with the boundaries of the Flat Ranch.

Falls River

Falls River is the largest Henry's Fork tributary and supports an excellent rainbow trout fishery managed under wild trout regulations. The lower four miles of the river are annually dewatered.

The remainder of the drainage is in excellent condition. There are miles and miles of fishable water, including tributaries, though access is somewhat limited. Resident species include rainbow, cutthroat and brook trout and mountain whitefish.

Warm River

A major Henry's Fork tributary, this river's main water source is a group of large springs six miles upstream from its junction with the Henry's Fork. Because it has plenty of gravel and fairly consistent water temperatures, and a lack of spawning areas from the Ashton Dam to Mesa Falls, many rainbow and brown trout from Henry's Fork migrate to the Warm River in the spring and fall to spawn. This is a critical area for the wild rainbow and brown trout that live in nearby in the Henry's Fork. The river is closed from its mouth to the railroad tunnel to protect spawning brown trout.

Island Park Reservoir (7,000 acres)

The water level in this reservoir fluctuates dramatically and it provides an important rainbow trout and kokanee fishery. The dam provides flood control, irrigation and electrical power for the region. Elev.: 6,309 feet.

Robinson Creek

This cold-water system has rainbow, brook, brown and cutthroat trout and mountain whitefish. It meets the Warm River just before that river enters the Henry's Fork.

Buffalo River

This cold-water stream enters the Henry's Fork below Island Park Reservoir. General rules apply for primarily brook trout.

Moose Creek

Moose Creek flows into the Upper Henrys Fork above Mack's Inn. Seasonal restrictions are in place to protect spawning kokanee salmon in the Island Park Reservoir. Other species include rainbow and brook trout.

Silver and Golden lakes (220 acres)

Located in Harriman State Park these lakes are a closed, cold-water preservation area, managed to protect waterfowl in the Targhee National Forest.

Sand Creek Reservoir (100 acres)

Located northwest of Ashton this put-and-grow fishery has rainbow, cutthroat, and brook trout managed with general regulations. The Sand Creek Wildlife Management Area is part of the larger Sand Creek Habitat Management Area, a joint project of private landowners, the Bureau of Land Management, IDF&G, and the U.S. Forest Service.

The Habitat Area was established to help elk, moose and mule deer in Fremont County. The animals summer in Island Park and Yellowstone, and winter in the sand dunes area west of St. Anthony. They need forage and solitude on their winter range, with minimal fencing and reasonable forage along their migration corridor. Elev.: 5,519 feet.

Gem State Dam to outflow at Idaho Falls power plant

Various rules apply, so check the current Idaho Fishing regulations. There is supplemental stocking of 26,000 catchable rainbow trout each year. Other important species include brown and cutthroat trout and mountain whitefish.

Idaho Falls Upper Power Plant to South Fork

This cold-water fishery is 39 miles long with cutthroat trout restrictions. Important species include cutthroat, rainbow and brown trout and mountain whitefish.

....

Lakes and ponds

There are 345 acres of lakes and ponds in this drainage available for general fishing. Stocked with rainbow and cutthroat trout fingerlings. Other species include brook trout and Arctic grayling in alpine lakes.

The Teton River Drainage

The Teton River begins on the westerly slopes of the Teton Mountains near Driggs and Victor. It travels nearly 100 miles before emptying into Henry's Fork south of St. Anthony.

There are two sections of river. The upper runs flat and smooth beneath the Teton peaks. Much of the lower canyon section is on private land so access can be tricky. Most of the takeout points are at bridges because few roads follow the river.

The most common practical method of fishing is with a watercraft of some sort. Drift boats or cata-rafts both have pros and cons. Ask a local shop about water levels and floatability.

The Teton River drains approximately 890 square miles in Teton and Madison counties. Prior to the construction and collapse of the Teton Dam in 1976, the river supported a self-sustaining native cutthroat trout fishery. Cutthroat trout were the most common game fish below the dam before the collapse. Wild and hatchery rainbow and brook trout and mountain whitefish were also found in the drainage.

In 1988 the Teton River Fishery Enhancement Plan began to improve habitat lost through both the flood and the gradual, cumulative changes from land-use practices. The objectives were to rehabilitate habitat so cutthroat trout could, once again, become self-sustaining in the drainage. So far, so good.

Rivers, Lakes and other Waters

Teton River
The Teton River system includes the North and South forks from their confluence with the Henry's Fork to Felt Dam. This is quality cutthroat trout water, wild trout water for rainbow with general rules for mountain whitefish. From Felt Dam to Trail Creek west of Victor, the river is managed as quality water for cutthroat, wild trout water for rainbow trout, as well as general water for brook trout and mountain whitefish.

Teton, Fox, Trail, Bitch, Badger, Moody and Canyon creeks
Access is limited, but worth the effort for these six creeks. It's quality water for cutthroat, wild trout water for rainbow with general regulations for brook trout and whitefish. Ask permission before going on private land. Teton, Trail and Fox creeks are closed until July 1 for spawning cutthroat. Access is limited to these areas.

All other tributaries
There are 84 miles of quality water for cutthroat trout and general management rules for brook trout. Some tributary water may not be fishable.

Trail Creek Pond FFW (two acres)
This pond is stocked with catchable rainbow trout.

Packsaddle Lake (four acres)
This lake is stocked with cutthroat trout fingerlings every three years. Elev.: 7,362 feet.

The Sinks Drainage

Below the rugged peaks of the Lost River Range, melting snowpack from these extreme heights drains down the valleys and draws to fill the Big Lost River in decent snow years. The river flows through the valley beneath Mt. Borah (state's highest peak), the active Lost River fault zone and into the Arco Desert. Somewhere south of Mackay the water disappears, into the porous basalt that was left by the most recent volcanic activity in the area.

The water sinks into the Snake River aquifer and migrates 150 miles to burst out of the steep canyon walls of the Snake River at Thousand Springs near Hagerman. The underground journey takes about two hundred years.

The Big Lost and Little Lost rivers, Birch, Camas, Beaver and Medicine Lodge rivers are the primary drainages, and all sink into the Upper Snake River Plain aquifer. Except for some headwaters and a few minor tributaries where brook trout are the most common fish, rainbow trout are.

Native cutthroat trout have fishable populations in some streams and mountain whitefish are found only in the Big Lost River drainage. Stream quality and fish populations range from excellent to poor. Do your homework and local shops can answer any questions.

Rivers, Lakes and other Waters

Big Lost River
The Big Lost River, which runs through Custer and Butte counties, is the largest of the sink drainages. It includes Mackay Reservoir and its major tributaries: Antelope, Summit and Wildhorse creeks; and the East, West and North forks of the Big Lost River.

Mackay Reservoir, built in 1916, is a widely fluctuating irrigation reservoir. During excessively high water years most of the trout and Kokanee are flushed into the Big Lost River. During low water years the fish pool up and then flow out the pipes at the dam. With the fish gone, fishing takes a serious hit the following year, making it impossible to manage Mackay Reservoir as a wild-trout fishery. During good water years when the reservoir is full the fish grow exceedingly fast and reproduce in the tributaries above the reservoir.

Hatchery rainbow comprise the majority of fish taken in the reservoir along with some brook trout, kokanee salmon and wild rainbow trout. The kokanee have become an important element, particularly in the winter, and established a foothold without stocking. The reservoir is a popular kokanee ice-fishing site in January and February. It is stocked more than other places because of its designation.

Below the reservoir a nice tail-water fishery has developed. Low water years affect the sink's drainages when water storage and natural stream flows do not meet irrigation demand. From the Moore Diversion upstream to Mackay Reservoir, the Big Lost River supports wild rainbow trout, brook trout and mountain whitefish populations. Though the Mackay Reservoir produces excellent fishing immediately downstream of Mackay Dam, large numbers of fish are lost annually to irrigation canals.

The Big Lost River from Mackay up to Chilly Bridge is dewatered yearly by irrigation, severely affecting long-term stream management plans. From Chilly Bridge upstream, the river and its tributaries support populations of wild rainbow, cutthroat, and brook trout, and some mountain whitefish.

Big Lost River tributaries, with the exception of Wildhorse Creek, offer good fishing for brook trout and some rainbow trout. Catchable rainbow trout are stocked regularly in Wildhorse Creek and other high-use sections of the North, East and West forks of the Big Lost River. Cutthroat have been stocked in the West Fork and the East Fork to try to establish a wild population.

Regulations for the Big Lost River drainage are general—six trout of any size may be taken. Cutthroat are protected throughout the region by a 16-inch minimum and two-fish limit.

In Copper Basin, on the East Fork of Big Lost River, the only remaining signs of past mining activity are the mine shafts and crumbling structures. Copper Basin is a beautiful, secluded area just above the confluence of the East and North forks of the Big Lost River. Primary species are rainbow and brook trout.

Little Lost River

In the Little Lost River drainage you will find mostly wild rainbow

trout, with brook trout being more abundant in the headwater areas. Populations of protected bull trout are present in Sawmill Creek and the upper Little Lost River and tributaries. The Little Lost River has been managed for wild trout production since 1983.

Much of the land in the Lemhi Range/Little Lost River drainage is BLM land. Most of the fences are there to manage livestock—not limit fishing access. For access information contact the Bent Rod Sport Shop in Mackay (208-588-3310). Ask first for access to private land.

Birch Creek

This popular stream north of Howe is maintained with stocked rainbow to add to the wild trout population. A cold-water stream it is quite heavily fished. It is 32 miles of tributary water managed as a put-and-take fishery to supplement its wild trout population.

Medicine Lodge Creek

Rainbow trout make up the majority of the fish in this waterway. Electrofishing of the creek showed good populations of cutthroat and brook trout in several of the tributaries, although wild rainbows were the dominant species. Medicine Lodge Creek has been managed for wild rainbow production since 1983.

Brook trout are managed with general regulations. Including its tributaries, the river covers 64 miles. It is managed for wild trout and quality fishing—so check your regulations. Fish and Game management plans call for a restricted cutthroat harvest.

Camas Creek

Mud Lake and Beaver and Camas creeks are all a part of the Camas Creek Drainage. You can find wild rainbow trout and brook trout in most headwater streams. Brown trout fingerlings have been planted here and some have grown to large size. Though few in number, there are native cutthroat trout to be found in the upper reaches. Because water conditions deteriorate in the lower reaches trout populations are limited.

Mud Lake (7,200 acres)

This large Jefferson County lake originally contained large numbers of cutthroat trout, but now supports a warm-water fishery with yellow perch, largemouth bass, brown bullhead and tiger muskie.

The lake supports a few hatchery rainbow trout that move down out of Camas Creek, but the high summer temperatures, fluctuating water levels and the low dissolved-oxygen levels have made it less likely to find trout here.

Experimental introduction of cutthroat began in 1990 and they are stocked when available. Tiger muskie have been stocked here in the past. Mud Lake covers more than 7,000 surface acres when it is full, and its primary species is perch and it is a wintertime draw for ice anglers. Elev.: 4,783 feet.

Mackay Reservoir (1,000 acres)

This impoundment is a put-and-take, put-and-grow fishery for rainbow trout. Major species also include brook trout and kokanee salmon. From the reservoir for 15 miles to the Chilly Bridge, the system is dewatered through natural sinks and irrigation diversion. When there is water, the river has rainbow and brook trout.

Tributaries include North, West, and Upper East forks, Wildhorse and Summit creeks, and total more than 232 miles with put-and-take regulations. Managed to maintain a wild trout population, available species include rainbow and brook trout, mountain whitefish and Arctic grayling. Some streams that flow through the valley are either on private land or are pay-to-fish streams. Elev.: 6,053 feet.

Beaver Creek

This river's lower end is dewatered annually by irrigation demands. Where there is water, the fishing is managed for wild trout, general and quality fishing.

Above Spencer near I-15 there are 18 miles of stream with supplemental stocking in areas of high use. Other species include rainbow, brook and cutthroat trout. Winter can be hard on this creek. As is typical with other shallow streams in the drainage, if there is not enough snow cover the river channel will freeze solid, causing water to flow over the banks, dramatically impacting the fish population.

Roberts Gravel Pond (35 acres)

Located near the village of Roberts this pond is managed with general fishing regulations. Species include stocked rainbow trout and yellow perch.

Alpine Lakes

There are 290 surface acres of alpine lakes in the drainage. They are planted with hatchery fry to maintain populations of rainbow, cutthroat, brook and golden trout, cuttbow hybrids and Arctic grayling. Contact the Bent Rod Sport Shop in Mackay for information on specific lakes.

Airstrips

Henry's Lake (state)

Henry's Lake Airport serves Lake, Island Park and Fremont County and is owned by the State of Idaho Transportation Department's Aeronautics Division. The turf runway extends for 4,600 feet. The facility is at an elevation of 6,596 feet and about 3 miles from Island Park Reservoir.

Copper Basin (backcountry)

Copper Basin Airport serves Mackay and Custer County and is owned by the State of Idaho Transportation Department's Aeronautics Division. The turf runway, southwest of Mackay, can be rough and extends for 4,700 feet and is 100 feet wide. The facility is at elevation of 7,920 feet and about 12 air-miles from Mackay.

SELECTING A DRIFT BOAT

A drift boat can be one of the best fishing aids you could ever buy. It allows you the freedom to fish an entire river rather than only the accessible points along the way. With a drift boat, you can quietly approach the best runs and areas where you can see fish rising.

There are a number of different models of drift boats available. A buyer needs to consider several different things before he or she buys. First, where is the boat going to be used? Will it be on relatively calm, flat rivers or will the boat be used on rivers that have white water, big drops and standing waves to negotiate? On calmer rivers, a low-profile boat is often a good choice, especially where high winds are a factor. On rivers with serious white water, a higher-sided boat is advisable.

Second, how will the boat be used? Fly fishing for trout? Pulling plugs for salmon or steelhead? Boats are available with front bench seating arrangements that will accommodate three passengers, a perfect configuration for pulling plugs. If the boat will be used solely for fly fishing on calm rivers, a low side boat might make the most sense. If you are thinking of fishing a variety of ways, look for a boat that will give you the needed flexibility.

Safety

The biggest thing to keep in mind while boating is to always wear your personal flotation device (PFD, or life jacket). Most boating accident fatalities could be avoided if the people in the boat were wearing PFDs. Accidents can happen in very unexpected places, and they happen very quickly.

With a drift boat you will usually be floating on moving water. Moving water has tremendous power. Should you allow the boat to hit a large mid-river boulder broadside, the force of the water could sink the boat within seconds. The rower must always keep the boat under control. If you have never rowed a drift boat, find an experienced and competent instructor to show you the basics. From there, slowly work your way up to more technical and demanding water.

Launching Your Drift Boat

Drift boats are light in comparison to other types of boats. There is no reason to back your boat trailer into the water. By keeping it out of the water, you will save wear and tear on the wiring and wheel bearings. A drift boat can be unloaded on a boat ramp or gravel bar and can be slid into the water with little or no effort.

Things to Keep in Your Drift Boat

Rope. Many rivers can change course during periods of high water. New channels can be created; trees can come down across the river. A lot of rivers do not have improved boat ramps. There may be a slide or a gravel bar that will not support a vehicle. A lining rope can help get you safely through these kinds of situations. Eight to 100 feet is a good length to carry.

Extra Drain Plugs. Drain plugs are inexpensive. One or two extras in the storage box could save your day.

Spare Oar. Would you leave on an automobile trip without a spare tire? You might never use a spare oar, but why take the chance?

First Aid Kit. When you launch your boat for a float, whether for a few hours or a few days, you are pulling away from easy access to any kind of aid. A basic first aid kit and familiarity with it is always a good idea.

Bailing Device. Hopefully you will not need this often, but on rainy days it is often nice to have. If you happen to take a big wave over the side, it is a necessity. A big sponge works fine for sopping up rainwater. A pump or small, square bucket removes larger amounts of water faster.

For more information on finding the right drift boat

call **ClackaCraft Drift Boats** at **800-394-1345**

See Sponsor Page in the Sponsor Index p. 239.

Yellowstone National Park

Yellowstone National Park

Licenses and Regulations

The general fishing season in Yellowstone National Park runs from the Saturday of Memorial Day weekend to the first Sunday in November. Fishing is allowed between 5 a.m. and 10 p.m. There are quite a few exceptions to the general season so be sure to check the specific regulations for where you intend to fish.

A valid Yellowstone National Park fishing license is required for all anglers 12 years old and older. Anglers less than 12 years old must be accompanied by a licensed adult. Licenses are available at local fly shops and at park ranger facilities. Make sure you get a park regulations booklet as it contains important and detailed information about fishing in the park.

All types of floating vessels, including motorized and non-motorized boats, canoes, kayaks and float tubes, require a permit for use in the park. The current fishing regulations will tell you where boat permits can be purchased. Floating vessels are not allowed on any river or stream in Yellowstone Park except for the Lewis River between Lewis and Shoshone lakes.

In Yellowstone, the health of the ecosystem takes precedence over angling. Fish are a major food source for animals such as ospreys, grizzly bears and otters. Fisheries management plans are designed to assure that there are enough adult fish to support the needs of these and other animals. Management plans also emphasize recreational angling for wild fish—stocking programs ended in the mid 1950s.

As a result of fisheries management statagies, regulations are often complex concerning fishing seasons, area closures, tackle restrictions and creel and size limits. Bait fishing is generally not allowed, some waters are designated fly fishing only or closed altogether, and only lead-free weight is allowed. It is your responsibility to know the regulations where you plan to fish when, and to be able to identify the various fish species.

When Should I Fish Yellowstone?

Good fishing can be found in Yellowstone throughout the season. Unless you are interested in fishing a specific river or lake, the best time to fish Yellowstone is whenever you are able. Generally, the rivers of the eastern part of the park (Firehole, Gibbon, Madison), and the lakes (Lewis, Shoshone, Yellowstone), fish best early and late in the season while the waters in the northeast corner of the park fish better from July through September.

Invasive, Non-native Species

(from the 2004 YNP Fishing Regulations)

Yellowstone fisheries are threatened by at least three invasive, non-native species. The whirling disease parasite has been implicated in the decline of wild trout populations in the Western United States. Widespread infection has been confirmed in Pelican Creek, one of the largest tributaries of Yellowstone Lake. New Zealand mud snails occur in many park streams, impact aquatic insect communities, and ultimately affect the angling experience. Also, non-native lake trout were discovered in Yellowstone Lake and pose a great threat to the future of the lake's native cuthroat trout.

Preservation of aquatic resources and quality angling depends on you. Help prevent further spread of these invaders by thoroughly cleaning mud, plants and debris from your fishing equipment and footwear before leaving your angling site. Drain live wells and clean fish only on the same body of water where they were caught. In an attempt to limit predation and competition between native cutthroat trout and the intorduced lake trout, all lake trout caught in Yellowstone Lake, its tributaries and the Yellowstone River must be killed.

Rivers, Lakes, and other Waters

Madison River

The Madison offers good access and a variety of angling opportunities for rainbow and brown trout, Arctic grayling and mountain whitefish. The river begins at Madison Junction, where the Firehole and Gibbon rivers meet, and it winds its way through a picturesque valley before exiting the park near West Yellowstone. Along the way anglers have easy access to about ten miles of the river. In some sections the Madison is like a large spring creek where the clear water, tranquil flows, and wary trout will challenge even the most accomplished angler. A stealthy approach and a knack for matching the hatch are required if you hope to hook one of the river's larger trout.

Other sections are dominated by shallow riffles that offer good fishing at certain times of the year. Using a dry-and-dropper rig is a great way to search these sections for feisty browns and rainbows. The Madison also has its share of good (and popular) runs and pools. Fishing a nymph or streamer through the depths of these sections can produce good action for whitefish and smaller trout when the rest of the river is fishing tough. Be ready though; on the right day any pool might produce a few surprises.

The Madison fishes best early and late in the season (opening day through early July and late September through close). The river may be closed to fishing during the middle of the summer due to high water temperatures.

The Madison River is fly fishing only. Spinning rods are allowed, but they must be used with a casting bubble or bobber and a fly.

Firehole River

The Firehole is truly a unique river, offering good access, fine dry fly fishing, and an opportunity to catch rainbow, brown and brook trout. Geothermal features line the river and animals such as elk and bison are seen in large numbers. The Firehole fishes best early and late in the season when water temperatures are below 70 degrees. The river may be closed to fishing during the middle of the summer due to high water temperatures.

Brook trout dominate in the reaches upstream of Old Faithful while rainbows and browns are common downstream of Biscuit Basin. Important hatches include several species of mayflies, caddis, stoneflies, midges, and even damselflies.

Check local fly shops to get up-to-the-minute information on the hatches. When the trout are rising, matching the hatch is the best way to fool them. Fishing small nymphs and soft hackles, dead drift or on the swing, may also produce a few grabs. Take note that the Firehole River is designated fly fishing only. Spinning rods are allowed, but they must be used with a casting bubble or bobber and a fly.

Many of the Park's thermal features are located on or near the Firehole and these thermal features are dangerous, so use caution when walking the banks. The area around Old Faithful is closed to fishing. The river may be closed to fishing during the summer due to high water tempertures.

Gibbon River

The Gibbon offers up a variety of fishing options and water types unmatched by many rivers 10 times its size. Available species include rainbow, brown, and brook trout, mountain whitefish and Arctic grayling. It is a small river, but one can find placid meadow reaches, fast and steep canyon water and classic riffle-run pools all mixed in with spectacular waterfalls and beautiful thermal features. The road runs along most of the Gibbon's length, making access relatively easy.

Typically, easier fishing can be had in the faster sections or in the headwater reaches, where the trout are a bit smaller and less picky. Attractor dries and nymphs work well. The meadow areas hold fish of all sizes, but landing any trout 14 inches or longer will prove a formidable challenge. Approaching the river stealthily and matching the hatch are critical.

The Gibbon River downstream of Gibbon Falls is fly fishing only. Spinning rods are allowed, but they must be used with a casting bubble or bobber and a fly. The river may be closed to fishing during the summer due to high water tempertures.

Gallatin River

This river offers good access and a mix of water ranging from willow-lined meadow reaches to quick, pocket-filled runs and riffles. Species present include rainbow, brown, and brook trout, mountain whitefish and Arctic grayling.

The Gallatin runs ice-cold and usually comes into fishing shape in early July when hatches of mayflies, caddis and stoneflies occur. Match the hatch if you can, or fish attractor dry flies with small dropper nymphs. Later in the season fish will take hopper, beetle and cricket patterns.

Spin fishers are rarely seen on the Gallatin, but a small, well-cast spinner is likely to produce a few grabs. The fish you are most likely to catch on the Gallatin are medium-sized rainbow trout. Larger fish are also present, usually in lesser-fished areas. The Gallatin can be a fickle river and it is often necessary to cover a lot of water before finding that day's honey hole.

Yellowstone River

The section of river from Yellowstone Lake down to Chittenden Bridge opens on July 15. Access is excellent as the road parallels the river for the entire stretch. This area offers the angler opportunities to fish for native Yellowstone cutthroats with dry flies as well as nymphs and spinning tackle. Rainbow and brown trout and mountain whitefish are also present. The hatches on this section of river are often complex so consult a local fly shop about hatches and river conditions.

Below Chittenden Bridge the mighty Yellowstone plunges over two spectacular waterfalls and begins its journey through Grand and Black canyons before exiting the park at Gardiner. Downstream of the lower falls you will find native Yellowstone cutthroats as well as a few rainbow and brown trout, and mountain whitefish. This section of river has very little easy access and is usually fished by adventurous anglers who enjoy hiking as much as fishing. Large attractor dry flies and nymphs are most effective in the turbulent canyon pocket water.

The Yellowstone is big water and anglers should exercise caution.

Lamar River

Located in the northeast corner of the park, this river offers both road and backcountry access to anglers for rainbow and cutthroat trout. Runoff often lasts until late July making this the last major river in the park to become fishable each year.

The Lamar is often muddied by thunderstorms in its headwaters so if you arrive and find it muddy check out nearby Slough Creek. Though hatches of mayflies and caddis bring fish to the surface when conditions are right the majority of fishing on the Lamar is done with large attractor dry flies, terrestrial insect imitations and standard nymphs.

The Lamar Valley is a favorite location for viewing wildlife as well as fishing. Bison, pronghorn antelope, grizzly bears and even wolves are seen in this area. Use caution while fishing and enjoy the wildlife from a safe vantage point.

Slough Creek

Slough Creek is a favorite of cutthroat and rainbow trout anglers because of its approachable size, and terrific scenery. It is a large meadow stream for most of its length with steep canyon stretches separating the meadow reaches. Road access is via the dirt road leading to Slough Creek Campground, but many anglers choose to hike from the trailhead near the campground upstream to the first, second or third meadow (one-hour, two-hour and three-hour hikes respectively).

Fishing is best when the runoff subsides and lasts until the first snows kill off the terrestrial insects. Delicate presentations and hatch-matching skills are often required. Spin anglers do best early in the season when the water is high.

Anglers should be cautious when fishing Slough Creek. The high banks that offer great views of the fish are often crumbly and precarious. Bear and other large animals are also common, especially in the back-country meadows.

Yellowstone Lake (87,000 acres)

Yellowstone Lake opens to fishing on June 15 and offers anglers opportunities to fish for native Yellowstone cutthroat trout and non-native lake trout. Fishing from shore with spinning or fly tackle is a great way to catch fish. Float tubing, canoeing and motor boating are other effective ways to fish the lake. Access to shore fishing is easy in many places where the road parallels the lake's edge. Woolly Bugger and leach patterns are all you really need to fly fish effectively, but the lake also offers some interesting dry fly fishing opportunities when conditions are right. Spin fishing can also be productive on Yellowstone Lake

The lake is big and cold and bad weather can appear without warning. If you decide to fish from a boat, canoe or float tube always wear a life preserver.

To protect the native cutthroat trout all lake trout must be killed, not released.

Lewis Lake (2,716 acres)

Lewis Lake is a popular angling destination for both fly and lure anglers. Species present include brown, brook, cutthroat and lake trout. The best fly fishing comes early and late in the season when the water is colder and the trout can be found in shallow water. Wading can be effective, but float tubing offers access to more water and makes for unhindered back casts. Hatches will bring fish to the surface when conditions are right, but fishing a large streamer or leach pattern is an all-around safer bet. Boaters use trolling lures such as gold spoons in search of brown and lake trout.

Shoshone Lake (8,050 acres)

Shoshone is the largest backcountry (no road access) lake in the continental U.S. Species there include brown, brook, cutthroat and lake trout. It fishes best early in the season, for about a month after ice-out and again in the fall when the surface water temperature cools down. Fly anglers use large streamers and leeches when not matching the early-season hatches. Gear fishers use standard spoons and spinners. Access is by foot via trails ranging from three to five miles in length or by canoe via the channel from Lewis Lake.

Like Yellowstone Lake, Shoshone is big and cold and bad weather can appear without warning. Use extreme caution and exercise good judgment if you decide to fish from a canoe or float tube, and always wear a life preserver.

....

Backcountry Waters

We have introduced the reader to ten of the most famous and easily accessible fisheries in Yellowstone National Park. These waters are popular because they offer excellent fishing opportunities while still providing challenges to anglers of all levels. With more than 400 fishable waters in Yellowstone you could spend a lifetime of summers learning these waters. For anglers with strong legs and a hearty sense of adventure, these backcountry fisheries bring them back to Yellowstone year after year.

In the Yellowstone backcountry you can fish a wilderness river for large native cutthroats or float tube a small lake for Arctic grayling. You can sneak up a tiny creek and cast dry flies to eager brook trout or match the hatch on a secluded meadow stream in hopes of fooling a monster rainbow. Part of the fun of fishing the backcountry is the sense of discovery that accompanies each new adventure.

For this reason, we will not name or describe any specific rivers or lakes in this section. However, the angling opportunities are endless. Pick up a detailed map of the park, give it a good look and remember that the majority of rivers, streams, lakes and ponds in Yellowstone hold trout of some kind. And when you visit the park spend a day or two on some water off the beaten path. You will be glad you did.

Your own safety is a priority in the backcountry. Yellowstone is a wild place, and many of the features that make it so special also make it fairly dangerous. Grizzly bear, black bear, moose, bison, elk, deer and even badgers can be dangerous if confronted or startled on the trail or stream. It is important that you act appropriately in the backcountry to avoid incidents with animals. Always travel in groups, make noise while you hike and carry pepper spray. Be informed and know what to do if you come in close contact with large animals.

Many of Yellowstone's thermal features are also located in the backcountry. While very beautiful, many springs are surrounded by thin or infirm ground that could collapse under a human's weight. Be careful and enjoy the thermal features from a safe distance.

Yellowstone's location and mountain topography make for unpredictable weather. A warm, sunny day can quickly turn into a cold, rainy or snowy one. Always be prepared and carry clothing that can be layered for warmth and retain body heat even when wet. Polar fleece and waterproof/breathable rain gear are a must.

Be sure to bring enough food and water to get you through the day and drink plenty of water. It is easy to become dehydrated during a long day on the trail. Because you will probably be on a river or lake, carry a portable water filter in your day pack. Store your food properly while fishing as animals have been known to dig into an unattended pack in hopes of scoring a peanut butter and jelly sandwich. Keep your food on you or hang it in a tree if there is a spot available.

Camping is allowed at designated sites only and backcountry camping permits (free) must be obtained in advance at one of the many park ranger facilities. Ask for more information on backcountry camping regulations at park entrances or ranger facilities.

Hatch Chart

Mayflies – baetis, PMDs, green drakes, gray drakes, and callibaetis
Specific imitations are important when fishing to selective trout that see a lot of fishing pressure.
Caddis - Designating the species is less important than with mayflies. Carry tan- green- and gray-bodied patterns in #14, #16 and #18.
Stoneflies – salmon flies, golden stones and "little yellow" stoneflies
Midges – various species in sizes #12-#24
Terrestrials – hoppers, crickets, Mormon crickets, beetles, ants, flying ants and termites.

Check with area fly shops for current information.

Matt Klara lives in Montana.

McGuire and the Moose

It was twenty-eight years ago this past February. McGuire and I were sitting in the last booth along the wall just outside the back room at Mack's Inn, a longtime watering spot in eastern Idaho not too far from Yellowstone. We were sipping a bit of the stuff that warms the innards, while outside more inches were being added to the snow piled road-sign high along the lonely highway. Sub-arctic temperatures held things pretty much in their icy grip. It had been a long winter, with no January thaw and no hint of a letup. A few citizens sat their stools at the long, solid mahogany bar, feet resting comfortably on the big brass rail, sipping beer and joined in quiet conversation. Now and then, a gravelly old-boy laugh would rise above the drone of their conversations.

Mack's Inn had opened in 1882 and not much had changed in the old, high-country saloon in the last hundred or so years. Not much, that is, except, for the addition of a huge moose head which owner Mack Jorgenson had hung on the wall in the mid-seventies. Along with the moose head, an ancient menagerie of nearly-mummified forest critters peered down on the patrons from their perches along the walls. Staring with unblinking eyes were squirrels, deer, elk, raccoons, rabbits, pheasants, grouse, the inevitable jackalope and a very large bison head. They were fusty enough to have been there since the place opened.

We were making plans for the most important day of the year—the opening of trout season. As we talked, McGuire kept studying the moose head hanging over the door to the back room. "I know that fella from somewhere," he would mumble. Staring bemusedly at the huge head, he would refill his glass, puff deeply on his pipe and rejoin our conversation. Despite these interruptions, by closing time, McGuire and I had firmed up plans for the Memorial Day weekend, but he still hadn't figured out where he and the moose had crossed paths. The next morning he headed back home to Ketchum.

McGuire was then and is now that rarest of creatures, a never-married bachelor. His mistress was fly fishing and he knew instinctively that no woman would put up with the whore that owned him. Good luck and good investing instincts provided him with the wherewithal to lustfully pursue the thing he loved most. And the Henry's Fork of the Snake River was his perennial choice for opening day in Idaho.

There was no mention of the moose in any of our phone conversations as March roared in on the wings of an Arctic blast and sent Island Park temperatures below zero for a week, then began slackening its grip. By the first week of May, the air was still nippy, but spring was definitely in the offing. The week before the opener, McGuire called to say he'd be up on Friday and that he had a surprise for me. I had a hunch it had something to do with the moose, but knew better than to ask. McGuire liked to surround events in mystery and the moose was the perfect vehicle.

The week before the opener was cold and murky with evening temperatures down in the twenties, but the outlook for Saturday was good: sunny with temperatures in the forties. Friday afternoon, the black and white Blazer rolled up our muddy driveway. McGuire stepped out. He was wearing his L.L. Bean travel chinos with pockets down to the cuffs, his soft-leather day hikers, an Orvis official opening day shirt, a three-hundred-dollar waxed cotton field coat, all topped with his olive drab Clancy hat. The Blazer was jammed with enough rods, reels, waders, fly boxes, vests and assorted gear to make an outfitter blush. Among other things, McGuire was pathological about owning every new piece of fly fishing equipment that came on the market and some before they got there.

A bit later, we were sitting in front of the fire in the Family room, sipping Southern Comfort manhattans with McGuire about to reveal his big news. But not before building the suspense by stirring the fire with the iron poker, digging into the wood box for another log and ceremoniously placing it onto the grate. By now, even my wife was interested and she stepped into the family room as our guest filled, tamped and lit his pipe. He blew a smoke ring the size of a bowling ball as the firelight played across his face, then cocking his head toward us, announced, "The head of that *Alces alces Americana* hanging in Mack's Inn is a world-class trophy." The smoke ring drifted slowly across the opening of the hearth, became caught in the draft and dissolved. "It's all that's left of the only moose ever taken on a fly rod."

"Yeah, right," I snorted, convinced he'd been sniffing head cement. But McGuire persisted. "Hear me out. When I was a kid, back in the 30's and 40's, my dad would take me to a lodge way up in British Columbia. He loved to fish those streams up there and so did I; he with a fly rod and me with an old metal casting rod and worms." McGuire worked his way over to the La-Z-Boy, sat down, raised the leg rest, leaned back and puffed his pipe load of tobacco back to life, then continued. "The main room of the lodge had a huge stone fireplace and above the mantle hung a very large moose head. The cook at the lodge was an old sourdough named Amos and he took a liking to me. One night Amos and I we're sitting on the porch and he got to talking about the moose head.

"Did ya ever notice that number fourteen Adams stuck in the mountin' board of that big feller? he asked. No, I told him. Well, says Amos, there's a feller comed up here every year for a long time name of George Watson. He was a fly fisherman, like yore old man. Nice feller, but he's passed now. Well, one evenin', ole George was fishin' Cadaver Creek, tryin' out some new fangled fly he'd heard about called an Adams. He was enjoyin' hisself just fine when a very large bull moose happened along. Now, no matter how big a moose gets, it can walk through the woods without crackin' a twig, so George had no idea the moose was behind him, just a munchin' and watchin'. On a long back cast, George snagged the number fourteen Adams he was usin' right smack in the butt of that there ole moose. When he turned around an' saw what he'd snagged, he headed for shore, pronto, leavin' that there fly stuck right where it was. Then the strangest dang thing happened: that there moose backed up to a big ole oak and started rubbing his butt up against it. He stood there snortin' and rubbin', snortin' and rubbin' until George, even taken as he was with all he was a seein', gave in to his system callin' fer a drink and dinner and headed back to the lodge. When he told the other fellers about the moose, they told him he better stop takin' his flask with him to the creek.

McGuire's pipe had gone out and his glass was empty. Dinner was ready, but my wife made him another drink. As McGuire relit his pipe, I threw another log on the fire and he continued with Amos's story:

Well sir, the next mornin' ole George heads over to Cadaver Creek for a look-see. He gets to the oak and there is bark and fur piled up all about, and the ground near the tree all torn up. Lyin' next to the tree is the moose's head. Everthin' else had been rubbed away, And there, caught in the bark of the that there tree was that there number fourteen Adams. Now ole George knew a trophy when he seen it so he hauled the moose head out of the woods, had it mounted and donated it to the lodge with that number fourteen Adams stuck right there in the mounting board. The lodge owner gave it the place of honor over the fireplace. The only moose ever taken on a fly rod.

My wife laughed and went back into the kitchen. I groaned as McGuire sat there with that gloating grin on his face. He had gotten me again.

Saturday morning we were on the river and, as usual, the opener was fun. We hooked four or five nice rainbows apiece, returned home satisfied, spent Sunday talking about Saturday and by mid-afternoon, McGuire was on his way home.

A few days after McGuire left, I stopped in at Mack's Inn and I took a close look at the moose. Near the base of the mounting board was a small hole. I took out the number fourteen Adams I had clipped inside my jacket. The hook fit perfectly into the hole and the Adams perched jauntily beneath the huge head. The last time I stopped in at the old saloon before the fire, the Adams was still there.

Mack's Inn burnt down a few years later. Some say it was a disgruntled employee that had been fired for being drunk on the job who started the blaze. Others say it was caused by embers from the huge fireplace that hit the tinder-dry oak floor and she was gone before you knew it. Today, all that remains is the three-story brick chimney and the empty fireplace.

Joe A. Evancho

Joe A. Evancho (aka the Hack), first discovered Idaho and Mack's Inn when stationed at Mountain Home AFB in 1951 when the author wasn't even a glint in his to-be-father's eye. That glint came nine years later. But what goes around comes around and the Hack, who lives in Traverse City, Michigan, now has two sons, a daughter-in-law and three grandchildren residing in Boise. He visits Idaho regularly to fish and visit his family, in that order.

Native Lands

Native lands in Idaho provide opportunities for a variety of fish throughout the state. When traveling on Native lands remember you are in a sovereign, self-governing nation so you must obey all tribal laws and regulations. Some areas are off limits to non-Natives and some have special regulations in place

On the Duck Valley Reservation, for example, the tribe asks that you not take photographs of teepees as they are used in religious ceremonies and tribal religious matters are very private and personal.

There are four major Native land holdings associated with fishing in Idaho. Fort Hall in eastern Idaho is home to the Shoshone and Bannock tribes. The Duck Valley Indian Reservation is located on the Idaho/Nevada border and home to Shoshone and Pauite tribes. The Nez Perce land is along the Clearwater River on the Nez Perce Reservation. and the Coeur d'Alene Tribe has land on the south end of Lake Coeur d'Alene in the Panhandle. All offer a quality fishing experience for those willing to follow the rules and special regulations that may apply to each area.

Fort Hall

Long before Lewis and Clark and the Corps of Discovery visited the West the Shoshone and Bannock Indian tribes roamed a vast area that is now parts of Wyoming, Utah, Nevada and southeastern Idaho. When the Corps returned east they reported of the riches of the region thus attracting hunters, trappers and traders to southeastern Idaho. In 1834 the Hudson Bay Company built the first permanent settlement here but it wasn't too long before trapping gave out and the fort converted to a supply stop for Oregon Trail travelers. Ruts of the historic trail can still be seen near an obscure monument to the original Fort Hall. Today the sovereign nation gets revenues from agriculture, tourism and other businesses operations.

At the western end of American Falls Reservoir a remarkable transformation has occurred to a fishery that was once over-grazed and heavily eroded. The work that has been done to restore the fishery has increased the number of fish and the quality of the fishery.

The Fort Hall Bottoms can be compared to any blue ribbon stream in the state for its excellent water quality and healthy fish. Springs from the surrounding region provide more than 6 billion gallons of gin-clear water to the Snake River. Wildlife in teh area includes coyote, pheasant, heron, ducks, porcupines, owls and deer. The two main fisheries are Clear and Spring creeks and permits are required for access.

Jimmy Creek

This creek is the northern-most of the three major creeks and it holds native Yellowstone cutthroat, rainbow, cuttbow hybrids and brown trout.

Spring Creek

The middle creek of the permit fishing water has about 12 miles of permit water that also contains native Yellowstone cutthroat, rainbow, cuttbow hybrids and brown trout. There is a boat ramp below Cable Bridge that allows boaters to fish some of the deeper holes below the bridge. Float tubers and waders above the bridge. No boats above.

Clear Creek

The seven-mile reach of river below Sheepskin Road is permit fishing for non-native anglers with native Yellowstone cutthroat, rainbow, cuttbow hybrids and brown trout.

Duck Valley

The Owyhee River enters the reservation in Nevada in the southeast corner and exits tribal land in the northwest section. The reservation's fishing reservoirs are located in the central valley.

The two main reservoirs Sheep Creek and Mountain View, are loaded with catchable trout and have campgrounds, grills and plenty of parking. Sheep Creek, Mountain View and the East Fork of the Owyhee River from the south boundary to the China Town Diversion Dam are open water. Tributaries to the East Fork of the Owyhee River are closed to the public.

Live bait is prohibited and fishing is allowed one hour before sunrise through two hours after sunset. Overnight camping is allowed in designated areas only. Since the reservoirs are on Native land no Idaho license is required. You must purchase a permit to fish the reservoirs.

Some of the water from Mountain view is used for irrigation by a local farmer, but in low water years he works with the tribe to make sure the resources is not adversely effected.

Other than the fishing the area offers excellent opportunities in the spring and fall for watching the migrating birds that travel through the reservation. Visitors can view tundra and trumpeter swans and a lot of other migrating waterfowl.

Every Arbor Day the tribe has a celebration with traditional drum groups playing their songs followed by a free barbecue. Every Fourth of July there is a rodeo and a powow.

There are boating restriction, no motors, on all reservoirs.

Sheep Creek Reservoir (788 acres)

This is the largest of the fishing reservoirs on the reservation and it is stocked with rainbow trout. Elev.: 5,294 feet.

Mountain View Reservoir (633 acres)

The northern most of the three reservoir is stocked with trout. Elev.: 5,322 feet.

Lake Billy Shaw (430 acres)

This newly built reservoir was created with funds derived through partial mitigation of lost fish (salmon) on the reservation. It is regularly stocked with 20- to 25-inch trout. Special regulations apply here. Catch-and-release is the rule with a single-point barbless hook. Elev.: 5,370 feet.

Nez Perce Reservation

Non-native anglers wanting to fish for steelhead on reservation land can purchase a permit from either the Nez Perce tribe or Idaho Fish & Game when on Nez Perce land. The Nez Perce permit does not extend to any other water or species.

A Nez Perce tribal steelhead license is not valid outside the reservation boundary on the Clearwater River or on the Salmon and Snake rivers. An Idaho fishing license is. Anyone possessing a valid tribal steelhead permit does not need an a state license when fishing within reservation boundaries.

Steelhead anglers that posses a valid Nez Perce Tribal steelhead fishing license may fish the Clearwater River only within the reservation, from near the mouth of Hatwai Creek to just above Kooskia.

IDFG and the Nez Perce Tribe agreed to honor either the tribal steelhead fishing license or an Idaho fishing license with steelhead permit on the Clearwater River within reservation boundaries.

Indian reservations hold fascinating history as well as excellent fishing opportunities

The Nez Perce portion of the Clearwater River on the Nez Perce Reservation, and its western and southern tributaries, are managed by the Nez Perce Tribal Council.

All of the main stem Clearwater River and South Fork Clearwater River within the Nez Perce Reservation, the North Fork Clearwater River below Dworshak Dam, and the Middle Fork Clearwater River upstream to the mouth at Clear Creek is open during the legal season.

The downstream boundary of the Nez Perce Reservation on the main stem Clearwater River is located near the mouth of Hatwai Creek adjacent to the Clearwater River Casino and the upstream boundary of the reservation on the South Fork Clearwater River is located near Harpster.

Tunnel Pond is a put-and-take, pay-to-fish fishery southeast of Orofino. These ponds were developed to mitigate salmon loss after the construction of Dworshak Dam. Daily and yearly permits are available. The season runs from the first weekend of April to October 31. Check with tribal offices for possession limits

Coeur d'Alene Reservation

The Coeur d'Alene Indian reservation cover 350,000 acres in Idaho's panhandle southwest of Coeur d'Alene and includes the towns of Benewah, DeSmet, Plummer, Tensed and Worley with the southern portion of the lake included on reservation land.

The Coeur d'Alene tribe manages the southern portion of Coeur d'Alene Lake. For the past 10 years both Benewah and Lake creeks have been closed to help restore the population of westslope cutthroat trout.

The tribe focuses their fisheries efforts on adfluvial westslope cutthroat that are born in the streams, move into the lake for a few years, then return to the streams to spawn.

State fisheries department focuses their hatchery efforts on chinook and kokanee salmon in Lake Coeur d'Alene.

A special tribal permit is needed to fish the southern portion of the lake.

High Mountain Lakes

High mountain lakes defined

Of all the IDF&G's fishery programs alpine lakes are the most successful. For more than 50 years the department has been stocking lakes on a regular basis—usually on a two- or three -year interval.

Throughout the state these lakes—some more accessible than others—have been stocked with salmonids, though they may not be native to a particular lake. Non-native species such as brook trout, Arctic grayling and brown trout have been stocked where the environment suits them.

There are four main guidelines used to manage mountain lakes:

- Alpine lakes are managed to limit or reduce negative impact on threatened or endangered species as well as other species in areas downstream of these headwater lakes.
- Because the majority of alpine lakes evolved without fish populations, some lakes will be maintained fishless for genetic and biological diversity as well as wilderness values. These areas also serve as research areas for other forms of aquatic life.
- Lakes in wilderness or national recreation areas will be managed in conjunction with federal authorities.
- Lakes with sustaining populations will be managed in ways that will reflect their needs.

Many forest lakes were naturally fishless, but are now stocked. Stocking is exclusively of various trout species. Most stocking is done by air about every three years. Maximum fish size occurs at about three years. Contact Idaho Fish and Game for their stocking histories. Because of their number we do not list individual lakes. They vary in location from an easy walk on maintained trails with developed camping nearby to remote lakes with no trails that are miles from mechanized access. Idaho Fish and Game manages several lakes under trophy regulations requiring the release of all but the largest trout. Carefully study the regulations.

Some lakes contain native species listed under the Endangered Species Act, so knowing how to identify those species is important. Take the time to learn how to identify these fish. Pick up a copy of the Idaho Fish & Game regulations and study the fish identification pages. If you aren't sure —release your catch.

The waypoints used in this section are approximations and have been recorded as reliably as possible. However, the accuracy of the coordinates is not 100 percent and efforts continue to update and verify the lake locations accurately. These coordinates are based on government and private surveys and are aimed at the geographic center of a particular body of water. They should not be relied upon where safety is an issue or used to steer a watercraft. This is general information only.

For more detailed information about alpine fishing opportunities refer to *Idaho High Mountain Lakes* to be published by Cutthroat Press in the spring of 2005.

Panhandle

Beehive Lake Use the Wigwams topo map @ N 48° 39.30 W 116° 39.24 to find the highest of the four lakes. Its elevation is approximately 6,460 feet. The lake receives 1,200 westslope cutthroat trout from the Cabinet hatchery on an even-year rotation. Harrison Lake is to the north and the lakes feed Beehive Creek.

Big Fisher Lake Use the Pyramid Peak topo map @ N 48° 50.38 W 116° 34.00 to find this Panhandle high mountain lake in the Kaniksu National Forest. The lake's elevation is approximately 6,725 feet and it covers almost eight acres. The lake is stocked on an even-year cycle with kamloops rainbow trout. The last planting was with 1,800 fry. Trout Lake lies to the south and Long Mountain Lake is west.

Caribou Lake Use the Mount Casey topo map @ N48° 25 W 116° 40 to find this high mountain lake in the Kaniksu National Forest in Bonner County. The lake's elevation is approximately 5,260 feet and covers more than five and a half acres. The lake is stocked on an even–year rotation with 2,100 Kamloop rainbow trout

Harrison Lake Use the Wigwams topo map @ N 48° 40.74 W 116° 39.33 to find this high mountain lake in the Kaniksu National Forest. The lakes elevation is approximately 6,181 feet and covers nearly 29 acres. The lake is on an even-year rotation and was last stocked with 5,800 westslope cutthroat trout from the Cabinet Gorge hatchery. Harrison Peak is to the north and Standard Lake is to the west.

Hidden Lake Use the Grass Mountain topo map @ N 48° 52.97 W 116° 45.44 to find this high mountain lake in the Kaniksu National Forest. The lake's elevation is approximately 5,440 feet and covers 40 acres. The lake is on an even-year rotation and was last stocked with 13,500 kamloops rainbow trout. Joe Lake is to the west. The fish are from the Cabinet Gorge hatchery.

Hunt Lake Use the Mount Roothaam topo map @ N 48° 34.69 W 116° 42.20 to find this high mountain lake in the Kaniksu National Forest. The lake's elevation is approximately 5,810 feet and covers 14 acres. The lake is on an even-year rotation and was last stocked with 4,200 westslope cutthroat trout from the Cabinet Gorge hatchery.

Lower Glidden Lake Use the Thompson Pass topo map @ N 47° 31.03 W 115° 43.75 to find this high mountain lake in the Coeur d'Alene National Forest. The lake's elevation is approximately 5,699 feet and covers nearly 18 acres near the Montana border. The lake is on an even-year rotation and was last stocked with 2,800 grayling fry.

Moose Lake Use the Benning Mountain topo map @ N 48° 21.24 W 116° 6.41 to find this high mountain lake in the Kootenai National Forest. The lake's elevation is approximately 5,437 feet and covers 10 acres. The lake was on an even-year rotation but it was removed in 2000. It had been stocked with 1,200 trout fry.

Myrtle Lake Use the Smith Peak topo map @ N 48° 45.25 W 116° 37.80 to find this high mountain lake in the Kaniksu National Forest. The lake's elevation is approximately 5,938 feet and it covers 20 acres. The lake is on an even-year rotation and was last stocked with 3,000 westslope cutthroat trout from the Cabinet Gorge hatchery. Ball Creek and Little Ball Creek lakes are to the north.

Standard Lake (Upper Standard Lake) Use the Wigwams topo map @ N 48° 41.03 W 116° 42.03 to find this high mountain lake in the Kaniksu National Forest. The lake's elevation is approximately 5,306 feet and it covers nearly 14 acres. The lake is on an even-year rotation and was last stocked with 3,900 westslope cutthroat trout from the Cabinet Gorge hatchery. Harrison Lake is east.

West Fork Lake Use the Caribou Creek and Smith Peak topo maps @ N 48° 50.29 W 116° 44.56 to find this high mountain lake in the Kaniksu

National Forest. The lake's elevation is approximately 5,764 feet and it covers nearly 11 acres. The lake is on an even-year rotation and was last stocked with 3,300 westslope cutthroat trout from the Cabinet Gorge hatchery. Caribou and Wilson lakes are northwest.

Clearwater

Bear Lake Use the Buffalo Hump topo map @ N 45° 34.98 W 115° 39.91 to find this high mountain lake in the Gospel Hump Wilderness in the Nez Perce National Forest. The lake's elevation is approximately 7,398 feet and it covers more than 13 and a half acres. The lake is on an even-year rotation and was last stocked with 1,000 westslope cutthroat trout from the McCall hatchery. Crescent Lake is north and Ruby Lake is south.

Bills Lake #4 Use the Mount Paloma topo map @ N 45° 58.23 W 114° 35.43 to find this high mountain lake in Nez Perce National Forest. The lake's elevation is approximately 6,752 feet and it covers 19 acres. The lake was removed from the stocking rotation and was last stocked with 1,000 westslope cutthroat trout from the McCall hatchery. Stingray and Brushy Fork lakes are northeast. Emerald Lake is southwest.

Canyon Creek Lake #13 Use the Mount Jerusalem topo map @ N 45° 51.80 W 114° 25.07 to find this high mountain lake in the Bitterroot National Forest. The lake's elevation is approximately 6,913 feet and it covers nearly 54 acres. The lake is on a three-year rotation and was last stocked with 2,000 westslope cutthroat trout from the McCall hatchery. Montana's Boulder Lake is east.

Chimney Lake (Florence) Use the Fenn Mountain topo map, @ N 46° 10.66 W 115° 12.94 to find this high mountain lake in the Clearwater National Forest. The lake's elevation is approximately 6,289 feet and it covers 31 acres. The lake was last stocked with 1,000 westslope cutthroat trout from the McCall hatchery. Link Lakes are east and Lloyd, Kettle and Elizabeth lakes are north.

Cub Lake Use the El Capitan topo map @ N 46° 00.94 W 114° 29.78 to find this high mountain lake in the Nez Perce National Forest near the Montana border. The lake's elevation is approximately 6,382 feet and it covers more than 38 acres. The lake has been removed from the stocking rotation and was last stocked with 1,000 westslope cutthroat trout from the McCall hatchery. Montana's Lake Capitan is east.

Duck Lake Use the Jeanette Mountain topo map @ N 46° 18.99 W 114° 36.25 to find this high mountain lake in the Selway Bitterroot Wilderness in the Clearwater National Forest. The lake's elevation is approximately 6,601 feet and it covers 15 acres. The lake is on a three-year rotation and was last stocked with 1,000 westslope cutthroat trout from the McCall hatchery. The Goat lakes are south and Jeanette Lake is northeast.

Emerald Lake #3 Use the Mount Paloma topo map @ N 45° 57.87 W 114° 36.27 to find this high mountain lake in the Selway Bitterroot Wilderness in the Nez Perce National Forest. The lakes elevation is approximately 7,011 feet and it covers 29 acres. The lake has been removed from the stocking rotation and was last stocked with 1,000 westslope cutthroat trout from the McCall hatchery. Bills and Brushy Forks lakes are northeast.

Gold Pan Lake Use the Magruder Mountain topo map @ N 45° 38.76 W 114° 48.37 to find this high mountain lake in the Frank Church Wilderness in the Bitterroot National Forest. The lake's elevation is approximately 7,292 feet and it covers 10 acres. The lake has been removed from the stocking rotation and was last stocked with 2,000 westslope cutthroat trout from the McCall hatchery. Elk Track Lake is south.

Hungry Lake Use the Hungry Rock topo map @ N 46° 19.59 W 114° 45.91 to find this high mountain lake in the Selway Bitterroot Wilderness in the Nez Perce National Forest. The lake's elevation is approximately 6,676 feet and it covers nearly 24 acres. The lake is on a three-year stocking rotation and was last stocked with 2,000 westslope cutthroat trout from the McCall hatchery. Upper and Lower Porphyry lakes are south.

North Lone Lake Use the Fenn Mountain topo map @ N 46° 13.54 W 115° 10.71 to find this high mountain lake in the Nez Perce National Forest. The lake's elevation is approximately 6,377 feet and it covers more than 13 acres. The lake is on an three-year rotation and was last stocked with 1,000 westslope cutthroat trout from the McCall hatchery. Lizard Lakes are south.

Moose Lake Use the St. Joseph Peak topo map @ N 46° 36.21 W 114° 21.45 to find this high mountain lake in the Selway Bitterroot Wilderness in the Clearwater National Forest. The lake's elevation is approximately 6,978 feet and it covers 19 acres. The lake was removed from the stocking rotation and was last stocked with 1,000 rainbow trout from the McCall hatchery. Lilly and Skookum lakes are north.

Parachute Lake Use the White Sands Lake topo map @ N 46º 24.90 W 114º 25.31 to find this high mountain lake in the Clearwater National Forest. The lake's elevation is approximately 5,918 feet and it covers 30 acres. The lake has been removed from the stocking rotation and was last stocked with 2,000 westslope cutthroat trout from the McCall hatchery. White Sand Lake is to the north and Garnet Lake is east.

Porphyry Lake #1 (South) Use the Hungry Rock topo map @ N 46º 18.06 W 114º 45.13 to find this high mountain lake in the Selway/Bitterroot National Forest. The lake's elevation is approximately 6,658 feet and it covers 11 acres. The lake is on a three-year stocking rotation and was last stocked with 1,000 westslope cutthroat trout from the McCall hatchery. Maple Lake is south and Hungry Lake is north.

Porphyry Lake #2 (North) Use the Hungry Rock topo map @ N 46º 18.54 W 114º 45.00 to find this high mountain lake in the Selway/Bitterroot National Forest. The lake's elevation is approximately 6,924 feet and it covers nearly five acres. The lake has been removed from the stocking rotation and was last stocked with 1,000 westslope cutthroat trout from the McCall hatchery. Maple Lake is south and Hungry Lake is north.

Siah Lake Use the Ranger Peak topo map @ N 46º 31.32 W 114º 26.62 to find this high mountain lake in the Clearwater National Forest near the Montana border. The lake's elevation is approximately 6,414 feet and it covers 12 acres. The lake was removed from the stocking rotation and was last stocked with 1,000 westslope cutthroat trout from the McCall Hatchery. Ranger Lake is east.

Central Mountains (West)

Baldy Lake (Big) Use the He Devil topo map @ N 45º 18.81 W 116º 34.26 to find this high mountain lake in the Hells Canyon Recreation Area. The lake's elevation is approximately 7,195 feet and it covers 46 acres. The lake is on a three-year rotation and was last stocked with 1,000 rainbow trout from the McCall hatchery. Triangle, Quad, He Devil and Echo lakes are north, Hanson Lake is east and Dog Lake is south.

Dog Lake Use the He Devil topo map @ N 45° 17.71 W 116° 33.33 to find this high mountain lake in the Payette National Forest. The lake's elevation is approximately 7,912 feet and it covers 12 acres. The lake has been removed from the stocking rotation and was last stocked with 1,000 westslope cutthroat trout from the McCall hatchery. Big Baldy Lake is northwest.

Echo Lake Use the He Devil topo map @ N 45° 19.70 W 116° 34.08 to find this high mountain lake in the Hells Canyon Recreation Area. The lake's elevation is approximately 7,242 feet and it covers nearly 10 acres. The lake is on a three-year rotation and was last stocked with 500 westslope cutthroat trout from the Cabinet Gorge Hatchery. Hunt Lake is to the north and McCormick Lake is to the south.

Gem Lake (Sheep Creek Lake) Use the He Devil topo map @ N 45° 20.19 W 116° 33.19 to find this high mountain lake in the Hells Canyon National Recreation Area in the Nez Perce National Forest. The lake's elevation is approximately 7,753 feet and it covers more than 15 acres. The lake is on a three-year rotation and was last stocked with 500 westslope cutthroat trout from the McCall hatchery. Sheep Lake is east and Rock Island Lake is south.

Hidden Lake Use the Alpha topo map @ N 44° 26.63 W 116° 06.74 to find this high mountain lake in the Payette National Forest. Its elevation is approximately 7,040 feet, with an area of ten acres. It is stocked on a three-year rotation with 500 westslope cutthroat trout fry from the McCall hatchery. Lost Lake is west.

Horton Lake Use the Blacktip topo map @ N 45° 07.76 W 116° 05.12 to find this high mountain lake in the Payette National Forest. Its elevation is approximately 7,432 feet, with an area of six acres. It is stocked on a three-year rotation with 500 westslope cutthroat trout fry from the McCall hatchery. Ellis Lake is west.

Lick Lake Use the Edwardsburg topo map @ N 45° 04.35 W 115° 18.18 to find this high mountain lake in the Payette National Forest. Its elevation is approximately 7,740 feet, and it is stocked on a three-year rotation and was last stocked with 2,000 westslope cutthroat trout fry from the McCall hatchery. Bear Lake is southeast.

Maloney Lake Use the Paddy Flat topo map @ N 44º 52.46 W 115º 54.02 to find this high mountain lake in the Payette National Forest. Its elevation is approximately 7,208 feet, with an area of nine acres. It is stocked on a three-year rotation with 3,000 grayling fry from the McCall hatchery. Buckhorn lakes are southeast.

Nut Basin Lake Use the John Day Mountain topo map @ N 45º 31.86 W 116º 09.92 to find this high mountain lake in the Gospel Hump Wilderness of the Nez Perce National Forest. The lake's elevation is approximately 6,775 feet and it is small. The lake receives fish when available and was last stocked with 1,000 rainbow trout from the McCall hatchery. You'll really have to want to get here as there are no landmarks around.

Central Mountains (East)

Blue Rock Lake Use the Warbonnet Peak topo map @ N 44º 03.87 W 115º 03.38 to find this high mountain lake in the Sawtooth Wilderness in the Sawtooth National Recreation Area. Its elevation is approximately 8,212 feet, with an area of five acres. It is on a three-year rotation and it was last stocked with 500 westslope cutthroat trout fry from the McCall hatchery. Little Warbonnet and Warbonnet lakes are east.

Dandy Lake Use the Mount Everly topo map @ N 43º 55.03 W 115º 05.16 to find this high mountain lake in the Sawtooth Wilderness in the Sawtooth National Recreation Area. Its elevation is approximately 8,494 feet, with an area of five acres. It is on a three-year rotation and it was last stocked with 1,000 westslope cutthroat trout fry from the McCall hatchery. Blue Jay Lake in north.

Flat Top Lake #1 (Lower) Use the Nahneke Mountain topo map @ N 43º 55 W 115º 08 to find this high mountain lake in the Sawtooth Wilderness in the Sawtooth National Recreation Area. This small lake's elevation is approximately 8,837 feet. It is on a three-year rotation and it was last stocked with 500 westslope cutthroat trout fry from the McCall hatchery. Diamond and Triangle lakes are northwest.

Glacier Lake Use the Mount Everly topo map @ N 43° 55 W 115° 05 to find this high mountain lake in the Sawtooth Wilderness in the Sawtooth National Recreation Area. Its elevation is approximately 8,476 feet, and it is on a three-year rotation and was last stocked with 1,000 golden trout fry from the McCall hatchery. Browns Lake is east.

Johnson Lake Use the Nahneke Mountain topo map @ N 43° 56 W 115° 08 to find this high mountain lake in the Sawtooth Wilderness in the Sawtooth National Recreation Area. Its elevation is approximately 8,808 feet, with an area of five acres. It is on a three-year rotation and it was last stocked with 500 westslope cutthroat trout fry from the McCall hatchery. Browns Lake is south.

Kate Lake Use the Warbonnet Peak topo map @ N 44° 00 W 115° 03 to find this high mountain lake in the Sawtooth Wilderness in the Sawtooth National Recreation Area. Its elevation is approximately 8,428 feet, with an area of five acres. It is on a three-year rotation and it was last stocked with 1,000 rainbow trout fry from the McCall hatchery.

Lake Creek Lake #2 Use the Edaho Mountain topo map @ N 44° 01 W 115° 08 to find this high mountain lake in the Sawtooth National Recreation Area. Its elevation is approximately 8,107 feet. It is on a three-year rotation and it was last stocked with 500 westslope cutthroat trout fry from the McCall hatchery. Pinchot Creek Lake #1 is south.

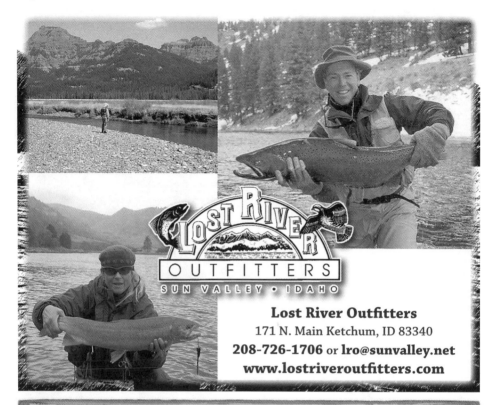

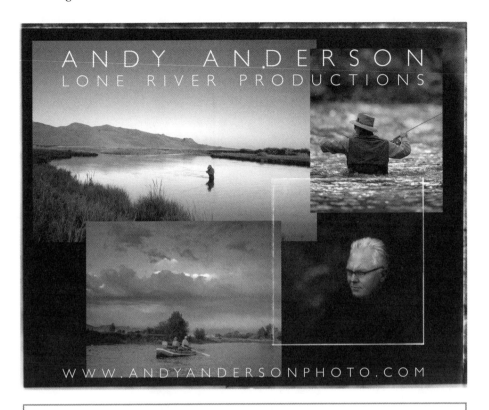

IDAHO
High Mountain
LAKES

Look for *Idaho High Mountain Lakes* to be published by
Cutthroat Press in the spring of 2005.

Cutthroat
PRESS

www.cutthroatpress.com • 208.343.8396 • jevancho@cableone.net
PO Box 1471 • Boise, Idaho 83701

Directory

Angler's-Full Orvis
7097 Overland Road
Boise, ID 83709
208.323.6768

Anglers Habitat
916 Blaine St.
Caldwell, ID 83605
208.454.8188

Arrick's Fly Shop
P.O. Box
1290 Canyon Street
West Yellowstone, MT 59758
406.646.7290

Bear Creek Fly Shop
5622 W. State
Boise, ID 83703
208.843.8704

Bent Rod
P.O. Box 358
211 Elm Street
Mackay, ID 83251
208.588.3310

Blue Ribbon Flies
305 Canyon Street
West Yellowstone, MT 59758
406.646.9045

Bud Lilly's Trout Shop
P.O. Box 530
West Yellowstone, MT 59758
406.646.7801

Castaway Fly Shop
350 West Bosanko
Coeur d'Alene, ID 83815
208.765.3133

Henry's Fork Anglers
3340 Hwy 20
Island Park, ID 83429
208.558.7525

Howard's Tackle Shoppe
1707 Garrity Blvd.
Nampa, ID 83687
208.465.0946

Idaho Angler - Boise
1682 S. Vista Ave
Boise, ID 83706
208.389.9957

Idaho Angler - McCall
305 E. Park
McCall, ID 83634
866.634.4004

Jimmy's All Season Angler
275 A Street
Idaho Falls, ID 83402
208.524.7160

Lost River Outfitters
171 N. Main
Ketchum, ID 83340
208.726.1706

The RiverKeeper Fly Shop
1224 Broadway Ave
Boise, ID 83706
208.344.3838

Silver Creek Outfitters
500 Main Street
Box 418
Ketchum, ID 83340
208.726.5258

South Fork Lodge
PO Box 22
Swan Valley, Idaho 83449
877.347.4735

Sportsman's Warehouse
Idaho Falls
2909 S. Hitt Rd.
Idaho Falls (Ammon), ID 83405
208.542.1900

Meridian
3797 E. Fairview Ave.
Meridian, ID 83642
208.884.3000

Twin Falls
1940 Bridgeview Blvd.
Twin Falls, ID 83301
208.737.9900

Spokane, Washington
14014 E. Indiana Ave.
Spokane, WA 99216
509.891.1900

Idaho Department of Fish and Game Regional Offices:

Panhandle
2750 Kathleen Avenue
Coeur d'Alene, ID 83814
208/769-1414

Clearwater
1540 Warner Avenue
Lewiston, ID 83501
208/799-5010

Salmon
1215 Hwy 93 N.
Salmon, ID 83467
208/756-2271

McCall
555 Deinhard Lane
McCall, ID 83638
208/634-8137

Southwest
3101 Powerline Road
Nampa, ID 83686
208/465-8465

Magic
868 E. Main St.
Jerome, ID 83338
208/324-4350

Southeast
1345 Barton Road
Pocatello, ID 83204
208/232-4703

Upper Snake
1515 Lincoln Road
Idaho Falls, ID 83401
208/525-7290

Headquarters
600 S. Walnut
Boise, ID 83707
208/334-3700

National Forests:

Boise National Forest
1750 Front Street
Boise, ID 83702
208/364-4100

Caribou National Forest
Federal Building, Suite 282
250 South 4th Avenue
Pocatello, ID 83201
208/236-7500

Challis National Forest
Highway 93 North
Challis, ID 83226
208/879-2285

Clearwater National Forest
12730 Highway 12
Orofino, ID 83544
208/476-4541

Coeur d'Alene, Kaniksu and St. Joe National Forest
1201 Ironwood Dr.
Coeur d'Alene. ID 83814
208/765-7223

Nez Perce National Forest
East U.S. Hwy 13
Grangeville, ID 83530
208/983-1950

Payette National Forest
106 West Park Street
McCall, ID 83638
208/634-0700

Salmon National Forest
Highway 93 North
Salmon, ID 83467
208/756-2215

Sawtooth National Forest
2647 Kimberly Road East
Twin Falls, ID 83301
208/737-3200

Targhee National Forest
420 North Bridge Street
St. Anthony, ID 83445
208/624-3151

State of Idaho:

Idaho Travel Council
700 West State Street
Boise, ID 83702
800/635-7820

Water Index

Alturas Lake 102
Alturas Lake Creek. 101
American Falls Reservoir......... 181, 182
American River...................... 87
Anderson Lake....................... 70
Anderson Ranch Reservoir 144
Antelope Lake 61
Arrowrock Reservoir 144

Badger Creek 204
Baker Lake......................... 170
Baldy Lake......................... 235
Banbury Springs 163
Battle Creek....................... 148
Bayhorse Lakes 100
Beach's Pond...................... 141
Bear Lake.................... 179, 191
Bear Lake (HML) 233
Bear Lake Tributaries.............. 191
Bear River......................... 188
Bear Valley Creek 117
Beaver Creek....................... 208
Beaver Creek (Middle Fork Salmon) ... 116
Beaver Creek (Priest Lake) 62
Beehive Lake 231
Benewah Lake 68
Ben Ross Reservoir................. 133
Big Boulder Creek.................. 150
Big Cottonwood Creek 173
Big Creek (Middle Fork Salmon) 115
Big Creek (Pahsimeroi) 98
Big Creek (St. Joe)................. 72
Big Fisher Lake.................... 231
Big Horn Crags Mountain Lakes....... 117
Big Jack Creek..................... 150
Big Lost River 205
Big Smoky Creek.................... 143
Big Trinity Lake................... 145
Big Wood River 164, 166, 170

Billingsley Creek 159
Bills Lake #4. 233
Birch Creek 207
Bitch Creek........................ 204
Blackfoot Reservoir 187
Blackfoot River.................... 186
Black Canyon Reservoir 134
Black Lake 70
Blair Trail Diversion Reservoir........ 160
Blanchard Reservoir 65
Bliss Reservoir 160
Bloomington Lake 190
Bloom Lake 58
Blue Creek 148
Blue Creek Reservoir............... 148
Blue Lake (Lateral Lake) 70
Blue Lake (Panhandle) 63
Blue Mountain Ponds................ 118
Blue Rock Lake..................... 237
Boise River.................... 40, 140
    Middle Fork Boise River 142
    North Fork Boise River 142
    South Fork Boise River........... 143
Bonner Lake....................... 57
Boulder Creek 136
Box Canyon Springs 163
Bray Lake.......................... 161
Breakfast Creek.................... 85
Brownlee Reservoir 129
Brundage Reservoir................. 110
Bruneau River.................. 146, 147
Brush Creek 187
Brush Lake (Boundary Co.)............ 57
Brush Lake (River of No Return) 118
Brush Lake (Treasure Valley) 137
Buffalo River...................... 202
Bull Run Lake 71
Bull Trout Lake 139
Burns Creek 197
Bybee Reservoir.................... 149

C.J. Strike Reservoir................ 130

Caldwell Ponds 141
Camas Creek (Magic Valley) 170
Camas Creek (River of No Return) 115
Camas Creek (Upper Snake) 207
Campbell's Pond 81
Canyon Creek (Treasure Valley) 139
Canyon Creek (Upper Snake) 204
Canyon Creek Lake #13 233
Cape Horn Creek 116
Cape Horn Lakes 117
Carey Lake 169
Caribou Lake 231
Carlson Lake 103
Cascade Reservoir 137
Cassia Creek 174
Castle Creek 131
Cave Lake 70
Cayuse Creek 86
Cedar Creek Reservoir 173
Cedar Draw Creek 160
Chase Lake 63
Chatcolet Lake 68
Chesterfield Reservoir 185
Chimney Lake 233
Clark Fork River 61
Clearwater River 37, 77, 79, 80
Little North Fork 85
Middle Fork 83
North Fork (above reservoir) 84
North Fork (below dam) 84
South Fork 86
Clear Creek (Clearwater River) 83
Clear Creek (Payette River) 139
Clear Lake 163
Clover Creek Reservoir 161
Cocolalla Creek 64
Cocolalla Lake 64
Coeur d'Alene River 68
Condie Reservoir 189
Corral Creek 187
Corral Creek Reservoir 137
Cove Arm 131

Crane Creek Reservoir 133
Crane Falls 131
Crooked River 86
Crowthers Reservoir 193
Crow Creek 197
Crystal Lake 162
Cub Lake 233
Cub River 192
Curlew Valley Reservoir 173

Dandy Lake 237
Daniels Reservoir 193
Dawson Lake 57
Day Rock Pond 71
Deadwood Reservoir 139
Deadwood River 139
Deep Creek (Magic Valley) 160
Deep Creek (Treasure Valley) 148
Deep Creek Reservoir 193
Deer Creek Reservoir 82
Devils Corral Spring 164
Devils Creek Reservoir 193
Diamond Creek 187
Dierkes Lake 162
Dike Lake 187
Dismal Lake 71
Divide Mountain Lakes 118
Dog Creek Reservoir 170
Dog Lake 236
Dry Bed Canal 196
Dry Creek 192
Duck Lake 234
Duff Lane Pond 141
Dworshak Reservoir 84

East River 62
Middle Fork 62
North Fork 62
Echo Lake 236
Elk Creek 85
Elk Creek Lake 117
Elk Creek Reservoir 85

Elsie Lake 71
Emerald Lake 163
Emerald Lake #3 234
Emmett Airport pond 134

Falls River 201
Featherville Dredge ponds 145
Fenn Pond 84
Fernan Lake 68
Family Fishing Waters (FFW) 10
 Bayhorse Lakes 100
 Caldwell Ponds 141
 Campbell's Pond 81
 Cedar Creek Reservoir 173
 Day Rock Pond 71
 Elsie Lake 71
 Emmett Airport pond 134
 Fenn Pond 84
 Fernan Lake 68
 Granite Lake 64
 Hayden Ponds 118
 Hyde Pond 118
 Iron Lake 99
 Jewel Lake 63
 Kelly Creek Pond 118
 Kelso Lake 63
 Magic Reservoir 167
 Meadow Lake 100
 Palouse River 79
 Rock Creek 162
 Roseworth Reservoir 173
 Round Lake 64
 Sinclair Lake 58
 Smith Lake 57
 Soldiers Meadow Reservoir 81
 Spring Valley Reservoir 81
 Stanley Lake Creek 101
 Star Road pond 134
 Tolo Lake 108
 Trail Creek Pond 204
 Wallace Lake 99
 Wilson Springs Ponds 141

Yankee Fork Ponds 118
Firehole River 216
Fish Creek Reservoir 168
Fish Lake 110
Five Mile Pond 87
Flat Top Lake #1 237
Foster Reservoir 189
Fox Creek 204
Frank Oster Lakes 161
Fred Warren Pond 82
Freedom Park Pond 163
Freeman Lake 63
French Creek 106

Gallatin River 217
Gamble Lake 65
Gamlin Lake 65
Gem Lake 236
Gibbon River 217
Giraffe Creek 192
Glacier Lake 238
Glendale Reservoir 189
Golden Lake 202
Gold Fork Creek 136
Gold Pan Lake 234
Goose Creek 172
Goose Lake 111
Grangeville Pond 108
Granite Creek (Clearwater) 89
Granite Creek (Panhandle) 62
Granite Lake (Panhandle) 64
Granite Lake (Payette River) 138
Grasmere Reservoir 149
Gravers Lagoon 169
Grimes Creek 142
Grove Creek 170

Hagerman Wildlife Management Area 161
Halverson Lake 129
Harrison Lake 231
Hauser Lake 68
Hawkins Reservoir 185

Hawley Creek 100
Hayden Lake 67
Hayden Ponds 118
Hazard Lakes. 111
Hells Canyon Reservoir. 128
Henry's Fork. 43, 198, 200
Henry's Lake 200
Henry's Lake Outlet. 201
Herd Lake. 103
Herrick Reservoir. 137
Hidden Lake (Central Mountains West) 236
Hidden Lake (Panhandle) 232
High Mountain Lakes. 230
    Baldy Lake. 235
    Bear Lake. 233
    Beehive Lake 231
    Big Fisher Lake. 231
    Bills Lake #4 233
    Blue Rock Lake. 237
    Canyon Creek Lake #13. 233
    Caribou Lake. 231
    Chimney Lake 233
    Cub Lake 233
    Dandy Lake 237
    Dog Lake 236
    Duck Lake 234
    Echo Lake. 236
    Emerald Lake #3 234
    Flat Top Lake #1 237
    Gem Lake. 236
    Glacier Lake 238
    Gold Pan Lake. 234
    Harrison Lake. 231
    Hidden Lake (Central Mountains West). . .
    236
    Hidden Lake (Panhandle) 232
    Horton Lake. 236
    Hungry Lake 234
    Hunt Lake. 232
    Johnson Lake 238
    Kate Lake. 238
    Lake Creek Lake #2 238

Lick Lake. 236
Lower Glidden Lake 232
Maloney Lake 237
Moose Lake (Clearwater). 234
Moose Lake (Panhandle) 232
Myrtle Lake 232
North Lone Lake 234
Nut Basin. 237
Parachute Lake 235
Porphyry Lake #1 235
Porphyry Lake #2 235
Sheep Creek Lake. 236
Siah Lake. 235
Standard Lake 232
West Fork Lake 232
Hoodoo Creek. 61
Horseshoe Bend Mill Pond 135
Horsethief Reservoir 136
Horse Creek. 106
Horton Lake 236
Hungry Lake. 234
Hunt Lake. 232
Hyde Pond. 118

Idaho's Big 10 32
Independence Lakes 174
Indian Creek (Middle Fork Salmon). . . . 116
Indian Creek (Priest Lake) 62
Indian Creek (Treasure Valley) 129
Indian Creek Reservoir 143
Iron Creek 103
Iron Lake 99
Irving Reservoir 170
Island Park Reservoir. 202

Jackknife Creek 197
Jarbidge River 150
Jewel Lake 63
Jimmy Smith Lake. 103
John's Creek. 86
Johnson Creek. 113
Johnson Lake 238

Johnson Reservoir 189
Jordan Creek 150
Josephus Lake 117
Juniper Basin Reservoir 148

Kalispell Creek 62
Karolyn's Pond 87
Kate Lake 238
Kelly Creek 33, 85
Kelly Creek Pond 118
Kelso Lake 63
Kerr Lake 58
Kids Creek Pond 98
Killarney Lake 70
Knapp Creek 116
Kootenai River 54, 55
Westside Tributaries 56

Lake Cleveland 174
Lake Coeur d'Alene 66
Lake Creek 99
Lake Creek Lake #2 238
Lake Fork Creek 136
Lake Lowell 142
Lake Pend Oreille 60
Lake Rock Lake 118
Lake Serene 111
Lake Walcott 180
Lamar River 218
Lamont Reservoir 190
Lanes Creek 187
Lapwai Lake 80
Lateral Lakes 70
Lava Lake 169
Lemhi Range Lakes 118
Lemhi River 98
Lewis Lake 219
Lick Lake 236
Lion Creek 62
Little Blue Creek Reservoir 149
Little Camas Reservoir 145
Little Lost River 206

Little Payette Lake 137
Little Redfish Lake 101
Little Round Lake 64
Little Salmon River 109
Little Smoky Creek 143
Little Trinity Lake 145
Little Valley Reservoir 190
Little Weiser River 132
Little Willow Creek 135
Little Wood Reservoir 168
Little Wood River 167
Lochsa River 35, 83
Logger Creek 142
Lolo Creek 82
Long Lake 118
Loon Creek 116
Loon Lake 113
Lost Valley Reservoir 133
Louie Lake 137
Loving Creek 169
Lower Box Canyon Lake 171
Lower Glidden Lake 232
Lower Goose Reservoir 173
Lower Palisades Lake 197
Lucky Peak Reservoir 144

Mackay Reservoir 208
Madison River 215
Magic Reservoir 167
Magic Valley 155
Malad River (Bear Lake) 192
Malad River (Magic Valley) 159
Maloney Lake 237
Mann Creek Reservoir 132
Mann Lake 81
Marble Creek (Middle Fork Salmon) . . . 116
Marble Creek (St. Joe) 71
Marsh Creek (Bear Lake) 184
Marsh Creek (River of No Return) 116
Mary's Creek Reservoir 149
McArthur Reservoir 56
McCoy Creek 197

McTucker Ponds................... 182
Meadow Lake (near Gilmore) 100
Meadow Lake (near Leadore) 103
Medicine Lake..................... 70
Medicine Lodge Creek 207
Mirror Lake 63
Montpelier Creek 192
Montpelier Reservoir................ 190
Moody Creek 204
Moose Creek...................... 202
Moose Creek Reservoir............... 81
Moose Lake (Clearwater)............ 234
Moose Lake (Panhandle) 232
Mores Creek 142
Morgan Creek..................... 100
Mormon Reservoir.................. 170
Morrow Reservoir 160
Mosquito Flat Reservoir.............. 100
Mountain Home Reservoir 145
Moyie River 56
Mud Creek........................ 160
Mud Lake (River of No Return)........ 110
Mud Lake (Upper Snake) 207
Murtaugh Reservoir................. 162
Myrtle Lake 232

Newsome Creek 87
Niagara Springs Ponds.............. 162
North Lone Lake 234
Nut Basin......................... 237

Oakley Reservoir................... 173
Owyhee River 146
Oxbow Reservoir................... 128
Oxford Reservoir................... 190

Packsaddle Lake 204
Paddock Reservoir.................. 135
Pahsimeroi River.................... 97
Palisades Creek.................... 197
Palisades Reservoir 197
Palouse River 79

Panhandle 53
Panther Creek 106
Parachute Lake.................... 235
Park Center Pond.................. 141
Partridge Creek 106
Payette Lake...................... 138
Payette Lake Complex.............. 137
Payette River 133, 134
   Middle Fork Payette River.......... 138
   North Fork Payette River........... 135
   South Fork Payette River 138
Payne Creek Reservoir 149
Pebble Creek..................... 185
Pend Oreille River 59, 61
Perkins Lake (Alturas Lake) 103
Perkins Lake (Kaniksu NF)............ 57
Petit Lake 102
Pine Creek 197
Pioneer Reservoir.................. 161
Pistol Creek 116
Pleasantview Reservoir 193
Porphyry Lake #1 235
Porphyry Lake #2 235
Portneuf River................ 183, 184
Potlatch River..................... 82
   East Fork....................... 82
Preuss Creek 192
Priest Lake 61
Priest River 62
Pritchard Creek 197

Raft River 172
Rainey Creek 197
Rapid Creek...................... 185
Rapid River....................... 110
Rawlins Creek 187
Redfish Lake...................... 101
Red River 87
Regions, The...................... 51
Reynolds Creek 129
Richfield Canal 167
Riddle Lakes Reservoir Complex....... 148

Riley Creek. 160
Ririe Reservoir 198
River of No Return 93
Roberts Gravel Pond 208
Robinson's Pond. 81
Robinson Creek 202
Robinson Lake 57
Rock Creek (Bear Lake) 181
Rock Creek (Magic Valley). 162
Roseworth Reservoir 173
Rose Lake. 71
Rose Pond 182
Round Lake (Benewah Co.) 68
Round Lake (Bonner Co.) 64
Round Prairie Creek. 56

Sagehen Reservoir 135
Salmon Falls Creek 171
Salmon Falls Creek Reservoir 172
Salmon River 89
    East Fork of the Salmon River 96
    Main Salmon River 94
        lower Salmon 107
        middle Salmon. 104
        upper Salmon 95
    Middle Fork Salmon River. . . 39, 114, 115
    North Fork Salmon River. 106
    South Fork Salmon River. 111
        East Fork of the South Fork 112
    Yankee Fork. 96
Sand Creek Reservoir 202
Sand Dunes Lakes 149
Sawtooth Mountain Lakes. 118
Sawyer Ponds 134
Scott Pond 162
Seafoam Lakes. 117
Secesh River. 112
Selway River 35, 83
Sheep Creek (Bruneau River) 149
Sheep Creek (Snake River). 89
Sheep Creek Lake 236
Shepherd Lake. 65

Shoofly Reservoir. 149
Shoshone Creek 172
Shoshone Lake. 219
Siah Lake 235
Silver Creek 42, 169
Silver Lake 202
Sinclair Lake. 58
Sinks, The. 205
Slate Creek 108
Slough Creek. 218
Smith Lake 57
Snake River 88, 128, 180
    Henry's Fork. 43, 198, 200
    South Fork 45, 195, 196
Snake River, Upper 195
Snake River (Bear Lake) 180
Snake River (Magic Valley) 157
Snake River (Treasure Valley) 131
Soldiers Meadow Reservoir 81
Solomon Lake 58
Spirit Lake. 65
Spokane River 66, 72
Springfield Lake. 181
Spring Valley Reservoir. 81
Squaw Creek. 135
Squaw Creek Pond 118
Squaw Creek Reservoir. 149
St. Joe River 32, 71
St. Maries River 72
Stalker Creek 169
Standard Lake 232
Stanley Basin Mountain Lakes 118
Stanley Lake. 101
Stanley Lake Creek 101
Star Road pond 134
Stoneridge Reservoir. 65
Stone Reservoir 173
Strongarm Reservoir 190
Stump Creek 197
Sublett Reservoir 173
Sulphur Creek 116
Swan Falls Reservoir 129

Swan Lake 70

Ten Mile Creek 86
Teton Creek 204
Teton River 203, 204
Thomas Fork River 191
Thompson Lake 70
Thorn Creek Reservoir. 170
Tincup Creek 197
Tolo Lake 108
Toponce Creek 185
Trail Creek (Magic Valley) 166
Trail Creek (Upper Snake) 204
Trail Creek Pond 204
Treasureton Reservoir 190
Treasure Valley 127
Tule Lake 118
24-Mile Reservoir 185
Twin Lakes
    Lower 67
    Upper. 67
Twin Lakes Reservoir 190
Two Mouth Creek 62

Upper Palisades Lake 197
Upper Payette Lake 137
Upper Priest Lake. 62
Upper Snake River. 195

Valley County Ponds 136
Valley Creek. 101
Valley Creek Lakes 102
Veterans Park Pond 141
Vinyard Creek 164

Waha Lake. 81
Wallace Lake. 99
Warm Lake. 113
Warm River 201
Warm Springs Creek. 166
Warm Spring Creek (Payette River) 139
Warm Spring Creek (Salmon River) 98

Weiser River. 131
    Middle Fork Weiser River 132
    West Fork Weiser River. 132
Weitas Creek. 85
Weston Reservoir. 193
West Fork Lake. 232
White Bird Creek. 108
White Cloud Mountain Lakes 118
White Sands Pond. 82
Wildhorse River. 129
Williams Lake. 99
Willow Creek (Treasure Valley) 135
Willow Creek (Upper Snake) 197
Wilson Lake 162
Wilson Springs Ponds 141
Winchester Lake 80
Winder Reservoir. 190
Wiregrass Reservoir 185
Wolverine Creek 187

Yankee Fork. 96
Yankee Fork Ponds. 118
Yellowbelly Lake 102
Yellowjacket Lake 117
Yellowstone Lake 219
Yellowstone National Park 213
    Firehole River. 216
    Gallatin River. 217
    Gibbon River 217
    Lamar River 218
    Lewis Lake 219
    Madison River 215
    Shoshone Lake. 219
    Slough Creek. 218
    Yellowstone Lake. 219
    Yellowstone River. 217
Yellowstone River. 217

Angler's Journal

Date _____

Location _____

Notes _____

_____

_____

_____

_____

_____

_____

_____

_____

Date _____

Location _____

Notes _____

_____

_____

_____

_____

_____

_____

_____

_____

_____

Angler's Journal

Date
Location
Notes

Date
Location
Notes

Angler's Journal

Date _____

Location _____

Notes _____

_____

_____

_____

_____

_____

_____

_____

_____

Date _____

Location _____

Notes _____

_____

_____

_____

_____

_____

_____

_____

_____